BEHAVIORAL SOCIAL WORK

BEHAVIORAL SOCIAL WORK

John S. Wodarski, Ph.D.

School of Social Work
University of Georgia, Athens, Georgia

Dennis A. Bagarozzi, Ph.D.

Kansas State University, Manhattan, Kansas

 **HUMAN SCIENCES PRESS**
72 Fifth Avenue   3 Henrietta Street
NEW YORK, NY 10011 ● LONDON, WC2E 8LU

Library of Congress Catalog Number 78-26356

ISBN: 0-87705-375-8

Copyright © 1979 by Human Sciences Press
72 Fifth Avenue, New York, New York 10011

Printed in the United States of America
9 987654321

Library of Congress Cataloging in Publication Data

Wodarski, John S.
  Behavioral social work.

  Bibliography: p.
  Includes index.
  1. Psychiatric social work. 2. Behavior modification. I. Bagarozzi, Dennis A., joint author. II. Title.
HV689.W62   362.2'04'25   78-26356
ISBN 0-87705-375-8

CONTENTS

Chapter 1

BEHAVIORAL SOCIAL WORK

In the chapters to follow behavioral social work will be formalized in an effort to help educators in schools of social work incorporate this empirically based area of knowledge into curricula where it has been neglected seriously in the past. This will aid both student and practitioner in the application of behavioral techniques in clinical practice. Treatment techniques based on the different theories of learning are reviewed, training procedures are outlined, and criteria for the assessment of competency for the practice of behavioral social work are discussed. The volume is based on the authors' experiences in the application of behavioral methods to different areas of social work practice, i.e., individual, family, and group practice, and institutional and societal intervention and in the supervision of students engaged in applying the methods.

The incorporation of treatment techniques based on behavior modification into social work practice has increased significantly during the last decade. A primary reason for social workers turning to behavioral methods is the accumulating evidence to indicate the limited effectiveness of traditional interpersonal helping methods (Bergin, 1963, 1966, 1967a, 1967b, 1971, 1975; Bergin & Suinn, 1975; Briar, 1968; Briar & Miller, 1971; Eysenck, 1952, 1961, 1965, 1966; Fanshel, 1966; Fischer, 1973b; Maas, 1966, 1971; Mullen & Dumpson, 1972; Newman & Turen, 1974; Schuerman, 1975; Segal, 1972; Stuart, 1971; Wodarski, Hudson, & Buckholdt, 1976). This shortcoming is due, in part, to the fact that traditional methods cannot be evaluated, and traditional research methodology cannot provide the data necessary to have these methods placed on an empirical basis; that is, few reliable and valid measurements exist for evaluating adequately treatment outcomes for more traditional forms of clinical intervention wherein the primary concern is change in personality structure through verbal interaction rather than overt behavioral patterns (Bloom, 1975; Bloom & Block, 1977; Gottman & Leiblum, 1974; Marks, 1972; Wodarski, Hudson, & Buckholdt, 1976). Another limitation has been the lack of adequate funding for projects to evaluate clinical intervention on a broad scale (Broadhead & Rist, 1976; Berk & Rossi, 1976; Mintz, Freitag, Hendricks, & Schwartz, 1976). Whatever the reasons, during the time the evidence accrued regarding the lack of effectiveness of traditional methods, there appeared numerous research studies showing the effectiveness of behavioral techniques with a variety of populations.

A concurrent development during this period has been the profession's increasing commitment to the basing of decisions regarding therapies and theories of human behavior on scientific principles and research data rather than on theoretical tradition and authority (Bloom, 1976; Fischer, 1971, 1973a; Thomas, 1964, 1967; Wodarski & Feldman, 1973). Since behavior modification is one of the few scientifically based therapies having substantial empirical support, the incorporation of this knowledge into social work practice was facilitated by the profession's increasing scientific emphasis.

Since many of our training programs in social work are based on globally defined objectives that cannot be operationalized in the classroom or in field work, social work educators have been searching for methodology that will enable formalization of the training for practitioners. Behavior modification methodology meets this need in that it operationalizes concepts that can be measured and thus enables evaluation of the training processes and provides indications of when practitioners have achieved a sufficient level of competence to practice effectively (Rose, Cayner, & Edleson, 1977).

Through external pressures at the federal and state levels, increasing emphasis has been placed on accountability in social work practice (Henderson & Shore, 1974; Newman & Turen, 1974; Rosenberg & Brody, 1974; Tropp, 1974). With the emphasis on precision of worker interventions, operationalization of concepts in terms of observables, collection of data to evaluate the treatment process, and inculcation of the scientific perspective in practitioners, behavior modification has developed methods that can be verified and thus provide the profession a means of responding to the external pressures for accountability. This emphasis on accountability should assure continued federal and state monetary support.

Finally, behavior modification methods are applicable to social work practice since the majority of clients seen lack social skills and require concrete and tangible services that behavioral practitioners can readily provide. Through the behavioral modification approach numerous explicit programs have been developed for finding jobs (Azrin, Flores, & Kaplan, 1975), improving parent and child relationships (Foxx & Azrin, 1973; Patterson, 1971; Patterson & Gullion, 1968; Patterson, Reid, Jones, & Conger, 1975), reducing alcoholism (Hunt & Azrin, 1973), reducing thievery (Azrin & Wesolowski, 1974), achieving appropriate classroom behavior (Azrin, Azrin, & Armstrong, 1977; Azrin & Powers, 1975), increasing marital harmony (Jacobson & Martin, 1976), setting realistic expectations for self and others (Mahoney, 1977), managing finances effectively (Knox, 1971), and so forth. The behavioral approach facilitates the acquisition of these requisite behaviors that improve clients' functioning in our society and places strong emphasis upon the acquisition of skills, their generalization to a variety of settings, and their maintenance once formal treatment has been terminated. It differs from traditional approaches which attempt to help clients acquire such necessary social behaviors primarily through verbal exchanges between the therapist and the client.

Virtually no systematic data exist to support the superior effectiveness of traditional modes of interpersonal helping. Some might argue that more time is needed to operationalize concepts or to develop adequate measurement procedures and experimental methods that capture the richness of clinical phenomena, that scientific methods cannot be applied to clinical phenomena, or that a substantial proportion of social work practice is an art that cannot be evaluated, and so forth (Hollis, 1976; Hartman, 1971). The authors leave the resolution of these issues to each reader. From our perspective, however, substantial data are being accumulated each year to support the successful history of behavior modification practice with children classified as *hyperactive* (Hamblin, Buckholdt, Ferritor, Kozloff, & Blackwell, 1971; Patterson, 1965; Patterson, Jones, Whitter, & Wright, 1965), *autistic* (Browning & Stover, 1971; Hamblin, et al., 1971; Graziano, 1971, 1975; Lovaas & Koegel, 1973; Margolies, 1977; O'Leary & Wilson, 1975), *delinquent* (Braukmann & Fixsen, 1975; Cohen, 1973; Graziano, 1975; O'Leary & Wilson, 1975; Patterson, 1973), and *retarded* (Bijou, 1973; Graziano, 1975; O'Leary & Wilson, 1975); and adults classified as *antisocial* (Cohen & Filipczak, 1971; O'Leary & Wilson, 1975; Yates, 1970), *retarded* (Forehand & Baumeister, 1976; O'Leary & Wilson, 1975; Tavormina, 1975; Yates, 1970), *neurotic* (Marks, 1975; O'Leary & Wilson, 1975; Wolpe, 1973; Yates, 1970), and *psychotic* (Ayllon & Azrin, 1968; Kazdin, 1975a, 1975b; Lewinsohn, 1975; O'Leary & Wilson, 1975; Yates, 1970), and so forth.*

*Only selected works are cited since hundreds of studies are available to document the effectiveness of behavioral techniques.

DIMENSIONS OF THE BEHAVIORAL SOCIAL WORKER

Behavioral social work involves the systematic application of treatment techniques derived from learning theory and supported by empirical evidence to achieve behavior change in clients. The behavioral social worker must possess both theoretical knowledge and an empirical perspective regarding the nature of human behavior and the principles that influence behavioral change. The worker also must be capable of translating this knowledge into concrete behavioral operations for practical use in a variety of clinical settings. In order to be an effective practitioner, therefore, the behavioral social worker must possess a solid behavioral science knowledge base as well as a variety of behavioral skills. Moreover, a thorough grounding in research methodology will enable the clinician to evaluate therapeutic interventions, a necessary requisite of behavior modification practice. Since the rigorous training of the behavioral social worker equips him to assess and evaluate any treatment procedure that he has instituted, there is continual evaluation that provides corrective feedback to the practitioner. For the behavioral social worker, theory, practice, and evaluation are all part of one intervention process. The arbitrary division of theory, intervention, and research which does not facilitate therapeutic effectiveness and improved clinical procedures is eliminated.

Knowledge Base

The central emphasis is on employing empirically supported procedures that are aimed at the solution of the client's difficulties. The body of knowledge that the behavioral practitioner needs to possess in order to be an effective agent of change includes:

　　1.　A thorough understanding of the scientifically derived theories of human learning as they relate to human behavior, personality formation, the development and maintenance of interpersonal relationships, and behavior change.

2.   An ability to conceptualize a client's difficulties in terms of observable behaviors and to make accurate behavioral assessments based upon learning theory concepts so that the appropriate techniques can be chosen and effective programs can be formulated to bring about the desired behavioral acquisitions or modifications or extinctions of unwanted behaviors for those clients who request such changes.

3.   An understanding of how knowledge of principles of learning can be utilized in a variety of contexts, for example, with individuals, in groups, among family members, and within large organizations and institutions as well as naturalistic settings.

4.   An ability to understand how these principles of learning and behavior change can be applied at the organizational and societal level to alleviate social problems and ensure the maintenance of behavior change through interpersonal strategies.

5.   A working knowledge of a wide variety of research designs, experimental approaches, and statistical procedures and the ability to utilize them appropriately for the critical evaluation of one's attempts at intervention whether they take place on the micro or macro levels of society.

Behavioral Skills

In addition to a knowledge base, the behavioral social worker must be able to exhibit a variety of behavioral skills and be able to demonstrate the following:

1.   The ability to establish a meaningful therapeutic relationship through the effective and appropriate use of the core conditions that will be discussed in Chapter 2: genuineness, accurate empathic understanding and nonpossessive warmth,

which research shows are necessary conditions but not sufficient in themselves for therapeutic change.

2.   The ability to make accurate behavioral assessments that include the specification of those conditions that are antecedent and consequential to the problem behaviors under consideration.

3.   The ability to formulate behaviorally relevant and specific treatment goals.

4.   The ability to implement effectively a treatment plan designed to modify those target behaviors identified by the client as problematic.

5.   The ability to evaluate objectively any treatment procedure and outcome and to formulate new treatment strategies when those which had been formulated originally have proven ineffective.

Value Base

The value orientation of a behavioral approach to social work intervention is in keeping with the humanistic tradition of the social work profession. The person's behavior is seen as being governed by scientific laws that are predictable and capable of explaining both functional as well as dysfunctional behavior. The person's behavior is seen as rationally motivated and not at the mercy of unseen, irrational, and unpredictable internal instinctual forces of unconscious origin. The behavioral approach emphasizes the person's ability to learn, adapt, change, and to exert control over his own behavior and the environment in which he lives.

THE PERSON AS AN INDIVIDUAL.   In adapting a learning approach to human development and behavior, the behavioral clinician abandons the archaic stigmatizing practice of diagnostic labeling and in so doing plays no role in perpetuating such labeling processes and their dehumanizing consequences. Each person is seen as unique and not as a member of a particular class, category, or personality subgroup. Individuals are seen in terms of individual differences and their behavior is understood as being the result of particular learning experiences which are unique for each person. Such an approach to the person enables the clinician to observe intraindividual continuities of personality and to understand how varied environmental contingencies foster differential responding. This type of person-in-situation approach to human behavior eliminates character stereotyping and allows for more accurate prediction of behavior that is essential for qualitative clinical intervention.

SELF-DETERMINATION.   The behavioral approach is in line with the traditional social work ethic of client self-determination. It supports the client's right to make his own decision as to what, if any, behaviors will be altered and what items are to be the focus of clinical intervention. That is, it supports his right "to participate in any plans made for his welfare" (National Association of Social Workers, 1967). In keeping with this orientation, the client is asked to identify specifically those behavioral responses he wishes to acquire, increase, or decrease. The decision as to how this end will be accomplished is a joint one made between the behavioral social worker and the client. Thus, in the behavioral approach the worker acts as a consultant in choosing behaviors to alter; however, the final decision rests with the client. In instances where such a process cannot be followed, as in work with children or incarcerated individuals, the behavioral social worker adheres to these principles as closely as possible. Each behavioral worker has to decide when organizational variables compromise the behavioral approach sufficiently so that it cannot be implemented according to moral and ethical codes.

BEGINNING WHERE THE CLIENT IS.   Since treatment goals are contractually agreed upon by both participants and outcome objectives are behaviorally detailed, there is little chance of the social worker redefining the client's goals. Training in the core conditions of warmth, genuineness, and accurate empathic understanding prevents the behavioral social worker from interpreting the client's behavior or imposing a taxonomy of hypothetical conflicts or problems that all clients must insightfully resolve in order to achieve behavior change. The behavioral social worker turns his attention to the presenting problem. It is these behaviors that the client has sought to change and it is therefore the behavioral social worker's responsibility to attend to their modification. Behavior, therefore, is not seen merely as a superficial manifestation of underlying conflicts but is the central focus of clinical intervention. The behavioral social worker focuses squarely on the presenting problem behaviors in specific observable terms and approaches them directly. This approach takes the control of the clinical process away from the clinician who now takes on the role of facilitator of the client's choice of available techniques to alter the behavior rather than as a manipulator of the interpersonal process. The principles and techniques of behavior change are shared openly with the client. Thus, in the behavioral approach, the power for behavior change is more evenly distributed between the client and the worker.

RESPONSIBILITY.   Although the client is given the knowledge and the tools with which to modify his own behavior, the behavioral social worker still takes full responsibility for his role in the helping process, because his contractual obligations require that he help the client to modify those specific behavioral problems for which professional assistance originally was sought. The behavioral social worker's knowledge of the principles of human development and behavior change and his training in clinical evaluation enable him to evaluate objectively the outcomes of any treatment program that he has devised for a particular client. If a particular behavioral program has proven to be ineffective in alleviating a client's distress, the behavioral social worker is ethically bound to investigate the possible reasons for its failure and to develop other means of altering the behavior based on substantive evidence.

The client, too, has a major role in the evaluation process. In this way, the helping relationship becomes a collaborative effort. The client is responsible for assessing his own role in any behavior change program that has been devised, and he must evaluate objectively whether he has fulfilled his part of the contractual agreement by carrying out the various behavioral assignments that are an integral part of any behavioral change program, such as completing a variety of homework assignments, keeping accurate charts and diaries, utilizing contingencies appropriately, and structuring the environment so that newly acquired behavioral patterns can be maintained.

The Preventive-Educative Role

A major dimension of the behavioral approach is the effect it has upon the role of the practitioner and the appropriate time when intervention is to be undertaken. The behavioral approach stresses the teaching-preventive component of social work intervention and deemphasizes the reparative-remedial role traditionally played by the clinical social worker. The behavioral social worker attempts to help the client learn how to exert control over his own behavior and over the environment in which he lives. In keeping with the preventive-educative role of active participant, the behavioral social worker shares his knowledge with his client, e.g., he may offer his expertise to prospective parents in the area of child rearing practices and behavioral management techniques drawn from social learning theory, or he may offer his services to individuals involved in intimate personal relationships who require guidance in the areas of financial management, problem solving, conflict negotiations, and communication skills. To educators and individuals who work with groups of children or institutionalized persons, the behavioral social worker can help implement programs for increasing group and individual performance, social participation, and acquisition of relevant prosocial behavior.

SCIENTIFIC TIES OF BEHAVIORAL SOCIAL WORK

It is common knowledge that learning theories rest upon a strong scientific base of empirical data. The learning approach to understanding human behavior began in the scientific laboratories where researchers employed animal experiments in order to test their beginning formulations about the possible causes of behavior. As experimentation progressed, empirically derived laws were developed according to the existing data base. Following the systematic collection of substantial data and the replication of numerous animal experiments which supported a law, learning experiments were undertaken with humans in order to test whether the principles that had been developed with animals would generalize (Powers & Osborne, 1976).

Such a sequential process in theory development and testing is dramatically different, however, from the manner in which other theories that social workers employ were developed. Such early theories began with global descriptions of human behavior without experimental data to support their postulates about human behavior. Adequate testing of these theories to alter human behavior has not occurred. This may be due to their structural unsoundness, lack of internal consistency, conceptual vagueness, and procedural weakness (Hall & Lindzey, 1970). Basic tenets and concepts of these theories have not been constructed in a logical, consistent, and testable fashion that would enable the prediction of human behavior. Moreover, appropriate behaviors that should be exhibited by the worker to facilitate client changes are not elaborated upon (Fischer, 1971, 1973a; Wodarski & Feldman, 1973). Although these theories do not lack descriptive richness and explanatory potency, they fail to offer highly specific and individualized treatment techniques, and their ability to reliably predict the future behavior of individuals remains to be demonstrated empirically. Predictive rather than descriptive theories give the behavioral worker the necessary conceptual tools to change behavior.

The behavioral social worker views practice as an experiment. Each technique is offered as a tentative hypothesis that awaits verification and global statements about causes of behavior, diagnosis, and treatment are avoided. The concepts used to explain and predict the behavior of both the client and the worker are always described in observable concrete terms so that communication is clear, open, and concise, not only between the worker and the client, but also between the worker and the other professionals who may be working concurrently with the client.

The behaviors of the social worker and the client always must have observable referents, i.e., any behavior must be described in such a manner that two or more persons can observe the behavior and agree that it has occurred. Such a procedure is essential if appropriate treatment procedures are to be devised. Data must be secured on all therapeutic interventions so that the worker can determine what effect the treatment attempts have produced. This provides the worker with the feedback necessary to assess whether a specific technique should be continued, treatment discontinued, or a given intervention program revised.

OVERVIEW OF THE APPLICATION OF BEHAVIORAL TECHNIQUES TO SOCIAL WORK PRACTICE

Opportunities for the application of techniques derived from behavior modification to social work practice are substantial. This section serves to highlight the possible applications. A further elaboration of theory, research, and illustrations of the application of the techniques is provided in each appropriate chapter. The roles that the behavioral social worker can play in a variety of agency settings are outlined below.

Children

FOSTER CARE.   The behavioral social worker develops behavioral management programs and appropriate parenting skills for both natural and foster parents. He trains parents of children to use contingency contracts, stimulus control and time out procedures to facilitate their development of social skills needed for effective adult functioning.

SCHOOLS.   He helps to decrease absenteeism; increase appropriate academic behavior such as reading comprehension, vocabulary development, and computational skills; increase interpersonal skills such as the ability to share and cooperate with other children and adults; and decrease disruptive behaviors.

JUVENILE COURTS.   The worker helps to decrease deviant behavior and increase prosocial behavior by contingency contracting. He programs significant adults to provide reinforcement for prosocial behavior, and develops programs for training children in those behavioral skills that will allow them to experience satisfaction and gain desired reinforcements through socially acceptable means.

CHILDREN PARTICIPATING IN COMMUNITY CENTERS.   He helps children to develop appropriate social skills, such as working together, participating in decision making, and making plans and decisions and successfully carrying them through.

OUTPATIENT CLINICS.   He helps clients to reduce anxiety, eliminate disturbing behavioral problems, define goals in terms of career and life-style, increase self-esteem, gain employment, solve problems both concrete and interpersonal, develop satisfying life-styles, and learn skills necessary for successful adult functioning in society.

Adults

FAMILY SERVICE.   The behavioral social worker helps in the development of marital interactional skills for effective problem solving and goal-setting behaviors, of better parenting behaviors, and of clearer communication structures to facilitate interaction among family members.

COMMUNITY MENTAL HEALTH CENTER.   He helps individuals to reduce anxieties through relaxation techniques; teaches self-control to enable clients to alter certain problematic behaviors; offers assertiveness training as one means of having personal needs met; helps in the acquisition of behaviors to facilitate interaction with family, friends, and co-workers.

PSYCHIATRIC HOSPITALS.   He uses token economies to help clients to acquire necessary prosocial behaviors for their effective reintegration into society, and structures clients' environments through the provision by significant others of reinforcement for the maintenance of appropriate social behaviors such as self-care, employment, social interactional skills, and so forth. Analogous emphasis is indicated for working with the retarded in institutions.

PUBLIC WELFARE.   He helps clients achieve self-sufficiency, learn effective child management and financial management procedures, and develop social behaviors, skills, and competencies that can be useful to gain employment.

CORRECTIONS.   He uses token economies to increase prosocial behaviors, to learn new job skills, to develop self-control, and problem-solving strategies which are not antisocial in nature, and so forth.

Summary

The behavioral approach to social work practice offers much promise for the social work profession. It provides an optimistic view of the person. It is based on empirical data and scientific findings. It makes available concrete tools for effective intervention, and, most importantly, it builds into the treatment process a problem-solving and evaluative component which is needed in the field of clinical social work at the present time.

In the chapters to follow we will indicate how behavior modification techniques can be incorporated into the practicing repertoires of clinical social workers. The necessary requisites for practicing behavioral social work also are elaborated. Chapter 2 provides a framework for understanding clinical interactional situations and how this relates to three major theories of behavior modification. Assessment, a necessary prerequisite to intervention, is covered in Chapter 3. In Chapters 4, 5, and 6, the three models of behavior modification: operant, respondent, and modeling are reviewed. In these chapters it is shown how techniques derived from these models can be applied to clinical practice. Techniques to modify marital interactions are covered in Chapter 7, where a variety of experimentally tested treatment techniques are reviewed and a stepwise procedure for conducting conjoint treatment with couples is presented. Cognitive behavior modification using self-control procedures, a relatively new approach to teaching self-control, is covered in Chapter 8. How behavioral techniques can be used in groups is covered in Chapter 9. The application of behavior modification at the macro level of intervention to alleviate social problems and to ensure the maintenance of behavior change through interpersonal strategies is reviewed in Chapter 10. A curriculum to train behavioral social workers is presented in Chapter 11. The

concluding chapter emphasizes the emerging trends in the field
of behavior modification.

REFERENCES

Azrin, N. H., Flores, T., & Kaplan, S. J. Job finding club: a group-assisted
program for obtaining employment. *Behavior Research and Therapy,*
1975, *13,* 17–22.

————, & Powers, M. A. Eliminating classroom disturbances of emotionally
disturbed children by positive practice procedures. *Behavior Therapy,*
1975, *6,* 525–534.

————, & Wesolowski, M. D. Theft reversal: an overcorrection procedure for
eliminating stealing by retarded persons. *Journal of Applied Behavior
Analysis,* 1974, *7,* 577–581.

Azrin, V. B., Azrin, N. H., & Armstrong, P. M. The student-oriented classroom: a method of improving student conduct and satisfaction. *Behavior
Therapy,* 1977, *8,* 193–204.

Ayllon, T., & Azrin, N. *The token economy.* New York: Appleton-Century
Crofts, 1968.

Bergin, A. E. The effects of psychotherapy: negative results revisited. *Journal
of Counseling Psychology,* 1963, *10,* 244–250.

————. Some implications of psychotherapy research for therapeutic practice. *Journal of Abnormal Psychology,* 1966, *71,* 235–246.

————. An empirical analysis of therapeutic issues. In D. Arbuckle (Ed.),
Counseling and psychotherapy: An overview. New York: McGraw-Hill,
1967. (a)

————. Further comments on psychotherapy research and therapeutic practice. *International Journal of Psychiatry,* 1967, *3,* 317–323.(b)

————. The evaluation of therapeutic outcomes. In A. E. Bergin, & S. L.
Garfield (Eds.), *Handbook of psychotherapy and behavior change: An
empirical analysis.* New York: John Wiley, 1971.

————. When shrinks hurt: psychotherapy can be dangerous. *Psychology
Today,* 1975, *6,* 96–104.

————, & Suinn, R. M. Individual psychotherapy and behavior therapy.
Annual Review of Psychology, 1975, *26,* 509–556.

Berk, R. A., & Rossi, P. H. Doing good or worse: evaluation research politi-
cally re-examined. *Social Problems,* 1976, *3*(3), 337–349.

Bijou, S. W. Behavior modification in teaching the retarded child. In C. E.
Thoresen (Ed.), *Behavior modification in education.* Chicago: The University of Chicago Press, 1973.

Bloom, M. *The paradox of helping: Introduction to the philosophy of scientific practice.* New York: Wiley, 1975.

——. Analysis of the research on educating social work students. *Journal of Education for Social Work,* 1976, *12*(3), 3–10.

——, & Block, S. R. Evaluating one's own effectiveness and efficiency. *Social Work,* 1977, *22*(2), 130–136.

Braukmann, C. J., & Fixsen, D. L. Behavior modification with delinquents. In M. Hersen, R. M. Eisler, & P. M. Miller (Eds.), *Progress in behavior modification* (Vol. 1). New York: Academic Press, 1975.

Briar, S. The casework predicament. *Social Work,* 1968, *13,* 5–11.

——, & Miller, H. *Problems and issues in social casework.* New York: Columbia University Press, 1971.

Browning, R., & Stover, D. O. *Behavior modification and child treatment.* Chicago: Aldine-Atherton, 1971.

Broadhead, R. S., & Rist, R. C. Gatekeepers and the social control of social research. *Social Problems,* 1976, *23*(3), 325–336.

Cohen, H. L. Behavior modification and socially deviant youth. In C. E. Thoresen (Ed.), *Behavior modification in education.* Chicago: The University of Chicago Press, 1973.

——, & Filipczak, J. *A new learning environment.* San Francisco: Jossey-Bass, 1971.

Eysenck, H. J. The effects of psychotherapy: an evaluation. *Journal of Consulting Psychology,* 1952, *16,* 319–324.

——. The effects of psychotherapy. In H. J. Eysenck (Ed.), *Handbook of abnormal psychology.* New York: Basic Books, 1961.

——. The effects of psychotherapy. *International Journal of Psychiatry,* 1965, *1,* 97–187.

——. *The effects of psychotherapy.* New York: International Science Press, 1966.

Fanshel, D. Sources of strain in practice-oriented research. *Social Casework,* 1966, *47,* 357–362.

Fischer, J. A. Framework for the analysis and comparison of clinical theories of induced change. *Social Service Review,* 1971, *45,* 110–130.

——. (Ed.) Interpersonal helping: Emerging approaches for social work practice. Springfield, Ill. Charles C Thomas, 1973. (a)

——. Is casework effective?: a review. *Social Work,* 1973, *18,* 5–22. (b)

Forehand, R., & Baumeister. Deceleration of aberrant behavior among retarded individuals. In M. Hersen, R. M. Eisler, & P. M. Miller (Eds.), *Progress in behavior modification* (Vol. 1). New York: Academic Press, 1976.

Foxx, R. M., & Azrin, N. H. The elimination of autistic self-stimulatory behavior by overcorrection. *Journal of Applied Behavior Analysis,* 1973, *6,* 1–14.

Gottman, J. M., & Leiblum, S. R. *How to do psychotherapy and how to evaluate it.* New York: Holt, Rinehart and Winston, 1974.

Graziano, A. M. (Ed.) *Behavior therapy with children.* Chicago: Aldine, 1971.

———. (Ed.) *Behavior therapy with children* (Vol. 2). Chicago: Aldine, 1975.

Hall, C. S., & Lindzey, G. *Theories of personality.* New York: John Wiley, 1970.

Hamblin, R. L., Buckholdt, D., Ferritor, D., Kozloff, M., & Blackwell, L. *Humanization process.* New York: John Wiley, 1971.

Hartman, A. But what is social casework? *Social Casework,* 1971, *52*(17), 411–419.

Henderson, R., & Shore, B. K. Accountability for what and to whom? *Social Work,* 1974, *19*(4), 387–388.

Hollis, F. Evaluation: clinical results and research methodology. *Clinical Social Work Journal,* 1976, *24,* 204–222.

Hunt, G. M., & Azrin, N. H. A community-reinforcement approach to alcoholism. *Behavior Research and Therapy,* 1973, *11,* 91–104.

Jacobson, N. S., & Martin, B. Behavioral marriage therapy: current status. *Psychological Bulletin,* 1976, *83*(4), 540–556

Kazdin, A. E. *Behavior modification in applied settings.* Homewood, Ill.: The Dorsey Press, 1975. (a)

———. Recent advances in token economy research. In M. Hersen, R. M. Eisler, & P. M. Miller (Eds.), *Progress in behavior modification* (Vol. 1) New York: Academic Press, 1975. (b)

Knox, D. *A behavioral approach to marital happiness counseling.* Champaign, Ill.: Research Press, 1971.

Lewinsohn, P. M. The behavioral study and treatment of depression. In M. Hersen, R. M. Eisler, & P. M. Miller (Eds.), *Progress in behavior modification* (Vol. 1). New York: Academic Press, 1975.

Lovaas, O. I., & Koegel, R. I. Behavior therapy with autistic children. In C. E. Thoresen (Ed.), *Behavior modification in education.* Chicago: The University of Chicago Press, 1973.

Maas, H. S. *Five fields of social service: Reviews of research.* New York: National Association of Social Workers, 1966.

———. *Research in the social services: A five year review.* New York: National Association of Social Workers, 1971.

Mahoney, M. M. Reflection on the cognitive-learning trend in psychotherapy. *American Psychologist,* 1977, *32*(1), 5–13.

Margolies, P. J. Behavioral approaches to the treatment of early infantile autism: a review. *Psychological Bulletin,* 1977, *84*(2), 249–264.

Marks, I. Behavioral treatments of phobia and obsessive-compulsive disorders: a critical appraisal. In M. Hersen, R. M. Eisler, & P. M. Miller (Eds.), *Progress in behavior modification* (Vol. 1). New York: Academic Press, 1975.

Marks, R. B. Has social work failed? *Social Service Review,* 1972, *46*(3), 427–431.

Mintz, M., Freitag, P., Hendricks, C., & Schwartz, M. Problems of proof in elite research. *Social Problems,* 1976, *23*(3), 314–324.

Mullen, E. J., & Dumpson, J. R. *Evaluation of social intervention.* San Francisco: Jossey-Bass, 1972.

National Association of Social Workers. *Code of ethics.* Washington, D.C.: N.A.S.W., 1967.

Newman, E., & Turen, J. The crisis of accountability. *Social Work,* 1974, *19,* 5–16.

O'Leary, D. K., & Wilson, G. T. *Behavior therapy applications and outcome.* Englewood Cliffs, N.J.: Prentice-Hall, 1975.

Patterson, G. R. An application of conditioning techniques to the control of a hyperactive child. In L. Krasner, & L. P. Ullmann (Eds.), *Case studies in behavior modification.* New York: Holt, Rinehart & Winston, 1965.

———. *Families: application of social learning to family life.* Champaign, Ill.: Research Press, 1971.

———. Reprogramming the families of aggressive boys. In C. E. Thoresen (Ed.), *Behavior modification in education.* Chicago: The University of Chicago Press, 1973.

———, & Gullion, M. E. *Living with children: New methods for parents and teachers.* Champaign, Ill.: Research Press, 1968.

———, Jones, R., Whitter, J., & Wright, M. A. A behavior modification technique for the hyperactive child. *Behavior Research and Therapy,* 1965, *2,* 217–226.

Patterson, L. R., Reid, J. B., Jones, R. R., & Conger, R. E. *A social learning approach to family intervention. Vol. 1: Families with aggressive children.* Eugene, Ore.: Castalia Publishing, 1975.

Powers, R. B., & Osborne, J. G. *Fundamentals of behavior.* New York: West, 1976.

Rose, S. D., Cayner, J. J., & Edleson, J. L. Measuring interpersonal competence. *Social Work,* 1977, *22*(2), 125–129

Rosenberg, M. L., & Brody, R. The threat or challenge of accountability. *Social Work,* 1974, *19*(3), 344–350.

Schuerman, J. R. Do family services help? an essay review. *Social Service Review,* 1975, *49*(3), 363–375.

Segal, S. P. Research on the outcome of social work therapeutic interventions:

a review of the literature. *Journal of Health and Social Behavior,* 1972, *13,* 3–17.

Stuart, R. B. Research in social casework and group work. In R. Morris, (Ed.), *Encyclopedia of social work* (Vol. 2). New York: National Association of Social Workers, 1971.

Tavormina, J. B. Relative effectiveness of behavioral and reflective group counseling with parents of mentally retarded children. *Journal of Consulting and Clinical Psychology,* 1975, *43*(1), 22–31.

Thomas, E. J. Selecting knowledge from behavioral science. In *Building social work knowledge.* New York: National Association of Social Workers, 1964.

———. (Ed.) *Behavioral science for social workers.* New York: The Free Press, 1967.

Tropp, E. Expectation, performance and accountability. *Social Work,* 1974, *19*(2), 139–148.

Wodarski, J. S., & Feldman, R. A. The research practicum: a beginning formulation of process and educational objectives. *International Social Work,* 1973, *16*(4), 42–48.

———, Hudson, W., & Buckholdt, D. Issues in evaluative research: implications for social work practice. *Journal of Sociology and Social Welfare,* 1976, *4*(1), 81–113.

Wolpe, J. *The practice of behavior therapy.* New York: Pergamon, 1973.

Yates, A. J. *Behavior therapy.* New York: John Wiley, 1970.

Chapter 2

BASIC THEORETICAL FRAMEWORK

Three theoretical frameworks form the foundation for behavioral social work; to wit, the respondent, operant, and modeling paradigms of learning. Recent research and theoretical thinking indicate that the lines between these paradigms and other learning theories are not as clear cut as was believed to be in the past (Franks, 1969; Franks & Wilson, 1975). It is now believed that a clinical situation contains elements of all three of these models that may be operating simultaneously and that new paradigms of learning are needed to explain and predict behavior. In the following chapters we will separate these models according to techniques derived from each theoretical framework to give the reader a historical perspective on the development of behavioral social work. In this chapter the behavioral exchange model is presented as one that can help us conceptualize more adequately clinical phenomena, and thus gain power to influence these phenomena. Initially we will review briefly the elements of the respondent, operant, and modeling theories and various theoretical principles that can be combined with behavioral

a cognitive map which is an internal representation of his environment and influences the behavior he exhibits. This mental map includes knowledge of relationships between various stimuli and behavior, reinforcement schedules, and expectations of reinforcement and punishment. Social learning theory places a special emphasis on the roles played by observation, and symbolic and self-regulatory processes in controlling behavior, that is, in the acquisition and maintenance of behavior. The leading social learning theorist, Albert Bandura, believes that traditional theories of learning generally depict behavior as a product of directly experienced behavioral consequences. He indicates that much of learning can occur on a vicarious basis through observation of other people's behavior and its consequences. It is interesting to note that social learning theory places greater emphasis on unobservable concepts than do the respondent and operant models (Parke, 1972).

For Bandura, reinforcement serves basically an informative and incentive function and has response-strengthening capabilities. He postulates that most human behavior is not controlled by immediate external reinforcement, but is learned, instead, through the influence of behavioral examples and observations, either deliberately or inadvertently, i.e., by observing others, individuals choose behavior that will bring them the greatest rewards at the least cost.

Reinforcement-focused theories of behavior assume that novel (original) responses must be reinforced in order to be learned. For social learning theories learning can occur through the observation of model behavior and accompanying cognitive activities without extrinsic reinforcement. Extrinsic reinforcement increases the probability that the individual will perform the behavior, however.

The social learning theory of Albert Bandura sees reinforcement as a facilitator rather than as a necessary condition for learning. It seeks to account for factors other than consequences of a response that can influence the organism's behavior. Social learning theory introduces higher mental processes and cognitive processing skills as viable concepts for behavior modification practice. The theory states that one does not have to be reinforced to acquire new behaviors. Thus, people can learn new behaviors through observation without direct reinforcement. Social learning theory forms many of the foundation blocks for cognitive behavior modification elaborated in Chapter 8. A greater discussion of social learning theory will occur in Chapter 6.

In summary, all three paradigms capture a part of the learning process. The respondent focuses on the association between events, the operant emphasizes the antecedents and consequences and their relationships toward controlling behavior, and modeling delineates cognitive processes and their role in the learning of new behaviors.

THEORETICAL PRINCIPLES

Many empirically based principles derived from other social science disciplines are closely related to behavior modification practice and enhance the application of behavioral techniques. The worker should apply these concepts along with the appropriate behavioral procedures. Such a combination increases the probability that the worker can alter the client's behavior. In the following sections we conceptualize the relationship formation and continuance process, which are essential elements of successful therapeutic practice, in terms of exchange theory, and we review principles involved in the formation and maintenance of the therapeutic relationship.

Basic Elements of the Clinical Situation

The clinical situation can be conceptualized as containing five basic elements:

1. Client behaviors. These include general interactional behaviors and behaviors that need modification.

2.   Worker behaviors. These include general clinical skills such as empathy, unconditional positive regard, interviewing skills, and so forth.

3.   The interaction that takes place between the client and the worker, i.e., the exchange of verbal and nonverbal behaviors.

4.   The context of the interaction. These include various items that influence the worker's and the client's behavior. The agency influences the worker's behavior in:

1.   how the worker perceives and evaluates the client's behaviors

2.   how much change the worker believes can take place in the client

3.   the structure of the interactions in terms of duration, frequency, and so forth.

Likewise, the agency influences the client's behaviors in terms of expectations for change, how the worker will proceed, behaviors the client is expected to exhibit, i.e., the client's understanding of the therapeutic process in regard to his role in the change process and his relationship with the therapist, and so forth.

5.   Influence attempts involving the operations employed by the worker to achieve behavioral change in the client, i.e., the application of techniques from the respondent, operant, and modeling paradigms.

Rationale for the Choice of the Exchange Model

The exchange model of human behavior provides a framework that can incorporate elements of all of the three basic learning paradigms. It provides a calculus for viewing the worker-client system as a reciprocal influence process that no other model provides. That is, the intervention process in social work practice heretofore has been conceptualized as a one way influencing process. The exchange model provides a proper emphasis in the reciprocal influence of client and worker's behavior. It views the organism as possessing cognitive processing attributes that influence behavior, and the organism learns through feedback it gains by operating on its environment (Greeno & Bjork, 1973; Schroder & Suedfeld, 1971; Slovic, Fischhoff, & Lichtenstein, 1977). Such a focus provides an umbrella for the new focus of behavior modification called cognitive behavior modification and does alleviate one of the criticisms levied against behavior modification, to wit, failure to focus on cognitive processes.

COMPONENTS.   All professionals agree that the relationship formed between a client and a change agent is an essential factor in producing behavior change whether the focus of change is at the micro or macro level of intervention. However, of all theories of human behavior, only the exchange theory focuses on the interactional process that occurs between the two parties in the formation of a therapeutic relationship. One of the positive benefits of employing exchange theory as a model for conceptualizing the process of relationship formation and its maintenance is this dual focus on the participants in the interactional situation (Gergen, 1969).

The interactional situation is viewed as being composed of a series of exchanges of behavior occurring between the client and the worker. Either participant can start the interactions and/or terminate them. During the interactions the patterns of exchange that can take place are unlimited. The diagram presented below contains the basic elements of the interactional situation.

Possible Pool of Behaviors for Both Worker and Client

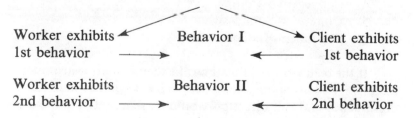

Each participant brings to the interactional situation a pool of potential behaviors, i.e., all of the behaviors in the client's and worker's repertoires. Every behavior of the worker and client has certain reward and cost values. Two sets of variables set limits on the type of behavior that can be exhibited by the client and worker. Endogenous variables consist of biological and psychological properties such as genetic make-up, past conditioning, and so forth. Exogenous variables are mainly sociological items such as norms, roles, and organizational constraints. Thus these variables limit the kinds of behaviors a client or worker can exhibit (Rosen, 1972). For example, a worker who has a strong aversion to abortion may not be able to help a client secure one.

FACTORS INFLUENCING THE FORMATION OF THE RELATIONSHIP

Range of Behavior

Compatibility of behaviors exhibited by worker and client definitely influences whether or not the relationship will be formed and continued. The range of possible behaviors which both client and therapist may exhibit can be conceptualized in terms of the following bi-polar dimensions:

1. Warmth–Hostility
2. Nondirective–Directive
3. Accepting–Rejecting
4. Cooperative–Competitive
5. Dominant–Submissive
6. Dependent–Independent

If the behaviors exhibited by the therapist are warm, nondirective, and accepting, complementary behaviors such as independence and self-direction would be required of the client in order for a working relationship to develop which is reinforcing for both participants (Carson, 1969). On the other hand, a dominant and directive therapist would require cooperative, submissive, and dependent behaviors on the part of the client in order for therapy to proceed satisfactorily. If a client were to exhibit independent and competitive behaviors, however, the therapeutic relationship would not be experienced as rewarding by either individual. Costs would outweigh rewards and it is likely that therapy would be terminated. Moreover, it is important to realize also that the exhibition of any set of behaviors will tend to elicit a similar behavioral response in the recipient (Gouldner, 1960). This is especially true for negative behaviors (Patterson & Reid, 1970). Therefore, a hostile, dominant, and rejecting set of behaviors exhibited by the therapist will most probably encourage a client to reciprocate similar responses in the therapeutic interview. If retaliatory hostility is made impossible by institutional constraints such as might occur in psychiatric hospitals, prisons, and half way houses, the client may resort to hostile submission in order to retaliate (Emerson, 1962, 1964), that is, to reciprocate the coercion and aversive control.

Aims of the Interactional Situation

The major goal of the participants in the interactional context is to engage in behaviors that bring them the greatest pleasure at the least cost (Thibaut & Kelley, 1959). Client and workers evaluate the behaviors exhibited on two reference points. The comparison level for the current interactional situation consists of evaluating the rewards and costs secured in the current interactional situation as compared to all others in which the client and/or worker has been involved in the past. Additionally, the interactional situation is evaluated against the hypothesized reinforcement value of other interactional situations available to the client and/or worker as alternatives. This evaluation process forms the foundation for practice since how the client and worker evaluate the current interactional situation influences: 1) their continuance or discontinuance in the formation of a therapeutic relationship, and 2) the power of each participant in future interactions.

Forming the Relationship

Whether or not the client and worker decide to form a therapeutic relationship depends on several processes. One critical process concerns the hypothesis that both form regarding the rewards that are possible from the interactional situation. The basic components of the hypothesis are:

1.   The interaction will continue if both participants can receive more rewards than other available interactional situations provide.
2.   How sure they are of no. 1.
3.   Behaviors of each participant have to be compatible in order for the interaction to be rewarding. Several factors which are elaborated below influence the formation of these hypotheses (Jones & Gerard, 1967).

Perception of Others

The perceptions of the worker and client are related to the concept of stimulus generalizability; that is, certain stimuli have positive or negative qualities due to their similarities to other stimuli that have been paired with negative or positive stimuli in the past. During the first few behavioral exchanges that occur, both participants are provided cues that influence how they perceive the other as a source of reinforcement. A variety of variables influence the formation of the hypothesis regarding the perception of the other's reinforcement potential. These primarily can be grouped into the past experiences of interactors with persons of similar verbal, physical, and social characteristics. For the client the therapeutic interactional situation contains many elements that are unlike real life interactional situations (Hastorf, Schneider, & Polefka, 1970). The client may characterize the interactional situation as being strange; that is, the acceptance, undivided attention, active listening, and so forth provided by the worker are atypical of their social interactions. The worker's ability to put the client at ease will increase the probability that the client will continue treatment.

Certain of the therapist's resources and attributes such as status, modeling of competent behaviors, ability to reduce anxiety, and ability to help the client solve initial concerns will influence the client's perception of the worker's power to help him secure additional rewards. Thus, as the worker's power increases, the probability that the client will stay in the interactional situation increases. For the worker different variables influence the perception of the client such as verbal ability, physical and social attractiveness, listening behaviors, and carrying out treatment plans, and influence the likelihood of the worker desiring to continue interacting with the client (Luborsky, Chandler, Auerbach, Cohen, & Bachrach, 1971).

Primacy

Research indicates that the first exchanges are of utmost importance in deciding whether or not a client or worker will be inclined to continue forming the relationship. The client's evaluation of the worker's behavior is probably more critical than vice versa since the worker has been trained to exhibit a certain amount of self-discipline. Through the first few behavioral exchanges the client cognitively develops a hypothesis about how reinforcing the interaction will be and how many costs are involved in continuing to form the relationship. Thus, beginning interactions should involve a minimal amount of punishing behaviors exhibited by the worker (Braun, 1976).

Attractiveness

The client will be more attracted to a worker who can secure rewards for him. Likewise, the worker will be more attracted to a client who will bring him rewards. Other items that control the amount of attraction between a worker and client are how similar they are on various physical and social characteristics, such as education, attitudes on relevant issues, age, verbal ability, social skills, and various interests. The worker will be seen as more attractive if treatment plans are developed and implemented and if the implementation alleviates the client's anxiety and difficulties. Moreover, the client's participation in the formulation of treatment and execution of plans will be rewarding to the worker thus increasing the client's reinforcement value (Byrne & Griffitt, 1973; Goldstein, 1971; Huston, 1974; Kanouse, 1971; Kelley, 1971; Levinger & Snoek, 1972).

Expectations

If both worker and client have positive expectations of change the probability is increased that both participants will remain in the interactional situation. Research indicates that the more positive the expectations between the interactional participants the higher the probability of positively reinforcing exchanges taking place. Likewise, the more negative the expectations, the more likely the relationship will be characterized as a series of negative behavioral exchanges thus reducing the attractiveness for each participant. The cues for the communication of positive or negative expectations occur through verbal and nonverbal channels. Recent research suggests that the worker's characteristics such as being likeable, dominant, relaxed, and competent, and his exhibiting low anxiety and hostility are variables that facilitate the communication of expectations. Thus, how each participant labels the clinical situation influences the continued formation of the relationship (Goldstein, 1973; Lewis, 1972).

FACTORS INFLUENCING THE MAINTENANCE OF THE RELATIONSHIP

A crucial element affecting the ability to alter a client's behavior is his decision to remain in therapy. Dropout rates are extremely high for all professions concerned with interpersonal helping. The following items are considered to increase the probability that the client will continue treatment so that behavioral techniques may be used for an ample period of time to allow for modification of his behaviors.

Minimal Use Of Punishment

If the worker wishes to increase participation and cooperation of the client the use of punishment should be minimal. A substantial use of punishment simultaneously may increase the probability that 1) the worker will lose reinforcing power, 2) the client will quit, and 3) the client may develop aggressive behavior toward the worker. Research conducted on lower organisms, as well as on children, indicates that punishment is an ineffective means of eliminating or modifying long-term behavior. Punishment frequently eliminates undesirable behavior, but it also tends to generalize to other desired behaviors, eliminating them as well. Moreover, the worker who punishes often becomes an aversive stimulus to his clients, thus hindering development of a positive therapeutic relationship. Finally, punishment may result in the emergence of new aggressive responses on behalf of the person being punished (Brush, 1971; Campbell & Church, 1969; Reese, 1966). Instead of punishment the worker should emphasize positive reinforcement of any behaviors that contribute to the enhancement of clients' prosocial repertoires. In this manner he can augment his referent power, demonstrate his ability to serve as a change agent, and increase the client's attraction to the therapeutic context.

Contracting (Providing Structure)

The worker should utilize the technique of contracting (structuring) with the client; that is, he should help the client develop clear and explicit treatment objectives. In the initial, and even in subsequent sessions, he should state clearly the objectives that are operative and the specific goals of the therapy, including how the client is expected to participate and what the worker's duties are. This process in itself is highly reinforcing for the client since it adds structure to the therapeutic situation (Reid & Epstein, 1972; Goldstein, Heller, & Sechrest, 1966). In addition, a situation in which the worker and client agree on a contract provides a context wherein the worker's influence over the client is greater than in low agreement contexts (Goldstein & Simonson, 1971). Periodically the worker and client should review what progress is being made toward the objectives. Such a process is reinforcing and provides the opportunity for new goals to be formulated.

Schedules of Reinforcement

Schedules of reinforcement delineate how, and with what frequency, clients' various behaviors will be reinforced. These schedules control both the acquisition and the maintenance of clients' behaviors. Initially, it is essential to reinforce a behavior continuously while it is being established but, conversely, in order to ensure its maintenance after therapy, not to reinforce it every time after it has been established. Otherwise, the behavior will be subject to rapid extinction. Likewise, initial goals that the client can achieve should be chosen. Choosing attainable goals and a proper schedule of reinforcement is a key to successful modification of behavior.

There are five basic schedules of reinforcement: continuous, fixed-ratio, fixed-interval, variable-ratio, and variable-interval. Only these five basic schedules will be discussed here. An elaboration of more complex schedules for social work practice, such as multiple schedules, await further conceptual development. On a continuous reinforcement schedule, the appropriate responses of an individual are reinforced every time that they occur. This schedule keeps an individual responding at a high rate for certain periods of time, even when he has been minimally deprived of the reinforcer because he has secured large numbers of them previously. However, by reinforcing each response satiation may occur and the reinforcer loses its reinforcing value to the organism. On the continuous schedule the target individual learns to expect a reinforcer every time that he exhibits the desired behavior. But once the behavior is established, if reinforcement does not follow display of the desired behavior, its rate of occurrence will decrease rapidly.

Fixed-interval reinforcement schedules make the reinforcement of an appropriate response contingent on the passage of a fixed interval of time since occurrence of the preceding reinforced response. An individual on this schedule will decrease temporarily his response rate after the reinforcement. His response rate will only increase as the next reinforcement interval approaches (Bachrach, 1962). Through use of such a schedule with normal children, Long and his associates (1958) were unable to maintain the stability of learned responses. Data indicate that this schedule is the least stable for the sustained control of human behavior. Moreover, behaviors that are produced by the first such reinforcements tend to decrease in frequency through time even when they are reinforced at fixed intervals (Reese, 1966). Variables which account for this instability are: 1) undue deprivation of reinforcement, i.e. length of time that the individuals have gone without reinforcement; 2) reinforcement quantity, i.e. the size or quantity of the reinforcer to be used; and 3) novel stimuli, i. e., characteristics of the environmental context which may deter effective response patterns.

An individual who is reinforced each time that he emits a certain number of responses is on fixed-ratio reinforcement schedule. Individuals on this schedule consistently perform at a high rate. However, certain problems such as a reduction in the frequency of the desired behavior, can occur when the ratio size is increased too quickly. Likewise, an individual can accumulate an extremely large number of reinforcements, thus decreasing the size of the response ratio and, ultimately, decreasing his response rate.

On a variable-ratio reinforcement schedule, the number of responses that must be emitted for an individual to secure a reinforcer tend to vary around a certain mean. Theoretically, this schedule should generate the highest rates of responding. Orlando and Bijou (1960) who used this schedule with retarded children found that their subjects responded at an exceedingly high rate. On a variable-interval reinforcement schedule, the interval of time during which reinforcers are available to an individual varies around a certain mean. When this schedule is correctly constructed it eliminates the cyclical variations characteristic of the fixed-interval schedule. Data collected by Long and his associates (1958) indicate that this schedule is effective in producing stable behavior in normal children. As a rule, behaviors that are conditioned on variable-ratio or variable-interval schedules are maintained longer than are behaviors conditioned on continuous, fixed-interval, or ratio schedules (Krasner & Ullmann, 1965).

Available data suggest that continuous reinforcement schedules should be used for the acquisition of behaviors in social work practice. However, once behaviors are acquired, reinforcements should be provided on an intermittent basis in order to ensure the maintenance of those behaviors. This is particularly important since continuous schedules are highly susceptible to extinction. Variable-ratio and variable-interval schedules should maintain prosocial behavior learned in social work treatment for a longer period of time than continuous, fixed-interval, or fixed-ratio schedules.

It should be noted that Schwitzgebel and Kolb (1964) used variable-ratio and variable-interval schedules to sustain stable patterns of prosocial behavior among delinquents with whom they worked and found that a fixed-ratio schedule maintained a given behavior for a shorter period of time than did a variable-ratio or variable-interval schedule. In applying this finding to the stabilization of certain verbal skills among delinquents, such as the proper use of verb tenses, one should vary the number of responses that are reinforced. Similarly, one should vary the amount and number of primary reinforcers used to reinforce prosocial academic behaviors. If one decides to use an interval schedule, the period of time that elapses between reinforcement and nonreinforcement of a particular emitted response should be varied. A word of caution is in order, however, about the relationships posited, especially those concerning how different reinforcement schedules influence the behavior exhibited by clients. Many of these postulates, like those for other formulations, await extensive empirical verification. Nonetheless, unlike many other formulations, most of the postulates have been derived from a logically consistent theoretical framework supported by an increasing body of experimental studies. Thus, the reinforcement schedule is one of the essential variables of the modification plan that determine how long the behavior will be maintained after the termination of treatment.

Verbal Communication

Verbal communication is one form of behavior that represents both a consequence of preceding contingencies and a determinant of future social interaction within a treatment context. As a discrete behavioral category it, too, is subject to examination in terms of the theoretical framework set forth above. Such an analysis can lead to more accurate specification of the relationships between verbal communication and the emergence of prosocial behavior in clients. Rosen (1972) and Rosen and Lieberman (1972), for example, have conceptualized two communication variables—verbal congruence and content relevance—and have indicated how outcome values associated with each can influence the probabilities of clients remaining in a given interactional situation.

VERBAL CONGRUENCE.   Verbal congruence is defined as the extent to which two or more persons' verbal exchanges are related to one another. The more congruence in verbal exchanges, such as between worker and client, the more positively will those parties evaluate their social interaction. Similarly, as verbal exchanges become more congruent the probability of members' continuation within treatment is likely to increase (Duehn & Proctor, 1977). The foregoing postulate, although referring only to a single communication variable, would suggest the efficacy of homogeneous grouping of clients and workers, especially as regards language capacity and corresponding antecedents such as age and social class. Should a given treatment modality favor heterogeneous grouping, this postulate, at the minimum, would point to the desirability of pretherapy tutoring or coaching for selected members and/or workers.

CONTENT RELEVANCE.   Content relevance refers to the extent to which the content of an interactive response is perceived by a participant as relevant and admissible to his definition of the interactional situation. It can be postulated that the presentation of expected content in an interactional situation is likely to be highly reinforcing to all concerned and, consequently, that the situation itself will be evaluated positively by the participants. This postulate has been supported by much social work literature concerning the compatibility between role expectations held by clients and therapists (Aronson & Overall, 1966; Mechanic, 1961; Oxley, 1966; Rosenfeld, 1964; Sapolsky, 1965; Thomas, Polansky, & Kounin, 1967).

A substantial body of research indicates that a worker can influence client's future verbal behavior, such as the number of utterances, pauses between verbal exchanges, rates of speech, number of interruptions, length of silence between verbal exchanges, and length of verbal statements. Hence, if a therapist wishes to increase any of these behaviors he should model them (Matarazzo & Wiens, 1972; Matarazzo & Saslow, 1968; Salzinger, 1969) and engage in other behavior increasing activities, such as shaping and selective reinforcement, i.e , reinforcing the client's closer approximations to the desired behavior. For example, if a relevant treatment goal is to increase the client's rate of utterances the worker can reinforce the client's appropriate verbal responses to achieve this objective and model such behavior.

Self-Disclosure and Self-Involving Statements

In order for the therapeutic relationship to develop successfully and maintain itself, the client must perceive his interactions with the behavioral social worker to be real and genuine. The behavioral social worker must be able to convey his humanism to the client by involving himself in a meaningful relationship with the client. Research has shown that a client's willingness to make self-disclosing statements and to express himself freely are positively related to the therapist's ability to actively participate in the helping process by sharing his own personal feelings and emotional reactions with the client (Bloch & Goodstein, 1971; Carkhuff, 1969a, b; Cozby, 1973; Goodstein & Reinecker, 1974; Goodstein & Russell, 1977; Ivey, 1971; Jourard & Lasakow, 1958; Stone & Gotlib, 1975; Stone & Stebbins, 1975). Danish and Hauer (1973) have offered simple illustrations of effective self-involving responses in the therapeutic process. Self-involving statements are described as being:

1. Usually feeling statements rather than beliefs or thoughts.
2. Direct reports of feelings and emotions as opposed to indirect reports.
3. Centered around feelings and emotions, not intellectualizations about feelings and emotions.

4.   Focused on present feelings and emotions rather than on feelings in the past.

It should be kept in mind that the expression of feeling on the part of the social worker always should be done to aid the client in his understanding of his difficulties and to facilitate and enhance the development of the therapeutic relationship and therapeutic discussions.

Necessary Conditions for Client Change

A number of researchers have found repeatedly that certain therapists help to facilitate positive changes in their clients while a substantive proportion of professionally trained therapists are either ineffective or cause their clients to deteriorate (Bergin, 1966, 1967a, 1967b, 1971, 1975). Three interpersonal skills have been isolated that are characteristic of effective therapists and are referred to as "core conditions" (Truax & Mitchell, 1971). These are genuineness, nonpossessive warmth, and accurate empathic understanding. These three core conditions will be discussed briefly in order to familiarize the reader with them. They not only influence the client's continuation in treatment, but increase the probability of behavior change when applied with the appropriate behavioral technique.

Genuineness

A therapist is said to be genuine when the basis for the entire therapeutic process is the establishment of a genuine and nonexploitative relationship between himself and the client. The degree to which the therapist can be honest with a client will equal the degree to which he can be honest with himself. The genuine therapist strives continually for an egalitarian and full-sharing relationship with his clients. He behaves as a real, living, and breathing human being, and he is not defensive or silent or a passive blank screen who is unresponsive to his clients' needs. He is aware of and sincere with himself about the responses the client is eliciting in him, and he experiences the clinical interview as a real and meaningful interpersonal encounter. He responds to the client's needs and feelings as real and not as though they are transferential distortions in need of interpretation. Above all, the genuine therapist is himself, but in being himself he employs his genuine responses constructively. In summary, he is as real in the therapeutic encounter as he is in all the activities of his everyday life. This point is illustrated graphically by Carkhuff and Berenson (1967) who state: "If there can be no authenticity in therapy, there can be no authenticity in life" (p. 29).

A valid rating procedure for accurately identifying and discriminating five distinct hierarchically ordered levels of facilitative genuineness has been developed by Carkhuff (1969a, 1969b). For example, a therapist at Level I will make verbal responses to his client that are totally unrelated to what he appears to be feeling at the moment, or if the therapist's responses are genuine, they are totally negative and tend to have a destructive effect upon the client. At Level V, however, the therapist is completely spontaneous in his interactions and open to experiences of all types, both pleasant and hurtful, with the client. In the event of hurtful responses, however, the comments made by the therapist are employed constructively in order to open up further areas of inquiry for both the client and the therapist.

Nonpossessive Warmth

Warmth can be considered the physical expression of empathy. When a therapist is warm he provides the client with a nonthreatening, safe, trusting, and secure atmosphere in which to express himself. This atmosphere is created through the therapist's acceptance, love, and positive regard for each client as a free individual who is capable of making his own decisions.

Each client is seen as being a unique individual who is accepted unconditionally and valued by the therapist. The effective therapist communicates this acceptance nonverbally by the respectful manner in which he treats his clients and in his sincere attempts to understand their plight.

A fine discussion of this facilitative dimension is offered by Gazda (1973) who devised a four-level rating scale that can be used to discriminate facilitative levels of warmth from those responses that do not communicate the physical expression of empathy. Since warmth is communicated generally through a wide variety of nonverbal media, nonverbal behaviors are the central focus of this scale of measurement. The lowest level of warmth can be observed, for example, in facial expressions that indicate boredom, disinterest, or disapproval, and in bodily postures that indicate a disregard for the client, such as, attending to other tasks while the client is talking, not establishing eye contact with the client, or turning away from the client as he speaks. The highest level of warmth may be characterized by the therapist who is wholly attentive and responsive to the interaction thus allowing the client to experience complete acceptance. The therapist is physically closer to the client and may even make physical contact with the client at appropriate moments during the interaction.

Accurate Empathic Understanding

A therapist who is accurately empathic is one who is able to understand the world according to each client's unique perspective. He is able to accurately feel and experience the world as the client does. He can grasp the meaning that a particular experience has for the client, and he does not base his understanding of a client's difficulties upon preconceived notions or theoretical formulations that postulate universal conflicts or complexes that everyone must resolve. He is with the client on a moment-by-moment basis throughout each therapeutic encounter. He responds with a full awareness of who the client is, and he is capable of a comprehensive and accurate understanding of his deepest feelings.

Similar to the rating procedure for accurately assessing and discriminating facilitative genuineness, Carkhuff (1969a, b) has standardized a five-level rating scale to measure accurate empathic understanding in therapists. At Level I, a therapist communicates no awareness of even the most obvious feelings expressed by the client. The therapist may be bored, disinterested, or simply interpreting what the client is saying from a preconceived frame of reference that totally excludes the client. A therapist who is functioning at the fifth and highest level of empathic understanding, on the other hand, will respond accurately to all the client's deeper as well as surface feelings. Accurate empathic understanding of this type will enable the client not only to express feelings that he was unable to express previously, but to explore previously unexplored areas of human existence.

Investigations of these core conditions, genuineness, nonpossessive warmth, and accurate empathic understanding, and their effect upon treatment outcome began with the early work of Halkides (1958) and has continued to the present (Betz, 1963; Carkhuff, 1969a, b; Rogers, 1951, 1957, 1962; Rogers, Gendlin, Kiesler, & Truax, 1967; Rogers & Truax, 1967; Truax, 1962a, b, 1963; Truax & Carkhuff, 1967; Truax & Mitchell, 1968; Truax and Wittmer, 1971; Whitehorn, 1964; Whitehorn & Betz, 1954). The effectiveness of these therapist characteristics has been found to hold for a wide variety of therapists, regardless of their therapeutic orientation, physical characteristics, or socioeconomic status. Moreover, these core conditions have been shown to be effective in treating a large variety of client populations ranging from college students to hospitalized schizophrenics (Luborsky et al., 1971; Truax & Mitchell, 1971). High levels of genuineness, nonpossessive warmth, and accurate empathic understanding have been found to relate consistently to positive therapeutic outcome while low skill levels on these dimensions are associated with no change in client condition or client deterioration (Bergin, 1971; Truax & Mitchell, 1971).

THE DEVELOPMENT OF THE THERAPEUTIC RELATIONSHIP

The authors do not conceptualize the development of a therapeutic relationship as much different from the development of interpersonal relationships in general because all interpersonal relationships are believed to proceed toward greater cohesiveness only if both participants experience their interpersonal exchanges as more rewarding than existing alternatives (Altman & Taylor, 1973; Levinger & Snoek, 1972). From the initial attraction between client and therapist in the first meeting and the mutually negotiated contractual agreements between the two participants the relationship escalates to a point where communications are open and both parties make positive evaluations of each other based upon a mutual satisfaction with the exchanges experienced thus far. Such an evaluation fosters continued interaction and the cohesion produced is the basis for successful therapeutic progress. Both therapist and client should see this relationship as a mutually cooperative endeavor which is characterized by increased intimacy, self-disclosure, and empathic understanding if the client is to reach the final stage of the therapeutic process, i.e., attainment of the desired behavior changes previously negotiated, continued ability to resolve behavioral problems by employing the skills learned in therapy, and an increasing capacity to achieve desired goals with minimal help from professional sources.

It should be understood that at each stage of the relationship the client is evaluating his outcomes. If the client feels that the exchanges have been equitable he perceives his rewards as proportional to his investment in the therapeutic process, that is, the therapeutic process will progress to the next level of interaction. When therapy is conceptualized in this fashion, each step in the process is seen as being preceded by a decision to continue or terminate the association. If the interaction is seen as more rewarding than costly, the therapeutic process will continue. If costs outweigh profits, however, termination is likely.

Resistance

A behavioral view of no change or avoidance of change, i.e., resistance on the part of the client, can be understood as the client's inability to make behavioral changes because he perceives the effort that he will have to exert in order to modify his problem behaviors to be more costly than the rewards that will be gained if such changes are made. For example, a client who receives public assistance checks may be reluctant to undertake remedial job training if the efforts he will have to make, studying and preparing for this new position, will allow him to earn little more than he is already collecting from public assistance. Similarly, depressed clients or individuals receiving secondary gains for exhibiting particular behaviors may be poor candidates for therapy if in modifying their behaviors they will lose a variety of social reinforcers or will be required to perform tasks that are experienced as punishments.

Summary

In this chapter we have reviewed the basic learning theories and characterized the relational system that forms between the client and the worker as an exchange system. The behavioral exchange theory has been utilized to conceptualize the process that is occurring between the worker and the client as a mutual influence process. We have introduced the reader to the additional basic concepts necessary to successfully implement behavioral techniques in social work practice and have covered the requisites for the establishment and continuance of the treatment relationship. The chapter emphasizes the need to continue developing the conceptualization and delineation of those variables that lead to effective behavioral change processes. When such specifications become possible then social work theory will be placed on a sophisticated empirically based body of knowledge.

REFERENCES

Altman, I., & Taylor, D. A. *Social penetration: The development of interpersonal relationships.* New York: Holt, Rinehart and Winston, 1973.

Aronson, H., & Overall, B. Treatment expectations of patients in two social classes. *Social Work,* 1966, *11*(1), 35–41.

Bachrach, A. J. *Experimental foundations of clinical psychology.* New York: Basic Books, 1962.

Bergin, A. E. Some implications of psychotherapy research for therapeutic practice. *Journal of Abnormal Psychology,* 1966, *71,* 235–246.

————. An empirical analysis of therapeutic issues. In D. Arbuckle (Ed.), *Counseling and psychotherapy: An overview.* New York: McGraw-Hill, 1967. (a)

————. Further comment on psychotherapy research and therapeutic practice. *International Journal of Psychiatry,* 1967, *3,* 317–323. (b)

————. The evaluation of therapeutic outcomes. In A. E. Bergin, & S. L. Garfield (Eds.), *Handbook of psychotherapy and behavior change: An empirical analysis.* New York: John Wiley, 1971.

————. When shrinks hurt: psychotherapy can be dangerous. *Psychology Today,* 1975, *6,* 96–104.

Betz, B. Bases of therapeutic leadership in psychotherapy with the schizophrenic patient. *American Journal of Psychotherapy,* 1963, *11,* 1090–1091.

Bloch, E., & Goodstein, L. D. Comments on "Influence of an interviewer's disclosure on the self-disclosing behavior of interviewees." *Journal of Counseling Psychology,* 1971, *18,* 595–597.

Braun, C. Teacher expectation: Sociopsychological dynamics. *Review of Educational Research,* 1976, *46*(2), 185–213.

Broadhurst, P. L., Fulker, D. W., & Wilcock, J. Behavioral genetics. In M. R. Rosenzweig, & L. W. Porter (Eds.), *Annual review of psychology.* Palo Alto, Ca.: Annual Reviews Inc, 1974.

Brush, F. R. (Ed.) *Aversive conditioning and learning.* New York: Academic Press, 1971.

Byrne, D., & Griffitt, W. Interpersonal attraction. In P. N. Mussen, & M. P. Rosenzweig (Eds.), *Annual review of psychology.* Palo Alto, Ca.: Annual Reviews Inc., 1973.

Campbell, B. A., & Church, R. M. (Eds.) *Punishment and adversive behavior.* New York: Appleton-Century-Crofts, 1969.

Carkhuff, R. R. *Helping and human relations: A primer for lay and professional helpers. (Vol. 1) Selection and training.* New York: Holt, Rinehart and Winston, 1969. (a)

————. *Helping and human relations: A primer for lay and professional helpers. (Vol. 2). Practice and research.* New York: Holt, Rinehart and Winston, 1969. (b)

———— & Berenson, B. G. *Beyond counseling and therapy.* New York: Holt, Rinehart and Winston, 1967.

Carson, R. *Interaction concepts of personality.* Chicago: Aldine, 1969.

Cozby, P. C. Self-disclosure: a literature review. *Psychological Bulletin,* 1973, *19,* 73–91.

Danish, S. J., & Hauer, A. L. *Helping skills: A basic program.* New York: Behavioral Publications, 1973.

Deese, J., & Hulse, S. N. *The psychology of learning.* (3rd. ed.) New York: McGraw-Hill, 1967.

Duehn, W. D., & Proctor, E. K. Initial clinical interaction and pre-mature discontinuance in treatment. *American Journal of Orthopsychiatry.* 1977, *47*(2), 284–290.

Elkind, D. (Ed.) *Learning: An introduction.* Glenview, Ill.: Scott, Foresman, 1971.

Emerson, R. M. Power dependence relations. *American Sociological Review,* 1962, *27,* 31–41.

————. Power-dependence relations: two experiments. *Sociometry,* 1964, *27,* 282–298.

Franks, C. M. (Ed.) *Behavior therapy appraisal and status.* New York: McGraw-Hill, 1969.

————, & Wilson, G. T. (Eds.) *Annual review of behavior therapy and practice, 1975.* New York: Brunner/Mazel, 1975.

Gazda, G. M. *Human relations development: A manual for educators.* Boston: Allyn & Bacon, 1973.

Geigen, K. J. *The psychology of behavior exchange.* Reading, Ma.: Addison-Wesley, 1969.

Glaser, R. (Ed.) *The nature of reinforcement.* New York: Academic Press, 1971.

Goldstein, A. P. *Psychotherapeutic attraction.* New York: Pergamon, 1971.

————. *Structured learning theory.* New York: Academic Press, 1973.

————, Heller, K., & Sechrest, L. B. *Psychotherapy and the psychology of behavior change.* New York: John Wiley, 1966.

————, & Simonson, N. R. social psychological approaches to psychotherapy research. In A. E. Bergin, & S. L. Garfield. (Eds.), *Handbook of psychotherapy and behavior change: An empirical analysis.* New York: John Wiley, 1971.

Goodstein, L. D., & Reinecker, V. M. Factors affecting self-disclosure: A review of the literature. *Progress in Experimental Personality Research,* 1974, *7,* 49–77.

————, & Russell, S. W. Self-reports and reports of others. *Journal of Counseling Psychology.* 1977, *24,* 365–369.

Gouldner, A. W. The norm of reciprocity. *American Sociological Review,* 1960, *25,* 161–178.

Greeno, J. G., & Bjork, R. A. Mathematical learning theory and the new "mental forestry." In P. H. Mussen, & M. P. Rosenzweig (Eds.), *Annual review of psychology.* Palo Alto, Ca.: Annual Reviews Inc., 1973.

Guttman, N. On Skinner and Hull: a reminiscence and projection. *American Psychologist,* 1977, *33,* 327–328.

Halkides, G. *An investigation of therapeutic success as a function of four variables.* Unpublished doctoral dissertation, University of Chicago, 1958.

Hastorf, H., Schneider, J., & Polefka, *Person perception.* Reading, Ma.: Addison-Wesley, 1970.

Huston, T. L. (Ed.) *Foundations of interpersonal attraction.* New York: Academic Press, 1974.

Ivey, A. E. *Microcounseling: Innovations in interview training.* Springfield, Ill.: Charles C Thomas, 1971.

Jones, E. E., & Gerard, N. B. *Foundations of social psychology.* New York: John Wiley, 1967.

Jourard, S. M., & Lasakow, P. Some factors in self-disclosure. *Journal of Abnormal and Social Psychology,* 1958, *56,* 91–98.

Kanouse, O. E. *Language, labeling, and attribution.* New York: General Learning Press, 1971.

Kelley, H. H. *Attribution in social interaction.* New York: General Learning Press, 1971.

Krasner, L., & Ullmann, L. P. (Eds.) *Research in behavior modification.* New York: Holt, Rinehart and Winston, 1965.

Kimble, G. A. *Hilgard and Marquis' conditioning and learning.* New York: Appleton-Century-Crofts, 1961.

Levinger, G., & Snoek, J. D. *Attraction in relationship a new look at interpersonal attraction.* New York: General Learning Press, 1972.

Lewis, W. C. *Why people change.* New York: Holt, Rinehart and Winston, 1972.

Lieberman, D. A. (Ed.) *Learning and the control of behavior.* New York: Holt, Rinehart, and Winston, 1974.

Long, E. R., Hammack, J. F., May, F., & Campbell, B. J. Intermittent reinforcement of operant behavior in children. *Journal of the Experimental Analysis of Behavior.* 1958, *1*(4), 315–339.

Luborsky, L., Chandler, M., Auerbach, A. H., Cohen, J., & Bachrach, H. M., Factors influencing the outcome of psychotherapy: a review of quantitative research. *Psychological Bulletin,* 1971, *75*(3), 145–185.

Marx, M. H. (Ed.) *Learning interactions.* New York: Macmillan, 1970. (a)

———. (Ed.) *Learning process.* New York: Macmillan, 1970. (b).

———. *Theories.* New York: Macmillan, 1970. (c).

Matarazzo, J. D., & Wiens, A. N. *The interview.* Chicago: Aldine-Atherton, 1972.

Matarazzo, R. G., & Saslow, G. Speech and silent behavior in clinical psychotherapy. In J. L. Shlien, H. F. Hunt, J. D. Matazarro, & C. Savage (Eds.), *Research in psycho-therapy.* Washington D.C.: American Psychological Association, 1968.

McLaughlin, B. *Learning and social behavior.* New York: The Free Press, 1971.

Mechanic, D. Role expectations and communications in the therapist-patient relationship, *Journal of Health and Human Behavior,* 1961, *2*(3), 190–198.

Orlando, R., & Bijou, S. W. Single and multiple schedules of reinforcement in developmentally retarded children. *Journal of Experimental Analysis of Behavior.* 1960, *3*(4), 339–348.

Oxley, G. B. The caseworker's expectations and client motivation. *Social Casework,* 1966, *47*(7), 432–438.

Parke, R. D. (Ed.) *Recent trends in social learning theory.* New York: Academic Press, 1972.

Patterson, G. R., & Reid, J. B. Reciprocity and coercion: two facets of social systems. In C. Neuringer, & J. L. Michael, (Eds.), *Behavior modification in clinical psychology.* New York: Appleton-Century-Crofts, 1970.

Reese, E. P. *The analysis of human operant behavior.* Dubuque, Iowa: William C. Brown, 1966.

Reid, W. J., & Epstein, L. *Task-centered casework.* New York: Columbia University Press, 1972.

Ribes, E. Relationship among behavior theory, experimental research, and behavior modification techniques. *The Psychological Record,* 1977 *2,* 417–424.

Rogers, C. R. *Client centered therapy.* Boston, Ma.: Riverside Press, 1951.

———. The necessary and sufficient conditions of therapeutic personality change. *Journal of Consulting Psychology,* 1957, *22,* 95–103.

————. The interpersonal relationship: the core of guidance. *Harvard Educational Review,* 1962, *32,* 416–429.

————, & Truax, C. B. The therapeutic conditions antecedent of change: a theoretic view. In C. R. Rogers, G. T. Gendlin, D. V. Kiesler, & C. B. Truax, *The therapeutic relationship and its impact: A study of psychotherapy with schizophrenics.* Madison, Wisc.: University of Wisconsin Press, 1967.

————, Gendlin, G. T., Kiesler, D. V., & Truax, C. B. *The therapeutic relationship and its impact: A study of psychotherapy with schizophrenics.* Madison, Wisc.: University of Wisconsin Press, 1967.

Rosen, A. The treatment relationship: a conceptualization. *Journal of Consulting and Clinical Psychology.* 1972, *38*(3), 329–337.

————, & Lieberman, P. The experimental evaluation of interview performance of social workers. *Social Service Review.* 1972, *46*(3), 395–412.

Rosenfeld, J. M. Strangeness between helper and client: a possible explanation of non-use of available professional help. *Social Service Review,* 1964, *38*(1), 17–25.

Sapolsky, A. Relationship between patient-doctor compatibility, mutual perception and outcome of treatment. *Journal of Abnormal Psychology,* 1965, *70*(1), 70–76.

Salzinger, K. The place of operant conditioning of verbal behavior in psychotherapy. In C. M. Franks (Ed.), *Behavior therapy: Appraisal and status.* New York: McGraw-Hill, 1969.

Schroder, H. M., & Suedfeld, P. (Eds.) *Personality theory and information processing.* New York: Ronald, 1971.

Schwitzgebel, R., & Kolb, D. A. Inducing behavior change in adolescent delinquents. *Behavior research and therapy,* 1964, *1*(4), 297–304.

Slovic, P., Fischhoff, B., & Lichtenstein, S. Behavioral decision theory. In M. R. Rosenzweig, & L. W. Porter (Eds.) *Annual review of psychology.* Palo Alto, Ca.: Annual Review Inc., 1977.

Stone, G. L., & Gotlib, J. Effect of instruction and modeling on self-disclosure *Journal of Counseling Psychology,* 1975, *22,* 228–293.

————, & Stebbins, L. W. Effects of differential pretraining on client self-disclosure. *Journal of Counseling Psychology,* 1975, *22,* 17–20.

Tapp, J. T. (Ed.) *Reinforcement and behavior.* New York: Academic Press, 1969.

Thibaut, J., & Kelley, H. H. *The social psychology of groups.* New York: John Wiley, 1959.

Thomas, E. J., Polansky, N. A., & Kounin, J. The expected behavior of a potentially helpful person. In E. J. Thomas (Ed.), *Behavioral science for social workers.* New York: Free Press, 1967.

Truax, C. B. Comparison between control patients, therapy patients perceiving high conditions, and therapy patients perceiving low conditions on measures of constructive personality change. *Brief Research Reports,* Wisconsin Psychiatric Institute, University of Wisconsin Psychiatric Institute, University of Wisconsin, 1962, *31.* (a)

————. Variations in levels of accurate empathy offered in the psychotherapy relationship and case outcome. *Brief Research Reports,* Wisconsin Psychiatric Institute, University of Wisconsin, 1962, *38.* (b)

————. Effective ingredients of psychotherapy: an approach to unraveling the patient-therapist interaction. *Journal of Consulting Psychology,* 1963, *10,* 256–263.

————, & Carkhuff, R. R. *Toward effective counseling and psychotherapy: training and practice.* Chicago: Aldine, 1967.

————, & Mitchell, K. M. The psychotherapeutic and the psychonoxious: Human encounters that change behavior. In M. Feldman (Ed.), *Studies in psychotherapy and behavior change.* Vol. 1., *Research in individual psychotherapy.* Buffalo, N.Y.: State University of New York Press, 1968, 55–92.

————, & Mitchell, K. M. Research on certain therapist interpersonal skills in relation to process and outcome. In A. E. Bergin, & S. L. Garfield (Eds.), *Handbook of psychotherapy and behavior change: An empirical analysis.* New York: John Wiley, 1971.

————, & Wittmer, J. The effects of therapist focus on patient anxiety source and the interaction with therapist level of accurate empathy. *Journal of Clinical Psychology,* 1971, *27,* 297–299.

Whitehorn, J. C. Human factors in psychiatry. *Bulletin of New York Academy of Medicine,* 1964, *40,* 451–466.

————, & Betz, B. A study of psychotherapeutic relationships between physicians and schizophrenic patients. *American Journal of Psychiatry,* 1954, *3,* 321–331.

Williams, J. L. *Operant learning: Procedure for changing behavior.* Monterey, Ca.: Brooks/Cole, 1973.

Chapter 3

ESSENTIALS OF BEHAVIORAL ASSESSMENT

The goal of this chapter is to equip the reader with the fundamental tools necessary for accurate behavioral assessment, an essential element of effective behavioral intervention at all levels of social work practice, whether it be at the individual, group, organizational, or societal level (Gingerich, Feldman, & Wodarski, 1976). Rigorous training in behavioral assessment is considered to be a *sine qua non* for qualitative training and social work practice. Insufficient time spent on this process, no matter what powerful techniques the change agents possess, results in ineffective or irrelevant intervention since an accurate assessment of the client's difficulties has not occurred.

A major documented shortcoming of traditional verbal therapies is their reliance on and utilization of assessment systems that fail to offer even minimal utility for the assignment of clients to different treatment procedures. Such nosologies have been evaluated by other writers in terms of their lack of explicitness, precision, reliability, and empirical validity (Eysenck, 1952; Franks, 1969; Harrower, 1950; Hock & Zubin, 1953; Menninger, 1955; Mischel, 1968, 1971, 1972, 1973 a, b, c; Roe, 1949; Rogers, 1951; Rotter, 1954; Scott, 1968; Wachtel, 1973 a, b; Zigler & Phillips, 1960, 1961 a, b). More serious considerations are raised by 1) the continued reliance upon traditional psychiatric classification systems that fail to predict violent and dangerous behavior on the part of the client (Dix, 1976; Schwitzgebel, 1972); 2) the classic Rosenhan research that illustrates the inability of the traditional classification systems to detect the sane individual from the insane (Bem & Allen, 1974; Crown, 1975; Davis, 1976; Farber, 1975; Mariotto & Paul, 1975; Millon, 1975; Reed & Jackson, 1975; Rosenhan, 1973, 1975a, b; Spitzer, 1975; Weiner, 1975); and, finally, 3) the preliminary research which indicates that the more training professionals have in traditional systems, the less they are able to make accurate assessments of behavior (Crow, 1957; Case & Lingerfelt, 1974; Gingerich, Feldman, & Wodarski, 1976).

POSITIVE ASPECTS OF BEHAVIORAL ASSESSMENT

Behavioral assessment is based on three essential operations: 1) the analysis of target behaviors chosen for modification in terms of observable events; 2) definition of the behaviors in a manner that enables two persons to consistently agree that the selected behavior has occurred; and 3) the systematic collection of data to determine if selected antecedent or consequent events (behaviors) significantly influence the rate of the client's behavior chosen for modification (Baer, Wolf, & Risley, 1968; Bijou, 1970; Bijou, Peterson, Harris, Allen, & Johnston, 1969). Thus, modification of behavior is attempted from 1) events that occur before a client's behavior (antecedents), or 2) events that occur after a client's behavior (consequences). Depending on the client's behavior, the context of therapy, characteristics of the change agent, and so forth, techniques for the modification of behavior are chosen from either or both categories.

The positive aspects of behavioral assessment are its emphases on specification and measurement of goals and objectives for the intervention process. For instance, when working with antisocial children it is possible to specify and operationalize antisocial behaviors in terms of the following actions: hitting others, damaging physical property, running away, climbing out of windows, making loud noises, using aggressive verbal statements, throwing objects such as paper, candy, erasers, and chairs, and so forth. Likewise, positive behaviors to be exhibited by workers in modifying client behaviors can be quantifiable as to the amount of praise, directions, positive attention, positive physical contacts, and so forth, as can such negative behaviors as holding, criticism, threats, negative attention, and time-out. The final operation is the acquisition of data to determine whether the worker's behavior actually played a part in the modification of the client's behaviors. These procedures involve measuring the behaviors of clients and worker according to some quantifiable format, an essential focus in an age of accountability.

COMPONENTS OF BEHAVIORAL ASSESSMENT

The task of any behavioral assessment process is threefold in nature and can be conceptualized as follows:

1.   What are the dimensions of behavior that require change in terms of their frequency of occurrence, their intensity, and their duration?
2.   What are the conditions under which the target behaviors are acquired and maintained?
3.   What are the most effective procedures that the social worker can utilize in order to help the client either increase, decrease or acquire the target behaviors?

The learning approach to behavioral assessment is similar to the traditional psychiatric diagnosis approach, i.e., the posited need for a close relationship between assessment and treatment. However, a functional analysis of the behavior is made in order to ascertain the explicit environmental variables that control the observed behavior. The focus of such a functional analysis is always observable phenomena in the form of antecedent events, behavioral manifestations and their consequences. The unit of such an analysis is always the interactive relationship between the client's overt behavior and the surrounding environment. All behaviors are considered to be maintained by their antecedents and by the consequences they produce for the client. An accurate appraisal of these effects can provide the social worker with an understanding of their instrumental value. As reviewed in Chapter 2, behaviors that produce positive and reinforcing consequences will tend to be repeated, while those which bring about punishments or fail to produce reinforcements will tend to become extinguished.

Although knowledge of the reinforcement history through which certain problematic behaviors have been acquired will help the clinician understand why some behaviors are more difficult to extinguish than others, this knowledge is purely academic since it is not essential to the development of an appropriate behavior change program for the client. Since data provided by various researchers indicate that the alteration of behavior is not related directly to how the client acquired the behavior, the focus of behavioral intervention is always centered on the control and manipulation of the environment and the contingent outcomes that each behavioral performance produces for the client. Traditionally many theorists and researchers have postulated that the variables involved in the alteration of behavior are analogous to the variables involved in its acquisition. Data have not supported such a view of human behavior, however. The behavioral approach is concerned with the assessment of the individual in the context of his environment; thus, intervention procedures are always tailored to modify the specific environmental forces that are maintaining the problematic behaviors, and treatment is always designed to deal with the unique behavioral manifestations presented by each client.

Moreover, clients are not assigned to sociological categories, which research shows are not related to treatment nor are a causative factor of behavior. Behavior can be assessed on frequency, duration, and intensity. Certain factors will influence the social worker's choice of the dimension to assess, such as the behavior chosen for alteration, availability of technical equipment, and the context of measurement (Bijou et al., 1969).

Dimensions of Behavior

Frequency refers to the number of times a behavior occurs within a specific interval of time. The frequency dimension can be assessed easily by having clients observe, count, and record the number of times they exhibit specific behaviors. When observations of a particular behavior are made and recorded by more than one individual such as a client and a social worker, a client and his spouse or a client and his parents, a reliability check can be established as a prerequisite for evaluating the success of the modification program. For example, records can be kept to reflect the frequency with which cigarettes are smoked, loving statements are addressed to one's spouse, prosocial acts are learned by an autistic child, a child hits another child, incorrect language is used, aggressive statements are expressed, sexual intercourse occurs, or job applications are submitted.

If a social worker should decide to use a frequency measure, a fixed interval of time should be selected to observe the behavior. If this does not occur, then an accurate account of the behavior may not be achieved due to the influence of time. If the behaviors are observed under varying time lengths, the frequency should be reduced to a percentage score with controls for the confounding of frequency of the behavior by time.

The *duration* dimension can be assessed by measuring the length of time a behavior is exhibited in terms of seconds, minutes, hours, and so forth. For example, how long does it take a client to finish one cigarette, how much time is spent by a spouse in positive interactions with his or her mate, what is the duration of prosocial play engaged in by an autistic child, what were the number of minutes a child sat still at the dinner table, and how many days passed without marital discord. Although duration can be measured reliably some critical events may not occur for more than a split second but, nevertheless, occur at a high frequency. Thus, the duration dimension is not the most appropriate measure and a frequency count may be more meaningful.

The *intensity* dimension is somewhat more difficult to work with because human assessment of this dimension may often prove inaccurate. For this reason, technical equipment has often been employed to aid in the assessment of intensity. Some investigators have measured the intensity of such behaviors as crying and laughing as well as sexual excitation (Butterfield, 1974; Freund, 1971; Masters & Johnson, 1966).

TIME SAMPLING

Since it is virtually impossible to observe a client for any extended period of time in order to secure an accurate description of those behaviors which are under consideration, the time sampling procedure becomes a useful method of data collection. Research has shown that time sampling observations can give an accurate and reliable representation of behavior if they are correctly structured and executed (Wodarski, Feldman, & Pedi, 1975). The type of time sampling procedures that are utilized by the social worker will depend on the type of behaviors chosen for observation, i.e., frequency, duration, and intensity of the targeted behavior; the availability of technical equipment, electrical counters, and videotapes; the cost of securing various types of data, i.e., employment of observers; and the context of the measurement, such as behaviors that occur at inconvenient times and/or where observation is not possible. After the behaviors of clients and worker are operationalized, a nonparticipant observer is usually placed in the treatment context to collect data for the worker in order that he may concentrate on his modification plan. The use of behavioral observers to secure data, however, will not be feasible in most agencies because it is too expensive. It is possible that other workers could serve as observers at selected time periods. The behavioral observations facilitate the worker's ability to operationalize client and worker behaviors and provide the data necessary for the worker implementing the treatment to judge its effectiveness.

The critical question is how to structure observations in order to get an accurate representation of behavior. For example, if a social worker should decide that a frequency measure is the most appropriate measure of a client's behavior, a fixed interval of time should be selected to observe the target behavior. Observations should be structured in a way that would allow the worker to sample the client's behavior during various periods throughout the day and in a variety of situational contexts. If this is not done, an accurate account of the behavior may not be achieved due to the influences of time and situation. If the behaviors are observed under varying time lengths, the frequency could be reduced to a percentage score to control for the confounding of time. When a client is observed in a variety of situations the social worker can assess which environmental circumstances exert their influences to either elicit, maintain, decrease, or increase the incidences of problematic behaviors. In this way a frequency times situation analysis can be made.

REQUISITES FOR MEASURING BEHAVIOR

Behaviors must be defined in terms of observables and in such a manner that two or more people can agree that the behavior has occurred. Such a process establishes the reliability of the behavior (Baer, Wolf, & Risley, 1968; Bijou, 1970; Bijou et al.,

1969). Problems may arise if the behaviors are defined too globally, i.e., a child is defined as hyperactive, retarded, antisocial, autistic, and adults are classified as schizophrenic, psychotic, neurotic, and so forth. These categorical classification systems consist of behaviors that are too heterogeneous for an adequate specification of behavior. In these instances the behaviors are not operationalized adequately enough to provide reliable observations which are prerequisite to the execution of an accurate behavior analysis.

THE TARGET OF CHANGE

In the initial analysis of the referral situation, the critical question that should be asked by the behavioral social worker is "what behaviors are objectionable and to whom are they objectionable?" After these behaviors are isolated the worker needs to gather enough information about the difficulties to isolate who will be the target of intervention.

In many instances the individual mentioned in the referral process may not be the target of intervention. For example, a child may be referred for exhibiting the following behaviors: throwing objects, making loud verbal statements, nagging, and so forth in order to secure the attention of his parents. In such instances the behavioral social worker would want to teach the *parents* to reinforce appropriate behavior and to not provide discriminative stimuli for misbehavior, such as not attending to the child when he is exhibiting prosocial behavior.

WHERE ASSESSMENT SHOULD TAKE PLACE

Assessment should occur in the context from which the referral was made. For example, if a child is referred to a child guidance clinic for general antisocial behavior at school the assessment procedure should take place at the school rather than at the clinic. Assessment in the general environment in terms of current discriminative stimuli and reinforcement contingencies that are controlling the behavior enables a worker to secure a clear and more accurate account of the behavior. If a worker is dealing with marital discord the assessment should take place where the couple happens to quarrel most frequently. Even current simulation exercises to judge marital discord, family interaction, fear levels of an object, assertiveness, and so forth may be inaccurate if they are different from the context in which the behaviors occur, and other variables may control the client's behavior such as expectations and demand characteristics of the measurement context (Bernstein & Nietzel, 1974; Borkovec, 1972, 1973; Borkovec & Nau, 1972; Borkovec, Stone, O'Brien, & Kaloupek, 1974; Kazdin, 1973; Smith, Diener, & Beaman, 1974; Speltz & Bernstein, 1976; Tasto & Suinn, 1972; Tryon & Tryon, 1974).

CHARACTERISTICS OF BEHAVIOR

The behavioral social worker in the clinical context can help the client change the following aspects of his behavioral repertory:

1. Behaviors can be increased in their frequency. For example, a husband may need to show his wife more affection through verbal praise and physical contact.

2. Behaviors can be decreased in their frequency such as negative self-thoughts, smoking, and assaultive behavior.

3. Behaviors can be acquired such as development of language skills in autistic children.

4. The form of an already acquired behavior can be altered. For example, it can be connected to other discriminative stimuli, or the duration or intensity can be reduced or increased.

Thus, after the worker decides what behaviors of the client need to be changed, he or she must isolate the discriminative stimuli and consequences which are controlling the behavior, and choose appropriate modification procedures. The appropriate modification procedures to employ will be elaborated upon in Chapters 4 through 9.

TWO CRITICAL QUESTIONS

Does the client want to change? What will happen if the behavioral change does occur? Substantial empirical literature exists to indicate that a worker will be unable to help a client change his behavior unless the client is motivated to do so (Feldman & Wodarski, 1975; Goldstein, Heller, & Sechrest, 1966; Goldstein & Simonson, 1971; Reid & Epstein, 1972). Thus, a prerequuisite to the successful use of behavior modification techniques with clients is their desire to change. This can be assessed by the amount of home reading completed, information provided on events controlling the behavior, and the client's general consistency in applying the techniques.

Once a behavior is changed, what are the implications for the client, others in their environment, and the worker? Can the environment support and maintain the new behavior? That is, can the client and worker program the environment to maintain the change? For example, in work with delinquent children various research reports indicate that substantial change in academic and social behaviors can occur under controlled conditions. However, few studies provide data that indicate that these acquired behaviors can be supported by the client's original environment (McCombs, Filipczak, Friedman, & Wodarski, 1978; Wodarski & Filipczak, 1977).

INCENTIVE ANALYSIS

Once behaviors are chosen for modification an incentive analysis should be undertaken. Three avenues provide information about the client's incentive profile. Information can be developed on the incentives that the client will work for by observing the client, by asking significant others, and by giving the client a reinforcement survey (Cautela, 1972). The next critical step is to isolate those incentives that can be employed and are powerful enough to produce the desired change. Various factors will control the incentive powers of the various items chosen, such as how much of the item the client presently has, how much of the item the client has had in the past, how much others around the client have of the item, can the item be presented every time the behavior occurs, what quantity of the incentive can be employed, are other incentives that maintain the behavior too powerful, can the worker control these other incentives or punishments provided by others for the desired behavior.

TREATMENT ANALYSIS

Once the target of intervention is chosen the worker has to decide if there are any biological factors that may prohibit the client from achieving the behavioral goals, such as a child who needs glasses before behavior modification techniques can be used to teach him to read. Sociological factors may impede the modification in terms of significant others providing reinforcers for undesirable behaviors. In such instances the worker must decide whether the reinforcers the worker can provide the client outweigh the reinforcers provided by others or he must implement a strategy to change the reinforcing patterns of these significant others.

If the client is being taught to manage his own behavior an analysis of self-control potential must occur, such as is this client motivated to change? will the client read the necessary materials? will the client diligently record his behavior? and will he consistently implement the techniques? Moreover, an incentive analysis of the worker's reinforcing potential for the client has to take place and the critical question becomes does the worker possess those qualities that are attractive enough to the client in order to use himself as a motivator for change. If the worker does not have these characteristics the most appropriate change agent must be isolated.

In the treatment analysis the worker will want to consider with the client how much energy the client will have to engage and how taxing the intervention will be. Such a cost effective analysis is crucial to determining whether therapy should be initiated. The final consideration in the treatment analysis should be whether the monitoring of the treatment intervention can occur to provide essential data on how well the treatment is being implemented and its effects on client behavior in order to alter the treatment plan if no behavioral change is occurring.

THE CHANGE AGENT

The choice of a change agent should be decided on between the client and the worker. Who in the client's environment is in the best position to effect the behavioral change? The person chosen should be sufficiently attractive to the client in order to facilitate the interpersonal influence attempt. Empirical literature suggests that individuals make good therapists when they can maintain eye contact, smile frequently, and display interpersonal warmth, unconditional positive regard, acceptance, empathy, positive expectation for behavioral change, and so forth (Carkhuff, 1969, 1971; Carkhuff & Berenson, 1967; Rosenthal, 1966; Rosenthal & Rosnow, 1969; Wells & Miller, 1973; Vitalo, 1975).

Additional research suggests that a behavioral change agent should have considerable verbal ability, should be motivated to help others change, should possess a wide variety of social skills, and should have adequate social adjustment (Berkowitz & Graziano, 1972; Gruver, 1971). There is virtually no social work literature available to indicate what type of characteristics a worker should possess in order to help clients. Even though other social science disciplines are beginning to gather preliminary data concerning the attributes and skills of helping agents, much more research is needed to delineate such characteristics. Following explication of these skills, schools of social work should be able to develop more appropriate student selection measures and to create more effective technologies to facilitate the acquisition of requisite skills and attributes.

AIDS IN ASSESSMENT

Five techniques that can be used as aids in assessment are self-inventories, behavioral interviews, behavioral samples, behavioral diaries, and baselines. The critical aspect of any measure chosen is the reliability of the data provided. Thus, the data provided by any of these sources should be collaborated by others (Goldfried & Sprafkin, 1974).

Self-Inventories

A number of questionnaires are being developed that should facilitate the acquisition of information necessary for the behavioral social worker to make an accurate assessment. For example, inventories that measure the following are available:

> *Anxiety*—(Jeger & Goldfried, 1976; McCullough & Montgomery, 1972; Richardson & Tasto, 1976; Wolpe, 1973)
>
> *Assertiveness*—(Galassi, DeLo, Galassi, & Bastien, 1974; Galassi, Hollandsworth, Radecki, Gay, Howe, & Evans, 1976; Gambrill & Richey, 1975; Hersen, Eisler, & Miller, 1973; Rathus, 1973; Vaal, 1975)
>
> *Fear*—(Bernstein, 1973; Geer, 1965; Hersen, 1973; Klorman, Weerts, Hastings, Melamed, & Lang, 1974; Landy & Gaupp, 1971; Rutner & Pear, 1972; Spiegler & Liebert, 1970; Tasto & Hickson, 1970; Tasto, Hickson, & Rubin, 1971; Wolpe & Lang, 1964).

Marital Functioning—(Butterfield, Thomas, & Soberg, 1970; Carter & Thomas, 1973a, b; Knox, 1971; Thomas, Carter, Gambrill, & Butterfield, 1970; Thomas, Walter, & O'Flaherty, 1974).

Incentive Preferences—(Cautela, 1972; Cautela & Kastenbaum, 1967). The individual social worker will have to choose those which are most appropriate.*

Behavior Interviews

The clinical interview can provide a suitable setting to observe the client's reaction to certain stimuli. The client's reaction, i.e., how the client presents himself physically and verbally, handles stress, and so on, gives the social worker a cue as to how the client approaches various life situations and provides the opportunity to gather information about reinforcement preferences, the possible antecedents and consequences that control the behaviors chosen for modification, how motivated the client is to change, and finally, who would be the best mediators of change (Holland, 1970; Kanfer & Grimm, 1977; Thomas, 1974; Wahler & Cormier, 1970; Wolpe, 1970, 1973).

Behavior Samples

No information can substitute for the actual observation of the client in the environment in which the problematic behavior occurs. The process gives the worker an accurate picture of the discriminative stimuli and consequences that are operating in such an environment. For example, observing a child on the playground provides the worker with firsthand knowledge of his social interactional skills, how many discriminative stimuli

*A text recently published contains a majority of the inventories behavioral social workers will want to use to facilitate their practices. See Cautela, J. R. *Behavior analysis forms for clinical intervention*, Champaign, Ill.: Research Press, 1977.

for such behaviors (such as approaching behaviors, eye contact, touching, and smiling) are provided by other children, who provides them, and what consequences are provided after the child exhibits an interactional behavior, at what frequency, and by whom. Videotapes provide another means by which the worker can observe the client's behaviors. If the worker is dealing with a couple, he may ask them to videotape interactions in the home or videotape their behavior during a simulation task in his office.

Behavioral Diary

In many instances the worker will not be able to observe the client. In these instances clients and/or significant others can keep a diary containing certain information on the antecedents and consequences which control the behavior that can prove to be a valuable asset in the modification of the behavior. In many instances the worker will have to help the client structure the process (how to observe, when to observe, how to record, and so forth) for securing the necessary data on antecedents and consequences that control the behavior.

Baselines: A Prerequisite

A prerequisite for adequate behavior analysis is to secure a baseline prior to implementation of treatment. The best type of baseline measure is secured by trained behavioral observers. Usually these observers have been taught to establish reliability on behavioral categories through an extensive training procedure. If observations on behaviors cannot be secured by trained observers, there are other less desirable data sources, such as baselines taken by the client himself or by significant others in his environment. These baselines are less reliable but many times their use is necessitated by various organizational or other environmental constraints. Some of these constraints may involve lack of money for trained observers or the investigation of behavior that occurs at a time when it is not readily observable by others. When baseline data are not secured by a trained observer, the data should be obtained from two or more independent sources in order to check on consistency.

There are various considerations that should be addressed before a behavioral social worker decides on the exact procedures for securing a baseline. The first consideration involves where the baseline should be taken. A context should be chosen in which the individual's behavior occurs at a high frequency. If the behavior occurs in more than one context, baselines may be secured for the various contexts. Such a procedure enables the assessment of a broader range of contexts where the behavior occurs, provides for the determination of whether or not behavioral changes in one context are analogous to those in another, and provides a more accurate measure of behavior. Additional considerations pertain to where the behavior occurs. If the behavior is readily accessible to observation, this will not be a problem. If it is inaccessible, such as one that occurs late at night or in contexts where observation is not possible, the investigator will have to use reports by the client, or others who are present when the behavior occurs, to secure the data. An important consideration is who can best secure the relevant data. As previously mentioned, it is preferable to have a trained observer record data. In any case, an individual who is consistent and reliable should be chosen.

CONTRACTS

After an adequate assessment is executed, contracts should be carried out between the worker and clients for the following reasons. Research indicates that contracts included as a major aspect of the therapeutic process act as powerful tools in that they provide the motivation and structure necessary for the initiation and facilitation of client change and legally protect the worker in terms of malpractice suits (Feldman & Wodarski, 1975; Goldstein, Heller, & Sechrest, 1966; Goldstein & Simonson, 1971; Martin, 1974, 1975; Reid & Epstein, 1972; Wodarski, 1976).

Private Agencies

Contracts involving clients who come to private agencies of their own volition involve fewer legal requisites for the behavioral social worker than do contracts wherein participation is involuntary and occurs in agencies supported largely by public funds (Friedman, 1975; Stepleton, 1975). Contracts executed in a private agency should include the following aspects which would be specified as clearly and concretely as possible to protect the worker and the client:

1. *Client and therapist duties.*   Included here should be the roles, expectations, and obligations of each participant.
2. *Purpose of the interaction.*   The goals should be clearly delineated.
3. *Target problems and areas of difficulty to be worked on.*
For example, preparing for an employment interview, discussing ways to alleviate marital discord, improving one's physical appearance, and learning new child management skills.
4. *Various goals and objectives that might be accomplished.*   Increase self-acceptance, decrease negative self-thoughts, improve anxiety management through the use of systematic desensitization or covert conditioning, and so forth.
5. *Administrative procedures or constraints.*   For example, payment of fees, contract renegotiation procedures, provision of data by client, and confidentiality.
6. *Techniques that will be used.*   Client centered therapy, behavior modification, group techniques, and so forth.
7. *Duration of the contacts.*   Such as number of sessions planned to accomplish specific goals and length of the sessions (Seabury, 1976).

These contracts should specify clearly the nature of the treatment in terms of the probable outcomes; that is, how effective are the treatment approaches according to the empirical evidence that exists, what risks and benefits are involved in participating in the treatment in terms of the percentage of individuals whose behavior deteriorates as compared to those who improve during the course of treatment, and other reasonably forseeable consequences of the treatment. In all instances these contracts should be written as explicitly as possible for the protection of the worker and the client.

Public Agencies

Contracts structured between public agencies and involuntary clients are more complicated than those of private agencies (Friedman, 1975; Martin, 1974). Out of a series of court cases involving conditions in state institutions for the mentally retarded, the mentally distressed, correctional offenders, and so forth was established the doctrine of the *right to treatment* (Asher, 1974; Ennis & Siegel, 1973; Schaar, 1976; Schwitzgebel, 1971; Spece, 1972). This legal precedent establishes the client's right to a treatment plan that is clearly related to his return to his community. No longer can an institution provide only custodial care to its clients. Furthermore, transfer of a client to another institution with a treatment program that does not provide a reasonable opportunity for him to be returned to the community is no longer permissible.

Institutional treatment procedures may not be described in vague terms. As in contracts of private agencies, the goals for the client must be stated in such a manner that it can be easily determined whether or not they can be attained. How the treatment program will help the client attain these goals must also be delineated. For example, if a treatment program involves a job that is routinely performed at an institution the task must be justified in terms of its relationship to treatment objectives and the client must receive appropriate remuneration according to the minimum wage standards set by the Office of Labor (Schaar, 1975).

No Behavioral Change: Problems to Look For

Behavioral Equation

Problems may arise in the following areas: the behavior is nonspecifically defined; the behavior is defined in a manner too global to enable specification of the discriminative stimuli and consequences which control its occurrence or to allow for its measurement to determine if the frequency, duration or intensity of the behavior has changed; the worker may not have isolated and changed or eliminated all of the discriminative stimuli that control the behavior; in some instances new discriminative stimuli may now control the behavior; the worker and the client may not have isolated and eliminated all of the consequences that control the behavior.

Reinforcement Analysis

The contingency contract may not be specified in such a manner that the client and others understand what is involved in the effort to modify the behavior (DeRisi & Butz, 1975). The type of reinforcer chosen for the client may not be appropriate for the individual. That is, the reinforcer is weak compared to other reinforcers that are currently maintaining the behavior. Three critical questions center on how appropriate the incentives are: How much of the reinforcer has the client had in the past, how much does the client currently possess, and how much of the reinforcer do others around him possess. The power of the reinforcer is inversely related to the answer to all three of these questions. The reinforcer may be appropriate but the amount is not proportional to the effort involved in changing the behavior. Likewise, the amount or the size of the reinforcer is appropriate but the reinforcer is not provided at a high enough frequency or the schedule of reinforcement is too erratic to override the cost involved in the client's changing the behavior. The appropriate reinforcers and delivery conditions are sufficient, but the worker has not isolated those significant others in the client's environment who are providing the reinforcement that maintains the behavior and who may in fact be punishing behaviors that are being reinforced. The significant others chosen to participate in the modification plan may be inconsistently applying the agreed upon plan of behavioral change or may not be attractive enough to facilitate the behavioral changes.

Summary

In this chapter we have reviewed the essentials of behavioral assessment. The emphasis has been on the worker's securing the most concrete information possible on the events that precede and occur after the behavior chosen for alteration. In the coming years behavioral assessment will focus on complex reinforcement contingencies, multiple discriminative stimuli, complex reinforcement matrices occurring between client and significant others, and so forth. Thus, the knowledge base will become increasingly complex but only then will we be able to reflect and cope with the intricacies of behavioral assessment in the natural environment.

REFERENCES

Asher, J. Supreme court agrees to hear landmark right-to-treatment case. *APA Monitor,* 1974, *5*(1), 4.

Baer, D. M., Wolf, M. M., & Risley, T. R. Some current dimensions of applied behavior analysis. *Journal of Applied Behavior Analysis,* 1968, *1,* 91–97.

Bem, D. J., & Allen, A. On predicting some of the people of the time: the search for cross-situational consistencies in behavior. *Psychological Review,* 1974, *81*(6), 506–520.

Berkowitz, B. P., & Graziano, A. N. Training parents as behavior therapists: a review. *Behavior Research and Therapy,* 1972, *10,* 297–317.

Bernstein, D. A. Situational factors in behavioral fear assessment: a progress report. *Behavior Therapy,* 1973, *4*(1), 1–21.

———, & Nietzel, M. T. Behavioral avoidance tests: the effects of demand characteristics and repeated measures of two types of subjects. *Behavior Therapy,* 1974, *5*(2), 183–192.

Bijou, S. W. What psychology has to offer education-now. *Journal of Applied Behavior Analysis,* 1970, *3,* 65–71.

———, Peterson, R. F., Harris, F. R., Allen, K. E., Johnston, M. W. Methodology for experimental studies of young children in natural settings. *The Psychological Record,* 1969, *19,* 177–210.

Borkovec, T. D. Effects of expectancy on the outcome of systematic desensitization and implosive treatments for analogue anxiety. *Behavior Therapy,* 1972, *3*(1), 29–40.

——— The role of expectancy and physiological feedback in fear research: a review with special references to subject characteristics. *Behavior Therapy,* 1973, *4*(4), 491–505.

———, & Nau, S. D. Credibility of analogue therapy rationales. *Journal of Behavior Therapy and Experimental Psychiatry,* 1972, *3*(4), 257–260.

———, Stone, N. M., O'Brien, G. T., & Kaloupek, D. G. Evaluation of clinically relevant target behavior for analogue outcome research. *Behavior Therapy,* 1974, *5*(4), 503–513.

Butterfield, W. H. Instrumentation in behavior therapy. In E. J. Thomas (Ed.), *Behavior modification procedure: A source book.* Chicago: Aldine, 1974.

———, Thomas, E. J., and Soberg, R. J. A device for simultaneous feedback of verbal and signal data. *Behavior Therapy,* 1970, *1*(3), 395–401.

Carkhuff, R. R. *Helping and human relations.* New York: Holt, Rinehart and Winston, 1969.

Carkhuff, R. R. Training as a preferred mode of treatment. *Journal of Counseling Psychology,* 1971, *18,* 123–131.

———, & Berenson, B. G. *Beyond counseling and therapy.* New York: Holt, Rinehart and Winston, 1967.

Carter, R. D., & Thomas, E. J. Modification of problematic marital communication using corrective feedback and instruction. *Behavior Therapy,* 1973, *4*(1), 100–109. (a)

———, & Thomas E. J. A case application of a signaling system (SAM) to the assessment and modification of selected problems of marital communication. *Behavior Therapy,* 1973, *4*(5), 629–645. (b)

Case, L. P., & Lingerfelt, N. B. Name-calling: the labeling process in the social work interview. *Social Service Review,* 1974, *48,* 75–86.

Cautela, J. R. Reinforcement survey schedule: evaluation and current applications. *Psychological Reports,* 1972, *30,* 683–690.

———, & Kastenbaum, R., A reinforcement survey schedule for use in therapy, training, and research. *Psychological Reports,* 1967, *20,* 1115–1130.

Crow, W. J. The effect of training upon accuracy and variability in interpersonal perception. *Journal of Abnormal and Social Psychology,* 1957, *55,* 355–359.

Crown, S. On being sane in insane places: a comment from England. *Journal of Abnormal Psychology,* 1975, *84*(5), 453–455.

Davis, D. A. On being detectably sane in insane places: base rates and psychodiagnosis. *Journal of Abnormal Psychology,* 1976, *85*(4), 416–422.

DeRisi, W. J., & Butz, G. *Writing behavioral contracts.* Champaign, Ill.: Research Press, 1975.

Dix, G. E. "Civil" commitment of the mentally ill and the need for data on the prediction of dangerousness. *American Behavioral Scientist,* 1976, *19,* 318–334.

Ennis, B., & Siegel L. *The rights of mental patients.* New York: Avon Books, 1973.

Eysenck, H. *The scientific study of personality.* London: Routledge & Kegan Paul, 1952.

Farber, I. E. Sane and insane: constructions and misconstructions. *Journal of Abnormal Psychology,* 1975, *84*(6), 589–620.

Feldman, R. A., & Wodarski, J. S. *Contemporary approaches to group treatment.* San Francisco: Jossey-Bass, 1975.

Franks, C. M. (Ed.) *Behavior therapy: Appraisal and status.* New York: McGraw-Hill, 1969.

Freund, K. A. Note on the use of the phallometric method of measuring mild sexual arousal in the male. *Behavior Therapy,* 1971, *22,* 223–228.

Friedman, P. R. Legal regulations of applied behavior analysis in mental institutions and prisons. *Arizona Law Review,* 1975, *17,* 39–104.

Galassi, J. P., DeLo, J. S., Galassi, M.D., and Bastien, S. The college self-expression scale: a measure of assertiveness. *Behavior Therapy,* 1974, *5*(2), 165–171.

———, Hollandsworth, Jr. J. G., Radecki, J. C., Gay, M. L., Howe, M. R., & Evans, C. L. Behavioral performance in the validation of an assertiveness scale. *Behavior Therapy,* 1976 *7*(4), 447–452.

Gambrill, E. D., & Richey, C. A. An assertion inventory for use in assessment and research. *Behavior Therapy,* 1975, *6*(4), 550–561.

Gardner, W. J. *Behavior modification in mental retardation.* Chicago: Aldine-Atherton, 1971.

Geer, H. J. The development of a scale to measure fear. *Behavior Research and Therapy,* 1965, *3,* 45–53.

Gingerich, W. J., Feldman, R. A., & Wodarski, J. S. Accuracy in assessment: does training help? *Social Work,* 1976, *21*(1), 40–48.

Goldfried, M. R., & Sprafkin, J. N. *Behavioral personality assessment.* Morristown, N.J.: General Learning Press, 1974.

Goldstein, A. P., Heller, K., & Sechrest, L. B. *Psychotherapy and the psychology of behavior change.* New York: John Wiley, 1966.

————, & Simonson, N. R. Social psychological approaches to psychotherapy research. In A. E. Bergin, & S. L. Garfield (Eds.), *Handbook of psychotherapy and behavior change: An empirical analysis.* New York: John Wiley, 1971.

Gruver, G. G. College students and therapeutic agents. *Psychological Bulletin,* 1971, *76*(2), 111–127.

Harrower M. (Ed.) *Diagnostic psychological testing.* Springfield, Ill.: Charles C Thomas, 1950.

Hersen M. Self-assessment of fear. *Behavior Therapy,* 1973, *4*(2), 241–257.

————, Eisler, R. M., & Miller, P. M. Development of assertive responses: clinical measurement and research considerations. *Behavior Research and Therapy,* 1973, *11*(4), 505–521.

Hock, P., & Zubin, J. (Eds.) *Current problems in psychiatric diagnosis.* New York: Grune & Stratton, 1953.

Holland, C. J. An interview guide for behavioral counseling with parents. *Behavior Therapy,* 1970, *1*(1), 70–79.

Jeger, A. M., & Goldfried, M. R. A comparison of situation tests of speech anxiety. *Behavior Therapy,* 1976, *7*(2), 252–255.

Kanfer, F. H., & Grimm, L. G., Behavior analysis: selecting target behavior in the interview. *Behavior Modification,* 1977, *1*(1), 7–28.

Kazdin, A. E. The effect of suggestion and pretesting on avoidance reduction in fearful subjects. *Journal of Behavioral Therapy and Experimental Psychiatry,* 1973, *4*(3), 213–221.

Klorman R., Weerts, T. C., Hastings, J. E., Melamed, B. G., & Lang, P. J. Psychometric description of some specific-fear questionnaires. *Behavior Therapy,* 1974, *5*(3), 401–409.

Knox, D. *A behavioral approach to marital happiness counseling,* Champaign, Ill.: Research Press, 1971.

Landy, F. J., & Gaupp, L. A. A factor analysis of the fear survey schedule III. *Behavior Research and Therapy,* 1971, *9*(2), 89–93.

Mariotto, M. J., & Paul G. L. Persons versus situations in the real-life functioning of chronically institutionalized mental patients. *Journal of Abnormal Psychology,* 1975, *84*(5), 483–493.

Martin, R. *Behavior modification: human rights and legal responsibilities.* Champaign, Ill.: Research Press, 1974.

—— *Legal challenges to behavior modification.* Champaign, Ill.: Research Press, 1975.

Masters, W., & Johnson, V. E. *Human sexual response.* Boston: Little, Brown, 1966.

McCombs, D., Filipczak, J., Friedman, R., & Wodarski, J. S. Long-term follow-up of behavior modification with high-risk adolescents. *Criminal Justice and Behavior,* 1978, *5,* 21–34.

McCullough, J. P., & Montgomery, L. E. A technique for measuring subjective arousal in therapy clients. *Behavior Therapy,* 1972, *3*(4), 627–628.

Menninger K. The practice of psychiatry. *Digest of Neurology and Psychiatry,* 1955, *23,* 101.

Millon, T. Reflections on Rosenhan's "On being sane in insane places". *Journal of Abnormal Psychology,* 1975, *84*(5), 456–461.

Mischel, W. *Personality and assessment,* New York: John Wiley, 1968.

—— *Introduction to personality.* New York: Holt, Rinehart and Winston, 1971.

—— Direct versus indirect personality assessment: evidence and implications. *Journal of Consulting and Clinical Psychology,* 1972, *38,* 319–324.

—— Facing the issues. *Journal of Abnormal Psychology,* 1973, *82*(3), 541–542. (a)

—— On the empirical dilemmas of psychodynamic approaches: issues and alternatives. *Journal of Abnormal Psychology,* 1973, *82*(2), 335–344. (b)

—— Toward a cognitive social learning reconceptualization of personality. *Psychological Review,* 1973, *80,* 252–283. (c)

Rathus, S. A. A 30-item schedule for assessing assertive behavior. *Behavior Therapy,* 1973, *4*(3), 398–406.

Reed, P. L., & Jackson, D. N. Clinical judgment of psychopathology: a model for inferential accuracy. *Journal of Abnormal Psychology,* 1975, *84*(5), 475–482.

Reid, W. J., & Epstein, L. *Task-centered casework.* New York: Columbia University Press, 1972.

Richardson, F. C., & Tasto, D. L. Development and factor analysis of a social anxiety inventory. *Behavior Therapy,* 1976, *7*(4), 453–462.

Roe, A. Integration of personality theory and clinical practice. *Journal of Abnormal and Social Psychology,* 1949, *44,* 36–41.

Rogers, C. *Client centered therapy.* Boston: Houghton Mifflin, 1951.

Rosenhan, D. L. On being sane in insane places. *Science,* 1973, *79,* 250–258.

—— The contextual nature of psychiatric diagnosis. *Journal of Abnormal Psychology,* 1975, *84*(5), 462–474. (a)

—— Letters to the editor. *Science,* 1975, *180,* 365–369. (b)

Rosenthal, R. *Experimenter effects in behavioral research.* New York: Appleton-Century-Crofts, 1966.

——, & Rosnow, R. L. (Eds.) *Artifact in behavioral research.* New York: Academic Press, 1969.

Rotter, J. *Social Learning and clinical psychology.* Englewood Cliffs, N.J.: Prentice-Hall, 1954.

Rutner, I. T., & Pear, J. J. An observational methodology for investigating phobic behavior: preliminary report. *Behavior Therapy,* 1972, *3*(3), 437–440.

Schaar, K. Minimum wage regs pose problems. *APA Monitor,* 1975, *6*(8), 11.

—— Community care ordered for D.C. mental patients. *APA Monitor,* 1976, *7*(1), 13.

Schwitzgebel, R. K. Development and legal regulation of coercive behavior modification techniques. Washington, D.C.: GPO 1971 (An NIMH monograph No. 73-9015; GPO HE 20.2420/2: C65).

—— Limitations on the coercive treatment of offenders. *Criminal Law Bulletin,* 1972, *8,* 267–320.

Scott, W. Research definitions of mental health and mental illness. *Psychological Bulletin,* 1968, *74,* 1–45.

Seabury, B. A. The contract: uses, abuses and limitations. *Social Work,* 1976, *21,* 16–21.

Smith, R. E., Diener, E., & Beaman, A. L. Demand characteristics and the behavioral avoidance measure of fear in behavior therapy analogue research. *Behavior Therapy,* 1974, *5*(2), 172–182.

Spece, R. G., Jr. Note, conditioning and other technologies used to "treat?" "rehabilitate?" "demolish?" prisoners and mental patients. *Southern California Law Review,* 1972, *45,* 616–682.

Speltz, M. L., & Bernstein, D. A. Sex differences in fearfulness: verbal report, overt avoidance and demand characteristics. *Journal of Experimental Psychiatry and Behavior Therapy,* 1976, *7*(2), 117–122.

Spiegler, M. D., & Liebert, R. M. Some correlates of self-reported fear. *Psychological Reports,* 1970, *26,* 691–695.

Spitzer, R. L. On pseudoscience in science, logic in remission, and psychiatric diagnosis: a critique of Rosenhan's "On being sane in insane places". *Journal of Abnormal Psychology,* 1975, *84*(5), 442–452.

Stepleton, J. V. Legal issues confronting behavior modification. *Behavioral Engineering,* 1975, *2,* 35–43.

Tasto, D. L., & Hickson, R. Standardization and scaling of the 122-item fear survey schedule. *Behavior Therapy,* 1970, *1*(4), 473–484.

——, Hickson R., & Rubin, S. E. Scaled profile analysis of fear survey schedule factors. *Behavior Therapy,* 1971, *2*(4), 543–549.

————, & Suinn, L. M. Fear survey schedule changes on total and factor scores due to nontreatment effects. *Behavior Therapy,* 1972, *3*(2), 275–278.

Thomas, E. J. (Ed.) *Behavior modification procedure: a source book.* Chicago: Aldine, 1974.

————, Carter, R. D., Gambrill, E. D., & Butterfield, W. H. A signal system for the assessment and modification of behavior (SAM). *Behavior Therapy,* 1970, *1*(2), 252–259.

————, Walter, C. L., & O'Flaherty, K. A verbal problem check list for use in assessing family verbal behavior. *Behavior Therapy,* 1974, *5*(2), 235–246.

Tryon, W. W., & Tryon, G. S. Desensitization and demand characteristics. *Behavior Therapy,* 1974, *5*(2), 297–298.

Vaal, J. J. The Rathus assertiveness schedule: reliability at the junior high school level. *Behavior Therapy,* 1975, *6*(4), 566–567.

Vitalo, R. L. Guidelines in the functioning of a helping service. *Community Mental Health Journal,* 1975, *11*(2), 170–178.

Wachtel, P. L. On fact, hunch and stereotype: a reply to Mischel. *Journal of Abnormal Psychology,* 1973, *82*(3), 537–540. (a)

———— Psychodynamics, behavior therapy, and the implacable experimenter: an inquiry into the consistency of personality. *Journal of Abnormal Psychology,* 1973, *82*(2), 324–334. (b)

Wahler, R. G., & Cormier, W. H. The ecological interview: a first step in out patient child behavior therapy. *Journal of Experimental Psychiatry and Behavior Therapy,* 1970, *1,* 279–289.

Weiner, B. On being in insane places: a process (attributional) analysis and critique. *Journal of Abnormal Psychology,* 1975, *84*(5), 433–441.

Wells, R. A., & Miller D. Developing relationship skills in social work students. *Social Work Education Reporter,* 1973, *21*(1), 60–73.

Wodarski, J. S. Recent Supreme Court legal decisions: Implications for social work practice. Paper presented at the 103rd Annual Forum, National Conference on Social Welfare, Washington, D.C., June, 1976.

————, & Filipczak, J. Long-term followup of behavior modification with high-risk adolescents: cohort two. Paper presented at the Johns Hopkins University Symposium on Alternative Educational Programs for Disruptive Secondary School Students, Baltimore, Maryland, May, 1977.

————, Feldman, R. A., & Pedi, S. J. Effects of different observational systems and time sequences upon non-participant observer's behavioral ratings. *Journal of Behavior Therapy and Experimental Psychiatry,* 1975, *6*(4), 275–278.

Wolpe, J. Transcript of initial interview in a case of depression. *Journal of Experimental Psychiatry and Behavior Therapy,* 1970, *1*(1), 71–78.

——— *The practice of behavior therapy.* New York: Pergamon, 1973.

———, & Lang, P. J. A fear survey schedule for use in behavior therapy. *Behavior Research and Therapy,* 1964, *2,* 27–30.

Zigler, E., & Phillips, L. Social effectiveness and symptomatic behaviors. *Journal of Abnormal and Social Psychology,* 1960, *61,* 231–238.

———, & Phillips, L. Case history data and psychiatric diagnosis. *Journal of Consulting Psychology,* 1961, *25,* 458.(a)

———, & Phillips, L. Psychiatric diagnosis: a critique. *Journal of Abnormal and Social Psychology,* 1961, *62,* 237–246. (b)

Chapter 4

THE APPLICATION OF THE OPERANT MODEL TO SOCIAL WORK PRACTICE

The theoretical framework of the operant model and its relevance to social work practice are reviewed in this chapter. Initially, a brief summary of the historical development of the theory and its philosophy is provided. Next, the discussion focuses on the elements of the model and its application to practice. Finally, some of the theoretical issues which should be resolved if the operant model is to become more valid, powerful, and relevant for social work practice are reviewed.

HISTORICAL DEVELOPMENT

The idea that human beings are motivated to seek pleasure and avoid pain, which is the central idea of the operant model, was postulated before Christ by the Greek philosophers Epicurus and Aristippus (Gergen, 1969). This principle historically formed the basis of the philosophical doctrines of hedonism and utilitarianism and became an integral part of Freud's psychoanalytic theory in terms of the pleasure-pain principle. Thorndike, a psychologist of the early 1900s, engaged in a series of investigations that supported this idea and subsequently resulted in his postulation of the law of effect (Kimble, 1961). This law specified that responses that are followed by satisfying events are more likely to recur; likewise, responses that are followed by unsatisfying events are less likely to recur. Skinner presents a modern version of the law of effect in his formulation of the law of the operant indicating that the kinds of consequences following a behavior determine the probability of that behavior occurring in the future. Thus, responses that are followed by consequences evaluated positively by the individual are more likely to occur in the future than responses followed by negative events (Skinner, 1953, 1966, 1969, 1971).

PHILOSOPHY

The basic concepts of the operant model are the probabilities of the behavior occurring and the events controlling the rate of its occurrence. The basic focus is on changing the rates of behavior. The model, therefore, is concerned with gaining knowledge over the antecedent events, i.e., the events in the client's environment occurring just prior to the behavior, and consequences, i.e., events in the client's environment occurring just after the behavior, which control the rate of certain behaviors. Depending upon the situation, either or both of these concepts are utilized in the modification of behavior. This focus is in opposition to many other models postulated for social work practice that posit the need for inner psychic change preceding behavioral change. The goal is to develop descriptive statements about events that affect rates of behavior. Thus, the behavior that is to be changed must be observable and countable (Kazdin, 1975; Skinner, 1969; Ullmann & Krasner, 1965).

The proponents of the operant model believe that it lends itself to a precise and reproducible account of why behaviors change. That is, since therapeutic processes are operationalized concretely an adequate account of interpersonal helping can occur. A social worker utilizing the operant framework with an antisocial child would want to specify those behaviors he wished to decrease, such as fighting, inability to concentrate on a given task, or verbal aggression and those he wished to increase such as academic and social behaviors, appropriate verbal statements, and/or self-care behaviors.

After determining the desirable behaviors that are to take the place of the undesirable behaviors, the worker would then proceed to determine the antecedent events and consequences controlling the behavior. Following isolation of these events the worker can employ a variety of techniques to modify the client's behavior, such as eliminating those stimuli that bring on the behavior, reducing the reinforcement available for deviant behavior, and/or reinforcing other desired behavior.

Until recently there has been an emphasis only on the determination of environmental events and their functional relationship in controlling or changing a person's behavior and a manipulation of these relationships to achieve behavioral change. Lately, behavior modification theorists have focused on the cognitive aspects of behavior, i.e., what clients are saying to themselves. This has led to an additional emphasis in behavior modification treatment in helping a client gain cognitive control over his behavior (Cautela, 1967, 1970a, b, 1971; Mahoney, 1977; Meichenbaum, 1974). This approach involves the client learning how to control his behavior through two techniques, structuring cognitive consequences for appropriate behaviors and eliminating or controlling the antecedent conditions that cause the behaviors. Thus, a mother who has been erratic in her child rearing practices could be taught to cognitively reinforce herself when her practices are consistent and to avoid those events, i.e., fights with her husband, excessive physical exertion, thoughts about her inadequacies as a mother, and so forth, which cause her to become erratic. This additional focus on cognitive control of human behavior, which is elaborated on in Chapter 8, will make the operant framework more viable.

Analogous development has been evident in social work as it has shifted its focus back and forth between emphasis on the individual and emphasis on the environment. Richmond placed considerable emphasis on the environment as a treatment vehicle in her explication of social diagnosis. Actually, her social diagnosis could have been considered a forerunner of the operant analysis of behavior (Richmond, 1965). Her ideas are compatible with the relationship postulated by the operant model which indicates that a change in an environmental event will lead to a change in the client's behavior. For example, the worker might determine that a couple should engage in more positive behaviors, such as exchanging compliments, practicing active listening, engaging in more pleasurable activities, and so forth. Both partners can be taught to exhibit more reinforcing behaviors that will increase the frequency of positive behaviors toward each other.

An integration of social work's historical emphasis on the individual's personality and environmental events at different time periods was accomplished in Florence Hollis' *Casework, a Psycho-Social Therapy.* Her conceptualization of diagnosis and treatment, which emphasizes that a person must be considered in the total stimulus environment in which he is operating (Hollis, 1965, 1972), is more encompassing than postulates set forth by other theorists. Hollis' emphasis parallels the development of behavior therapy which now not only emphasizes assessing the individual's external environment but also looks at the individual's internal environment.

COMPONENTS OF THE MODEL

The three basic elements of the operant model are *discriminative stimuli, the operant,* and the *consequences* that follow the operant. Each one of these elements may be dealt with individually, but they usually compose a unit called the unit of analysis. When the operant model is the paradigm that is applicable to practice situations, the worker will want to examine these elements in order to be able to help a client change his behavior. Actually, this conceptual framework is similar to Hollis' conceptualization of behavior as the result of the forces inside the individual called stresses and the forces of the environment called presses and the interaction that takes place between them to produce behavior. Depending on the life situation of the client, stresses and presses could be discriminative stimuli or consequences. Discriminative stimuli, i.e., antecedent events that occur in the individual's environment before the behavior, indicate to the individual what the conditions of reinforcement are for the context he is in; that is, what is the probability of his receiving reinforcement for exhibiting a particular behavior in that setting. These stimuli gain a controlling function over the behavior an individual exhibits since, due to past experiences, the client learns that certain behaviors will be reinforced when particular stimuli are present, and when other stimuli are present either a neutral, negative, or adversive consequence will be received.

The operant is synonymous with the particular verbal, physical, and cognitive behaviors that an individual exhibits. Consequences are the events that either increase or decrease the probability of an operant behavior occurring in the future. Thus in analyzing why a particular couple quarrels, the worker would want to know what antecedent events such as negative commands, disapproval, and/or teasing occur before the quarreling and the consequences such as securing a desired reinforcer, termination of an aversive event, and so forth that occur afterwards. This represents a significant departure from the traditional diagnostic framework that tends to focus primarily upon the antecedent determinants of behavior.

Discriminative Stimuli

In social work practice the worker serves as a discriminative stimulus for the client and vice versa. The client's presence and certain behaviors such as stating problems and exhibiting anxiety through verbal and nonverbal channels serve as discriminative stimuli for the worker and indicate that he should be warm, accepting, and reassuring, convey confidence and encouragement, exhibit trust, interest, and sympathetic listening, convey concern for the client's well-being, and gather information about the antecedents and consequences that control the behaviors chosen for modification. Actually one of the functions of graduate social work education is to train workers to respond accurately to different discriminative stimuli clients present. Likewise, disruptive behaviors exhibited in the therapeutic context would indicate that the worker should set limits. After a number of sessions the therapist's behaviors become signals for the client to exhibit certain types of behaviors as he interacts with the therapist, e.g., talking about problematic areas such as sex, drugs, school performance, or getting along with others, providing data on the frequencies of certain behavior and so forth. Time, day of week, length of session, physical aspects of the therapeutic context, type of agency, and office furnishings also serve as discriminative stimuli for the worker's and client's behaviors (Dinges & Oetting, 1972; Kazdin, 1975; Lauver, Kelley, & Froehle, 1971; Seabury, 1971; Widgery & Stackpole, 1972).

For example, through discussions a worker can help an antisocial child to see how certain behaviors directed toward his parents, i.e., raising his voice, losing eye contact, throwing things down or slamming doors, muttering unintelligible statements under his breath, or not doing tasks agreed upon, serve as discriminative stimuli for his parents to exhibit consequences that are evaluated negatively by the child. These verbal descriptions of possible future consequences for appropriate or inappropriate behavior increase the likelihood of more successful behavior occurring. In order to help a child and his parents acquire new and more satisfying negotiation repertories, the behavioral social worker may want to teach both the parent and the child to state problems in an inoffensive manner, state options, and negotiate in a reciprocal way so that reinforcers for both parties are exchanged and increased. Thus programs that are designed to teach new, appropriate, and successful behaviors utilize discriminative stimuli components such as modeling of appropriate behavior, verbal and nonverbal instructions, behavioral demonstration, instructional practice, feedback and reinforcement to precisely refine a response, and verbal descriptions of possible future consequences for appropriate or inappropriate behavior. It is the dual focus on the control of discriminative stimuli and consequences that is instrumental in developing and maintaining appropriate behavior that is characteristic of the sophisticated and effective behavior modification treatment program.

Operant Behaviors

All verbal, cognitive, and physical behaviors have operant components. The basic theme delineating an operant behavior is that its rate is changed by altering the antecedent events occurring before the behavior and/or consequences occurring after the behavior. Social work practice focuses primarily on verbal behavior. It is through verbal behavior that we hope to accomplish changes in cognitive and physical behaviors. Thus, the most relevant literature from the operant model concerns verbal conditioning which indicates that certain positive reinforcers such as a smile or nod of the head, various expressions of the face, hands and body, positive body position (leaning forward attentively or maintaining a comfortable distance), eye contact, and standard statements of a positive nature occurring after verbalizations, such as "please elaborate" or "tell me more about that," tend to increase verbalization in the therapeutic interview. Likewise, certain consequences such as interruptions, lack of appropriate inflection in speech, inadequate interpersonal distance, negative body position, and so forth tend to decrease verbalization.

For example, a client with a history of failure to keep a job, marital discord, and inability to manage his children might be encouraged through positive statements of praise to discuss the difficulties he is having in these areas and by the same process increase discussion on the resolution of these difficulties. The question that social work practice must ask is whether this type of verbal conditioning is beneficial and does in fact carry over into the verbal, cognitive, and physical behaviors a client exhibits after he leaves the interview context (Matarazzo, Wiens, Matarazzo, & Saslow, 1968; Salzinger, 1969; Verplank, 1955). This is a question to be resolved by future research.

Consequences

Behavior is controlled not only by discriminative stimuli but by the environmental events, or consequences, occurring after the behavior. The central assumption of the operant model is that consequences affect the probability of the behavior occurring in the future. Consequences are defined in terms of reinforcing properties of events which either increase or decrease the future probability of a behavior. Positive reinforcers which increase the probability of the behavior occurring later are usually considered to be of three types: primary, secondary, and generalized (Keller, 1954).

The *primary positive reinforcers,* food, water, and sexual activities, are reinforcing due to their biological bases, and their reinforcing power is intensified as deprivation increases. For example, often candy (a primary positive reinforcer) is used with autistic children to establish eye contact and to increase social and linguistic behaviors (Hamblin, Buckholdt, Ferritor, Kozloff, & Blackwell, 1971). Even though their use in social work practice is not often intentional, primary reinforcers are used and have many side effects. A general mode of operation is for social work practitioners to make themselves more attractive by dispensing reinforcers. Think of the times you have taken a child for a Coke, helped a mother with a task, or helped a client with an operational difficulty in securing employment. It is through such reinforcing operations and through the dispensation of primary reinforcers that we make ourselves acquire secondary reinforcing properties.

Secondary reinforcers acquire reinforcing properties through repeated association with a stimulus having positive reinforcing properties. Secondary reinforcement occurs when a teacher dispenses candy bars to children for working mathematics problems toward a certain level of performance and then pairs this distribution of the candy bars with a verbal expression such as "good." After a number of associations the children will work for the expression of "good" since, through the pairing, it has gained reinforcing properties (Hamblin, et al., 1971). Another illustration of the process of secondary reinforcement is the teacher's extensive use of privileges that are paired with statements of praise such as "John, I like the way that you have cleaned your desk. You may line up for recess." Hence, students do work for the positive statements and affection of teachers since they become conditioned reinforcers.

Social workers utilize various types of reinforcers in clinical interviews. The fact that during the first interview the social worker goes through a series of anxiety-reducing operations probably accounts for the client's decision to return for subsequent interviews (Bersheid & Walster, 1969; Houston, 1974). The entire process of defining the problem and discussing means of remedying it lead to the reduction of anxiety. The procedure proves reinforcing for the client and thus leads to the social worker's acquisition of reinforcing properties. Reinforcing the client for his participation by smiling, nodding the head, and using positive verbal statements throughout the process helps to ensure his continued participation. If a client has been given a preliminary plan or some type of behavior to accomplish before the next interview we might positively reinforce him through a positive verbal statement such as "you did well" when he reports back that he ascertained the goal. Such a procedure increases the probability that the person will carry out other treatment plans and adds to the attractiveness of the practice context, thus increasing the chances that the client will continue seeing the worker.

A stimulus that 1) follows a behavior and 2) enables the individual to secure other reinforcers is called a *generalized reinforcer* (Ayllon & Azrin, 1968). In certain treatment milieus "tokens" have been used as generalized reinforcers. These are exchangeable for valued items such as cigarettes, food, and home furloughs. In everyday life, resources such as money, prestige, and social status are common generalized reinforcers since they can be exchanged readily for other desired items. We do not utilize these reinforcers extensively with clients. However, through our practice endeavors we enable them to secure generalized reinforcers more readily. For example, when we help a child secure social skills such as getting dressed without help, making his own bed, developing proper eating habits, and increasing conversational competence the child not only gains self-worth but, through exhibition of these behaviors, he also secures additional reinforcers such as social approval from peers and significant adults. Thus, each time such a process occurs it increases the value of positive behavior and decreases the value of negative behaviors.

INTERVENTIONS TO DECREASE UNDESIRABLE BEHAVIORS

There are six types of intervention that can be utilized in social work practice to decrease behavior: punishment, avoidance conditioning, escape conditioning, time out, extinction, and stimulus control (Bandura, 1969). These procedures are discussed by themselves for the purpose of conceptual clarity to illustrate how they may operate in practice. However, these techniques should always be paired with procedures that increase the frequency of prosocial behavior to be exhibited by a client. The sole use of these interventions to decrease undesirable behaviors increases the likelihood that the client will evaluate the treatment context as negative which in turn increases the probability that the client will terminate the treatment process. These interventions may decrease behavior temporarily; however, unless the client develops appropriate behaviors which are reinforced by his environment the behavior will possibly return to its former level of frequency (Wodarski, Feldman, & Flax, 1974).

Punishment involves applying an aversive stimulus after a behavior occurs which decreases the probability of that behavior occurring in the future. When a client introduces a certain topic we may punish him by changing the topic to another, pointing out deficiencies in his behavior, probing an area before he is ready, or not providing the appropriate positive reinforcer for the accomplishment of a behavioral task. It is important to note that there are a number of instances when we may want to decrease certain behaviors, such as an inability to address oneself to a discussion of a problematic area, the commitment of antisocial acts, and failure to carry out a treatment objective (Campbell & Church, 1969).

Avoidance conditioning involves exhibiting some behavior that prevents an aversive stimulus from occurring. In interviews with the client he may avert probing questions and topics of conversation he evaluates negatively. If a client characteristically chooses to withhold information necessary to work on his difficulties, the worker may choose to ask a number of probing questions. After a period of time the client learns that by giving the worker desired information he can avoid the aversive stimulus of probing questions such as "Why can't you talk about your father?" Avoidance behavior is also exemplified by the antisocial child who is referred by the court for casework and avoids the stimulus of incarceration by going to the treatment context as the judge has ordered.

In *escape conditioning* the aversive stimulus does occur and the client terminates the stimulus by exhibiting a certain type of behavior. A welfare worker may threaten to remove a child from an inadequate home if the parents do not improve their care of the child. Hence, the parents may remove the aversive stimulus (threatened removal of the children) by improving their child rearing habits. A spouse may nag in order to secure a desired item and his or her partner may provide the item to reduce the nagging.

Time-out involves removing the person from a reinforcing situation for a period of time in order to decrease a behavior. When a worker terminates an interview prematurely because he feels the client has not participated adequately he is employing the time-out technique. The worker may indicate to the client that an interview will be rescheduled for a later date at which time he hopes that the client will use the time beneficially. Similarly, when clients do not return for interviews it serves as a time-out to the worker who, in turn, may modify his own interviewing behaviors. Time-out has worked especially well in situations that are highly reinforcing to the individual.

Withholding reinforcers when a client exhibits a certain behavior is designated as *extinction.* In social work practice certain types of verbal responses are extinguished through withholding reinforcement when the client exhibits these behaviors. Thus, if the goal of an interview is to discuss how to refuse drugs and the child spends a large portion of this time talking about how disagreeable his parents are we might choose to ignore this behavior by breaks in eye contact, silence, and increasing the distance between ourself and the child.

Stimulus control refers to the process of removing a stimulus that elicits certain undesirable behaviors. If one of the behaviors to be changed is the consumption of alcohol the worker should help the client remove from the environment as many stimuli that elicit the behavior as possible, such as, removing alcohol from his dwelling, reducing the interaction with individuals who consume large quantities of alcohol, and reducing the frequenting of places where the consumption of alcohol is acceptable.

The foregoing intervention techniques should be used in conjunction with positive reinforcement for prosocial behavior. Such a combination of techniques provides workers with a very potent means of changing behavior. However, if they are used singularly such negative consequences as the following can occur: the avoidance of the worker, undesirable side effects in terms of an emotional response, termination of treatment by the client, and negative reactions generalizing to positive behavior.

SHAPING

Shaping, another useful technique, involves reinforcing closer and closer approximations to the desired behavior. This process facilitates the acquisition of behavior for clients who cannot initially exhibit terminal treatment goals. For example, a worker might want to shape problem-solving attempts. Initially, he would reinforce elementary attempts at problem solving. Gradually he would make reinforcement contingent upon more elaborate problem-solving attempts until the terminal behavior is reached. The key to successful utilization of this concept is in stating a goal which is achieved readily by the client at the onset of treatment. Likewise, once the terminal behavioral goal is reached, the behavior should be placed on a schedule of reinforcement (see Chap. 2) that will maintain it and provide the possibility of the behavior generalizing to other contexts. Analogous to this concept is "sequence of responses" that involves helping a client learn a series of behaviors required for completion of a complex task, such as securing employment. A knowledge of where to go, skill in presenting oneself physically and verbally, and preparation and capabilities for the job are prerequisites to fulfillment of such a task.

ISSUES TO BE RESOLVED

The operant model requires that we thoroughly delineate and specify variables. When the model is employed in the animal laboratory it is a simple matter to define a discriminative stimulus, behavior, and consequences. However, when the same concepts are used to analyze behaviors of concern to practitioners, ambiguities develop. Specifically, what are the dimensions of a discriminative stimulus? How does it differ from behavior? How does behavior differ from reinforcement? From our experience in trying to apply this model in group practice, we have struggled to isolate the discriminative stimuli and the consequences that control the antisocial behaviors of children in a group. We found this problem stemmed from the numerous behavioral exchanges taking place in any practice context that increase the complexity of specifying the behavioral concepts and our interventive strategies. For example, when a worker reinforces a child for exhibiting a prosocial behavior, does this reinforcing behavior of the worker also serve as a discriminative stimulus for the child that if he wants additional reinforcers he should continue exhibiting prosocial behavior? Likewise, the worker's statement, "don't do that or a punishment will occur," could be a reinforcement of certain behavior or could serve as a discriminative stimulus. Thus, in clinical practice behavioral concepts need more delineation. This observation is not meant to detract from the proven benefits of the operant model's use in helping many clients, but to indicate what needs to be developed if the model is to be more relevant for social work.

It is generally agreed that certain reinforcers such as praise, candy for children, and money for adults have properties that seem to be very effective with most individuals, but even this proposition depends on other functional variables such as deprivation, or the extent of time that the individual has been without the reinforcer, the relative quantity he has received in the past and the amount of the reinforcer others possess. There is very little systematic knowledge of which reinforcers are effective for certain client groups and further study in this area is warranted. For example, it would be beneficial to have an inventory of reinforcers that could be utilized with antisocial children, clients in mental hospitals, outpatient clients, and so forth. Obviously, this classification of reinforcers will be a formidable task since there will be differences in preferences among various populations. Nonetheless, the delineation of appropriate reinforcers is necessary for effective theory building and practice applications since the manipulation of reinforcers is central to the operant model.

One cannot negate the fact that there is a question of values involved in the decision regarding behaviors to be increased or decreased. With adults in the free environment this is rarely problematic since behavior modifiers plan the treatment in conjunction with the adults. It does seem to be a problem, however, with clients who are within closed or semi-closed institutions, such as mental hospitals, prisons, and schools where the operant model has been employed most extensively. In most instances it seems that behavior modification theorists have addressed themselves to the issue by suggesting that the increased behaviors are productive for the individual and the environment, e.g., teaching mathematics behaviors to children in order that they may be able to tell time and make change, helping hospitalized patients learn self-care behaviors, and helping adults and juvenile offenders learn new vocational and social skills for their integration into society (Bandura, 1969, 1975; O'Leary, Poulos, & Devine, 1972; Winett & Winkler, 1972). An issue for further exploration is how to ensure that people who learn to work the operant contingencies of their environments also retain enough individuality to challenge contingencies with which they disagree. In other words, how do we prevent the technology from being used solely to make people conform, especially those persons classified as socially deviant. Insurance against the misuse of behavior modification knowledge is in the adequate preparation of the professionals who apply the operant model and direct client participation in the choice of treatment goals. Whether this preparation takes place in a school of social work, a training institute, or an agency it should include knowledge of how the values of worker, supervisor, and agency influence what behaviors are chosen to be increased or decreased. Professional associations should develop standards against which practitioners could judge their work and have the ability to impose sanctions for misuse of the model.

It is evident that most of the interventions behavior modifiers have utilized in the past have been on a one-to-one basis with a specific focus on modifying the individual's behavior. This procedure, if continued, may allow for few transfer effects to the client's general environment (Koegel & Rincover, 1977; Wahler, 1969). This situation could be altered if we analyzed how we can modify the social system in order to maintain the behaviors altered in therapy. It is interesting to note that a social system can be conceptualized as a series of interconnected reinforcers that can be utilized to maintain prosocial behaviors. Thus, the question to be resolved is how can we modify the system after the person has altered his behavior and/or how can we help the individual learn how to modify the system. It is evident that such systems as psychiatric hospitals, prisons, and institutions for the retarded in many instances maintain the behaviors that they are structured to modify and, in addition, teach other maladaptive behaviors to clients. Again, the question is how to alter these systems; this will be elaborated on in Chapter 10.

Another issue raised by concerned colleagues is the application of the operant model in an open setting. Open settings do not readily provide the control necessary to implement behavior modification technology. Difficulties are encountered in monitoring the client's behavior and having him carry out aspects of his treatment plan. However, these concerns are characteristic of most treatment processes. To alleviate these difficulties clients will have to be taught how to keep daily charts of their behavior and how to record what happens before and after their problematic behaviors occur. In addition, successful applications of this knowledge to open environments will require the ability to develop adequate monitoring systems implemented by significant persons in the client's environment. If treatment is taking place in a closed environment, education of certain staff members in the basic treatment plan is essential in order that they may coordinate and participate in the structuring of proper reinforcement contingencies to aid treatment. Similarly, this principle is applicable to the open environment in that the involvement of significant others such as family members in the treatment process increases the probability of successful treatment (Sarri & Vinter, 1967; Wodarski, 1976).

Akin to this issue is the problem of who is adequately equipped to implement the operant model. For a period of time social workers have talked about MSW's performing functions that could well be carried out by others. It would seem that behavior modification technology lends itself nicely to execution of tasks by para-professionals with MSW's as supervisors. However, a note of caution is advised. Research in other fields indicates that certain characteristics such as motivation, self-adjustment, and verbal ability are essential for para-professionals who execute treatment (Gruver, 1971; Guerney, 1969). It is imperative that we determine what other characteristics are essential for effective treatment in order that we choose para-professionals who successfully can implement the treatment technology.

The role of expectations in the operant model deserves consideration. There is substantial research now to indicate that a most crucial variable in the achievement of therapeutic change is that the therapist communicates to the client that he feels the client will get better (Braun, 1976; Goldstein, 1962; Rosenthal, 1969). A personal observation of behavior modification techniques being implemented over the last few years seems to substantiate that expectations may indeed be critical to the success of these techniques with certain client populations. The noted success of the method may be due in part to the enthusiasm with which people apply the model, e.g., the number of positive reinforcers they apply in therapeutic work such as eye contact, voice qualities, body positions, gestures, touching, smiling, and other body language. Further research must clarify the role of expectations in the model and determine how expectations are communicated.

Summary

In this chapter, the operant model has been presented as a practice tool for social workers. Techniques such as positive reinforcement, time-out, and shaping that have an accumulated data base have been illustrated and discussed in relation to social work practice situations. The aim is to give the practitioner a clear explication of the model and issues involved in its application to practice. The application of the model to social work practice no doubt will increase substantially in the coming years since a majority of the difficulties clients present can be alleviated by working on behaviors that have operant components. Moreover, the influence of operant conditioning in the behavioral exchanges that occur between worker and client during the interpersonal helping process cannot be underestimated.

REFERENCES

Ayllon, T., & Azrin, N. *A token economy: A motivational system for behavior rehabilitation.* New York: Appleton-Century-Crofts, 1968.

Bandura, A. *Principles of behavior modification.* New York: Holt, Rinehart and Winston, 1969.

―――. The ethics and social purposes of behavior modification. In C. M. Franks, & G. T. Wilson (Eds.), *Annual review of behavior therapy theory and practice.* New York: Brunner/Mazel, 1975.

Berscheid, A., & Walster, E. H. *Interpersonal attraction.* Reading, Ma.: Addison-Wesley, 1969.

Braun, C. Teacher expectation: sociopsychological dynamics. *Review of Educational Research,* 1976, *46*(2), 185–213.

Campbell, B. A., & Church, R. M. (Eds.), *Punishment and aversive behavior.* New York: Appleton-Century-Crofts, 1969.

Cautela, J. R. Covert sensitization. *Psychological Record,* 1967, *20,* 459–468.

―――. Covert negative reinforcement. *Behavior Therapy and Experimental Psychiatry,* 1970, 2, 273–278. (a)

————. Covert reinforcement. *Behavior Therapy,* 1970, *1,* 33–50. (b)

————. Covert extinction. *Behavior Therapy,* 1971, *2,* 192–200.

Dinges, N. G., & Oetting, E. R. Interaction distance anxiety in the counseling dyad. *Journal of Counseling Psychology,* 1972, *19,* 146–149.

Gergen, K. J. *The psychology of behavior exchange.* Reading, Ma.: Addison-Wesley, 1969.

Goldstein, A. P. *Therapist-patient expectancies in psycho-therapy.* New York: Pergamon Press, 1962.

Gruver, G. G. College students as therapeutic agents. *Psychological Bulletin,* 1971, *76,* 111–127.

Guerney, B. G., Jr. *Psychotherapeutic agents: New roles for nonprofessionals, parents and teachers.* New York: Holt, Rinehart and Winston, 1969.

Hamblin, R. L., Buckholdt, D. R., Ferritor, D., Kozloff, M. A., & Blackwell, L. J. *The humanization process: A social behavioral analysis of children's problems.* New York: John Wiley, 1971.

Hollis, R. *Casework: A psycho-social therapy.* New York: Random House, 1965.

————. *Casework: A psycho-social therapy,* (2nd ed.) New York: Random House, 1972.

Houston, T. *Foundations of interpersonal attraction.* New York: Academic Press, 1974.

Kazdin, A. E. Behavior modification in applied settings. Homewood, Ill.; Dorsey Press, 1975.

Kimble, G. A. *Hilgard and Marquis' conditioning and learning,* (2nd ed.) New York: Appleton-Century-Crofts, 1961.

Keller, F. S. *Learning: reinforcement theory.* New York: Random House, 1954.

Koegel, R. L., & Rincover, A. Research on the difference between generalization and maintenance in extra-therapy responding. *Journal of Applied Behavior Analysis,* 1977, *10,* 1–12.

Lauver, P. J., Kelley, S. D., & Froehle, T. C. Client reaction time and counselor verbal behavior in an interview setting. *Journal of Counseling Psychology,* 1971, *18,* 26–30.

Mahoney, M. M. Reflection on the cognitive-learning trend in psychotherapy. *American Psychologist,* 1977, *32*(1), 5–13.

Matarazzo, J. D., Wiens, A. N., Matarazzo, R. G., & Saslow, G. Speech and silent behavior in clinical psycho-therapy. In J. L. Shlien, H. F. Hunt, J. D. Matarazzo, & C. Savage (Eds.), *Research in Psycho Therapy,* Washington, D.C.: American Psychological Association, 1968.

Meichenbaum, D. *Cognitive behavior modification.* Morristown, N.J.: General Learning Press, 1974.

O'Leary, K. D., Poulos, R. W., & Devine, V. T. Tangible reinforcers: bonuses or bribes? *Journal of Consulting and Clinical Psychology,* 1972, *38,* 1–8.

Richmond, M. E. *Social Diagnosis.* New York: Free Press, 1965.

Rosenthal, R. Interpersonal expectations: Effects of the experimenter's hypothesis. In R. Rosenthal, & R. L. Rosnow (Eds.), *Artifact in behavioral research.* New York: Academic Press, 1969.

Salzinger, K. The place of operant conditioning of verbal behavior in psychotherapy. In C. M. Franks (Ed.), *Behavior therapy appraisal and status.* New York: McGraw-Hill, 1969.

Sarri, R. C., & Vinter, R. D. Organizational requisites for a socio-behavioral technology. In E. J. Thomas (Ed.), *A social behavioral approach and application to social work,* New York: Council on Social Work Education, 1967.

Seabury, B. A. Arrangement of physical space in social work settings. *Social work,* 1971, *16,* 43–49.

Skinner, B. F. *Science and human behavior.* New York: Macmillan, 1953.

———. Contingencies of reinforcement in the design of a culture. *Behavioral Science,* 1966, *11,* 159–166.

———. *Contingencies of reinforcement.* New York: Appleton-Century-Crofts, 1969.

———. *Beyond freedom and dignity.* New York: Bantam, 1971.

Ullmann, L. P., & Krasner, L. *Case studies in behavior modification.* New York: Holt, Rinehart and Winston, 1965.

Verplank, W. S. The control of the content of conversation: reinforcement of statement of opinion. *Journal of Abnormal and Social Psychology,* 1955, *51,* 668–676.

Wahler, R. G. Selling generality: some specific and general effects of child behavior therapy. *Journal of Applied Behavior Analysis,* 1969, *2,* 239–248.

Widgery, R., & Stackpole, G. Desk position, interviewee anxiety and interviewer credibility: an example of cognitive balance in a dyad. *Journal of Counseling Psychology,* 1972, *19,* 173–177.

Winett, R. A., & Winkler, R. C. Current behavior modification in the classroom: be still, be quiet, be docile. *Journal of Applied Behavior Analysis,* 1972, *5,* 499–504.

Wodarski, J. S. Procedural steps in the implementation of behavior modification programs in open settings. *Journal of Behavior Therapy and Experimental Psychiatry,* 1976, *7,* 133–136.

———, Feldman, R. A., & Flax, N. Group therapy and anti-social children: a social learning theory perspective. *Small Group Behavior,* 1974, *5*(2), 182–210.

Chapter 5

THE APPLICATION OF THE RESPONDENT MODEL TO SOCIAL WORK PRACTICE

In the social work literature there are lacking detailed explanations of the respondent model and the treatment techniques derived from it. Thus, the practitioner's understanding of the empirical rationale upon which the techniques rest and his application of the techniques are hindered. In order to facilitate the application of these techniques the historical development and basic elements of respondent conditioning are presented first. Next are reviewed the techniques of progressive relaxation, systematic desensitization, and assertive training, all of which are based on the respondent model. Following the presentation of each technique is a review of problems that might occur in implementing the techniques.

HISTORICAL DEVELOPMENT

The original theoretical rationale for progressive relaxation, systematic desensitization, and assertive training is derived from classical conditioning theory. In order to lay the groundwork for this chapter it is necessary to elaborate upon the classical conditioning paradigm briefly reviewed in Chapter 2. Classical conditioning, often referred to as Pavlovian conditioning, was discovered in the course of a series of studies, conducted by the eminent Russian physiologist, I. P. Pavlov, on the physiology of digestion in the early 1900s. Pavlov was concerned originally with the preparatory reflexes of the stomach, that is, how the stomach prepares itself, by secreting digestive juices, for food that is placed in the mouth.

The salivary reflex, like all other reflexes, consists of a stimulus, food in the dog's mouth, that elicits a response, salivation. Pavlov discovered if a previously neutral stimulus occurs just before food is placed in the dog's mouth, the neutral stimulus itself gradually can elicit salivation. In Pavlov's terms, the food in the mouth is an unconditioned stimulus that elicits the unconditioned response of salivation. After being repeatedly paired with the unconditioned stimulus, the previously neutral stimulus acquires the eliciting powers of the unconditioned stimulus and is called the conditioned stimulus. In Pavlov's original conditioning experiment he rang a bell (a neutral stimulus) just prior to placing food (unconditioned stimulus) in a dog's mouth. The unconditioned food stimulus elicited saliva (unconditioned response) and, after repeatedly pairing the neutral bell stimulus with the unconditioned food stimulus, the neutral stimulus by itself gained the power of eliciting the saliva, thus, in the parlance of conditioning theory, becoming a conditioned stimulus.

Although Pavlov first demonstrated the classical conditioning process using laboratory animals, it was left to John B. Watson and Rosalie Rayner to demonstrate the applicability of classical conditioning theory to humans. In a now classical study by Watson and Rayner (1920), a baby less than a year old by the name of Albert was conditioned to "fear" a rat. Every time the child was in the presence of the rat, a piece of metal was struck which produced a loud noise near the child. Soon the child began to cry vigorously when the rat alone was present. The following schematic diagram and narrative illustrates the classical conditioning paradigm used to condition Albert's cry at the mere sight of the rat.

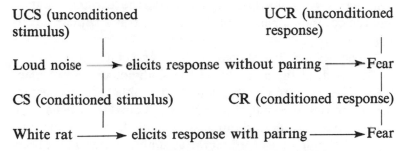

The loud noise (unconditioned stimulus) produced by vigorously striking a steel bar placed directly behind the infant's head elicited a fear response (unconditioned stimulus). A white rat (neutral stimulus) was repeatedly paired with the loud noise until by itself the white rat (now a conditioned stimulus) was able to elicit a fear response (conditioned response).

Two other theoretical principles of relevance to relaxation, systematic desensitization and assertive training, also have been derived from classical conditioning theory. First, the principle of *generalization* states that stimuli similar to but different from conditioned stimuli develop eliciting powers. Thus, not only did Albert, in the Watson and Rayner study, respond with fear to the conditioned white rat stimulus, but his fear generalized to other stimuli such as a rabbit, dog, cat, or simply a ball of wool that resembled the rat. Second, the principle of *extinction* states that the conditioned stimulus will lose its elicitation power unless periodically paired with the unconditioned stimulus. Thus, if the white rat were continuously presented to Albert without being intermittently paired with the loud noise, the fear response would eventually extinguish. The neutral stimulus through being paired a number of times with an eliciting stimulus thus acquires properties similar to the unconditioned stimulus. After the neutral stimulus acquires such properties it must be paired occasionally with the original stimulus to maintain them. For example, a client can develop a fear of airplane travel through the pairing of the travel with bad weather, unpleasant reasons for air travel such as sickness or death, and so forth. This fear is maintained through avoiding the learning situation and the occasional pairing of the airplane travel with an adversive stimulus.

The maintenance of anxiety, fears, and nonassertive behavior is based on the assumption that individuals do not place themselves in learning situations that enable them to acquire new responses to stimuli that currently elicited these behaviors. Progressive relaxation training, systematic desensitization, and assertive training are based on the assumption that these procedures facilitate the establishment of responses that are incompatible with anxiety, fear, and nonassertive behaviors. Various explanations of why these techniques change behavior such as expectations (Brown, 1973; Wilkens, 1971), reciprocal inhibition theory (Yates, 1975), counter conditioning (Davison, 1968), operant shaping (Kazdin & Wilcoxon, 1976), relationship factors such as warmth (Andrews, 1966; Krapfl & Nawas, 1969; Morris & Suckerman, 1974 a, b; Woldwitz, 1975), cognitive factors (Borkovec, 1973; Davison & Valins, 1969; Lott & Murray, 1975; Rosen, 1976), modeling (Kazdin & Wilcoxon, 1976), and muscular activities (Craighead, 1973; Farmer & Wright, 1971) have all been entertained. However, the empirical data to support any one of these explanations over another is lacking. A review of the literature seems to indicate that all factors are operative.

PROGRESSIVE RELAXATION

Introduction

Relaxation may be one of the most important techniques a practitioner can learn if we entertain the assumption that the majority of clients who seek counsel are highly anxious. This technique can be employed initially to reduce anxiety levels in order to facilitate the application of other procedures to resolve difficulties. Relaxation is used primarily as a method of teaching the client a coping skill that can be used to deal with daily anxieties. The procedure consists of teaching clients to relax certain muscle groups to reduce their level of anxiety and/or tension (Bernstein & Borkovec, 1973).

Theory

Edmond Jacobson originated the ideas and techniques for relaxation training through his investigations of anxiety (Jacobson, 1938). He reasoned that complete muscular relaxation was the direct physical opposite of anxiety which is indicated by the presence of a high degree of muscular tension. Therefore the logical treatment for anxious behavior is muscle relaxation. This follows the basic assumption that all of the techniques reviewed in this chapter rest upon, that is, the development of a response incompatible with the behavior being altered. His treatment plan never received much attention due to the large amount of time it required, approximately 200 training sessions to learn the procedures. The techniques of relaxation became popular after Joseph Wolpe reworked and abbreviated the method to make this application more practical (Wolpe, 1973). Wolpe streamlined the procedures to involve approximately 10 training sessions (plus home practice) and purported that by the 10th session the individual should be capable of developing deep relaxation in under a minute.

Progressive relaxation can be easily confused with systematic desensitization, a technique to diffuse specific anxiety- or fear-producing stimuli. In systematic desensitization the client is first taught the methods of relaxation. The therapist then helps the client maintain the state of relaxation while being presented with a hierarchy of anxiety- or fear-producing stimuli. Thus, the use of relaxation in the application of system-

atic desensitization is for the purpose of diffusing specific anxi-
ety- or fear-producing stimuli.

Criteria for the Application of Progressive Relaxation and Systematic Desensitization

The application of progressive relaxation and systematic desensitization can be differentiated on three continua. These must
be used flexibly and are presented here only as a rough guide
since more concrete guidelines await empirical development. In
general, progressive relaxation is used where stimuli are less
specific and not as highly charged. The continuum of specificity
suggests that the more specific the anxiety-producing event, the
more appropriate is the use of systematic desensitization. Thus,
progressive relaxation can be used to reduce general anxiety
states where stimuli are less specific and not as highly charged
and systematic desensitization used to reduce the fear-producing potential of specific items.

    Another continuum is the level of anxiety that the client
is experiencing. If the client is experiencing a high level of
anxiety, systematic desensitization should be used as the treatment of choice if stimuli can be isolated and hierarchies constructed.

    The last continuum is the frequency of exposure. The more
the client is exposed to the anxiety-producing situation, the
more likely it is that some of the anxiety will be extinguished.
Thus someone who faces insomnia every night would probably
experience less anxiety than someone who manages to avoid the
anxiety-producing situation for long periods of time and relaxation therefore would be the appropriate treatment for the in-
somniac.

    Another consideration to be made centers around the
cause for tension. The relevant question is to what extent is the
anxiety appropriate. If the client's tension is in response to an
actual dilemma, a more appropriate treatment goal would be

for the therapist to help the client modify the environment in terms of developing strategies to alleviate the conditions.

Requisites for Progressive Relaxation

Progressive relaxation should be preceded by medical clearance. Initially, all possible organic causes for tension should be ruled out. Second, it should be kept in mind that the use of drugs inhibits the effectiveness of progressive relaxation. Medical advice should be obtained regarding the possibility of discontinuing any drug use while a client is being trained in relaxation techniques. Finally, the worker must make sure that the tensing of certain muscle groups is not physically harmful to the client.

In order to be effective, progressive relaxation requires that the client be able to do three things. First, he must be able to focus on specific muscle groups. Second, he must be able to tense and relax these muscle groups. Finally, he must be willing to practice the exercises regularly, for without practice the effectiveness of the skill is limited.

It is important in progressive relaxation training that everything possible is done to increase the ability of the client to focus his attention on the relaxation procedures. The therapeutic setting should be quiet and comfortable. As much external stimulation as possible should be eliminated such as phones, distracting noises such as typewriters and so forth. Windows and doors should be closed and shades drawn. Room lighting should be dim to the point where it is comfortable for the client. In making the client comfortable it is desirable that his body be completely supported. The ideal chair is a well-padded recliner. Loosely fitting and comfortable clothing is the most suitable for the client to participate in relaxation training.

A useful skill for the therapist to have is the ability to instill in the client a feeling of enthusiasm and confidence in the effects of relaxation. Above all the worker should impress the client

with his own competence. The worker should pay close attention to those conditions that act as unique stimuli to the client
and which may not facilitate relaxation training. For example,
if an individual gets upset (tense) in the dark or when his eyes
are closed it may be best to start the training process another
way. If the individual reports getting upset while lying down,
say due to the intrusion of sexual thoughts, then sitting
back may be a more appropriate way to begin. Generally,
to the extent possible, the idea is to decrease tension producing stimuli (both environmental and individual) of the therapeutic context.

At the beginning of the first session, the therapist educates
the client, explaining to him the role of tension in the total
problem situation and indicating that from a social learning
point of view tension or anxiety is seen as a learned behavior.
The client is informed that he has been exposed to experiences
that originally caused him anxiety or fear. After one or more
such exposures the client has learned to associate the anxiety
response with a variety of stimuli original and similar to those
present in former learning contexts. These stimuli in themselves
should no longer elicit the anxiety response. However, due to
the laws of learning the anxious behavior still occurs when the
client thinks about or interacts with such items. The therapist
then informs the client that the empirical data show that progressive relaxation training methods are the best available to
help him reduce the anxiety-producing properties of the
stimuli.

Before the therapist attempts to engage the client in relaxation training he needs to explain carefully the rationale for its
use. The worker should outline the treatment plan, explain the
relationship of progressive relaxation to other treatment procedures, and give an estimation of the amount of tension or
anxiety that can be expected to be reduced and the length of
time that will be required. Before beginning, the client should
have a communicated understanding and acceptance of progressive relaxation as an aspect of treatment. All of this, of

course, is no different from responsible procedure preceding any therapeutic interaction.

Technique

Training in progressive relaxation starts by first familiarizing the client with the basic procedure. After the client has an idea of what he can expect the client and worker actually go through the progressive relaxation exercises. The first progressive relaxation training session involves the relaxation of 16 muscle groups. They are:

1. Dominant Hand and Forearm
2. Dominant Biceps
3. Nondominant Hand and Forearm
4. Nondominant Biceps
5. Forehead
6. Upper Cheeks and Nose
7. Lower Cheeks and Jaws
8. Neck and Throat
9. Chest, Shoulders, and Upper Back
10. Stomach/Abdomen
11. Dominant Thigh
12. Dominant Calf
13. Dominant Foot
14. Nondominant Thigh
15. Nondominant Calf
16. Nondominant Foot

After the client has mastered relaxation of these 16 muscle groups, the client can be taught to consolidate them into seven. For example, the muscles of the arm are tensed and relaxed as a single group; thus the hand, lower arm, and biceps muscles are combined. After this is mastered the seven can be consolidated to four. When relaxation is mastered with four muscle groups, the client can begin to learn exercises that do not involve the tensing and the relaxing of muscles, but instead recall the feeling of relaxation.* In conditioned relaxation the client can learn to associate a cue word or counting with relaxation to bring about the relaxed state. This makes it possible to use relaxation in a variety of situations.

The beginning phases of progressive relaxation consist of a basic five-step procedure:

1. Focusing attention on a specific muscle group
2. Tensing the muscle group for 5 to 10 seconds, while focusing attention on the sensations
3. Immediate relief of the muscle group on the verbal cue, relax
4. Focusing on the sensations that accompany relaxation for about 30 seconds
5. Maintaining the relaxed or tension free state

The alternation between tension and release (relaxation), and the concentration on ensuing sensation, helps the individual develop a feedback system that facilitates:

1. Recognition and monitoring of tension and relaxation
2. Perceptual isolation of areas of muscle tension
3. Bringing the induction of tension and relaxation under voluntary control

Beginning sessions should involve 16 groups, the recommended procedure being to begin with the first muscle group, the dominant hand and forearm. The tension release procedure

*This description is only to provide the worker with a beginning description of what is involved in the use of progressive relaxation training. Before implementing the technique the clinician will want to consult Bernstein and Borkovec (1973) and Wolpe (1973). Moreover, many records and tapes are available that facilitate the clients practicing in contexts other than the therapist's office (Bernstein & Borkovec, 1973; Budzynski 1977).

is repeated twice in succession. If relaxation is achieved, then the same procedures are repeated with the next muscle group, the dominant bicep, while maintaining a relaxed state in the first muscle group. Maintaining relaxation in previously exercised muscle groups, while acting on another specific group, of course, contributes to the overall feeling of relaxation. It also has the advantage of further complementing the objective of being able to manipulate regular muscle groups on an individual basis (relaxation in certain ones and tension in others). This process is simply repeated until all muscle groups have been tensed and relaxed, and all are reported by the client to be in a state of relaxation.

If relaxation in the muscle group is not reportedly achieved in the course of two tensing and release sequences, then the process can be repeated until it has been accomplished. However, the literature suggests not exceeding four or five sequences since muscle strain and frustration might result, both of which are counterproductive in relaxation.

Beginning with the stomach muscles, the client is instructed next to take a deep breath and hold it in and then to release the breath at the same time he releases the muscle tension. This begins an important association between breath release and relaxation, which is useful at the more advanced level of progressive relaxation training, cue conditioned relaxation. The therapist can also begin to time his verbal relaxation suggestion with the client's breath release, which further reinforces the relaxation reflex that is being developed, i.e., the word "relax" now is being associated with the actual experience of relaxation.

Descriptions in the literature reveal that many therapists institute progressive relaxation with less than the 16 muscle groups recommended by Wolpe. There is no indication that they experienced any particular difficulties in starting on a group plan of eight or more, and the implication is that there is more than one way to approach the process. Moreover, if the recommended procedures are followed as described in the literature the guarantee is that all of the muscles of each group will be involved thereby ensuring maximum possible relaxation.

Once the relaxation process is completed, the therapist reviews sequentially (last to first) the muscle groups that have been relaxed, reinforcing, through suggestion, continued and deeper relaxation. The therapist then asks the client to signal if all the muscle groups are relaxed. If not, he reviews the muscle groups asking the client to signal the group that is not relaxed. Once that group is identified the worker can repeat the relaxation process with that particular group of muscles.

If all the groups are relaxed, the therapist continues to focus the client's attention on these sensations of general relaxation for a couple of minutes, which allows the client to experience the pleasant sensation a little longer. With the successful completion of the relaxation process, the worker begins a gradual four-count termination process. He instructs the client that on the count of four, he is to begin to move his legs and feet; at three he is to begin to move his arms and hands; at two he is to begin to move his head and neck; and at one to begin to open his eyes.

As some clients may feel a little disoriented at first the worker can make a casual reference to this state being analogous to the feeling of waking up from a nap and so forth, essentially relabeling the experience so as to stem any anxiety that might ensue from transitory disorientation.

The last few minutes of the session should involve some post relaxation questioning. The worker begins with a generally oriented open-ended question "how do you feel," and so forth and moves to more specific questions about any particular:

1.   difficulty with one or another muscle group in relaxation,

2.   difficulty with anything the therapist said, or

3.   any particular success with some phrase or wording that the therapist used.

This procedure provides feedback that can help the worker practice more effectively with the client. Additionally if the worker has the client describe how the sensations felt, the therapist can then include the same descriptions (verbatim) in the next relaxation session, thereby facilitating and reinforcing relaxation even more.

The 16 muscle group tension relaxation exercises take around three weeks to master (provided the client practices two or three times a week at home). The second phase, which may be appropriately engaged during the fourth and fifth sessions, involves combining some of the 16 muscle groups so that seven muscle groups are now tensed and relaxed. The procedure is exactly the same as before, only some of the muscle groups are combined for expediency.

The third phase involves further combinations so as to reduce the number of muscle groups to four. It is important to understand that all of the muscles involved in the first phase (16 groups) are involved in this phase (four groups); the difference is that now they are combined into a smaller number of units. This phase is appropriate for sessions six and seven, and the overall time needed to go through the relaxation procedure should now be reduced to about 10 minutes.

The fourth phase involves relaxation of four muscle groups through recall and should begin around the eighth session. This procedure differs markedly from the first three in that it does not involve deliberately tensing muscles. Instead the general procedure is to:

1.   Focus attention on the muscle group.

2.   Focus attention on any tension in that muscle group for about five seconds.

3.   Focus attention on recalling feelings associated with the relief of that tension for about 30 seconds.

4.   Focus on the feelings of relaxation associated with tension release.

If the procedure induces relaxation then the worker goes on to the next muscle group; if not, the procedure is simply repeated. If there is a particular difficulty with one muscle group, to induce relaxation the therapist can go back to the tense/release exercise for that particular group.

Phase five involves four muscle groups for recall and counting. This essentially involves going through the phase four procedure, plus an additional vocal counting to 10 that is timed with the client's breath exhalations. Although there should probably be some fixed ratio breath count, it need not be one to one. During this ten count, the therapist reviews the four muscle groups while suggesting deeper relaxation.

Phase six involves relaxation through counting alone. The worker once again counts time with breath exercises and in the process suggests deep relaxation. This brings the total time needed to induce relaxation down to approximately a minute. If there is any particular muscle group that is resistant to relaxation, through this method the therapist can simply go back to an earlier method (recall, tension/release) for that particular group.

Phase seven is conditioned relaxation. The goal is to enable the client to achieve relaxation in response to a self-produced cue. This type of procedure presents a significant advantage over the general relaxation procedure. The original procedure tends to be rather time consuming, which of course affects costs and limits the implementation of the technique. Thus, there are particular contexts that render the technique relatively impractical, i.e., the client may become anxious but cannot institute exercises to reduce the level of tension at that particular time or place.

In conditioned relaxation the client is first trained in progressive relaxation and then taught an association between the state of relaxation and a cue word. The cue word thus becomes an effective device in alleviating tension any time the client experiences anxiety. The client merely invokes the cue word and returns to a state of relaxation. This makes progressive relaxation highly adaptable to many social situations (Philipp

& Wilde, 1972; Russell & Sipich, 1973; Sirota & Mahoney, 1974). The basic two-step process for developing this cue conditioned relaxation consists of the following:

1. The client is instructed to repeat a silent cue word with each breath release that is paired with muscle release. This helps an association to occur between the cue word and relaxation. The cue word can be "relax," "be calm," "cool," and so forth. Words should be chosen that have tension-reducing properties due to cultural conditioning.

2. The client is told to imagine several stressful scenes until some anxiety is felt, take a deep breath, and then repeat the cue word silently. If the anxiety is reduced the association between the cue word and relaxation is sufficient.

Problems

The worker may encounter the following problems in the application of the relaxation procedure. First, muscle cramps, spasms, and tics may result. Muscle cramps can be dealt with by lowering the level of tension in a training phase that calls for the muscles to be tensed. Since spasms and tics are not unusual, the worker can reassure the client that they are only a normal response to effective relaxation and after the first few sessions they should no longer occur.

Second, problems include intrusive thoughts, such as strange feelings, losing control, and an arousal of minor tensions. Intrusive thoughts are troublesome in that they are tension producing in themselves. The worker can increase the amount of talking in order to avoid silent periods, or suggest an alternative relaxing set of thoughts for the client. Thoughts of sexual arousal are often disturbing for the client. It is recommended that the worker explain that their reaction is normal and not a cause for anxiety.

Many unusual and new positive feelings may be experienced by the client in the first relaxation training sessions. Again, the worker should respond to these feelings with the reassurance that they are not unusual. The client can be encouraged to enjoy rather than fear these new experiences. For some clients following the regular relaxation program may result in a restimulation of certain disturbing experiences that cause them to feel they are losing control of their emotional states or their behaviors. In these cases the relaxation program should be modified so as to introduce each component in a step-by-step fashion. This could be done by starting the progressive relaxation procedure with the lights on, having the client sit in an upright position with his eyes open, and maintaining progressions at a slow pace.

Other problems include the client's failure to practice the procedures outside of the treatment context. The client who fails to practice should be reassured by the therapist as to the importance of following instructions and of regular practice itself. The client may confront an inability to relax specific muscle groups. Alternative muscle-tensing strategies should be developed by the worker to help the client relax. Problems may center around the sleep-inducing properties of the relaxation procedure. If a client responds to relaxation procedures by sleeping, the worker can progressively increase the volume of his voice until the client awakens. Another problem may involve a client who is talking or laughing during the procedure. The client should be instructed as to the necessity of remaining quiet unless this is an anxiety-producing state. When coughing or sneezing occurs, the client should be told that it is acceptable to do so since holding back may cause more tension and would not facilitate the application of relaxation procedures.

SYSTEMATIC DESENSITIZATION

Systematic desensitization is the most empirically based technique that social workers can employ to reduce specific fears and anxieties (Franks & Wilson, 1975). Generally criteria for its application are when anxieties are localized on objects; situations are external to the individual; the client's fears can be described and clearly defined as to time, place, and setting; and the client has adequate personal social functioning in other areas. Poor candidates for systematic desensitization include those with a history of psychosis and those with ill-defined and free-floating anxiety. Fears that are the product of specific interpersonal anxieties such as fear of social interactions may be treated through assertive training in conjunction with systematic desensitization. There will also be problems in using systematic desensitization when baseline behavioral analysis shows secondary gains and reinforcement of phobic fears from significant others in a person's life and/or the client exhibits extreme personality and social disorganization (Wolpe, 1973; Yates, 1970, 1975).

Technique

Systematic desensitization consists of four components. First, there is training in deep muscle relaxation. Second, there is the establishment of subjective anxiety through the use of various scales. Third, there is the construction of hierarchies, and finally, there is pairing of relaxation with anxiety-producing items that compose the hierarchy. The essential components of the systematic desensitization procedure consist of a strong anxiety-competing response, i.e., relaxation, a hierarchy of anxiety-producing stimuli, and the pairing of the anxiety-provoking stimuli with the competing response of relaxation (Cooke, 1968; Sue, 1972).

Following an initial interview and an assessment of the client's phobic behaviors, the worker begins by explaining and providing the rationale for the use of systematic desensitization. The first step in the process is to clear up misconceptions concerning the rationale behind systematic desensitization and to decide if the technique is the most appropriate or whether changes in the client's life situation are necessary. Depending on the source, anxiety can be reduced sometimes through the technique of stimulus control, that is, by changing the client's life situation or reducing or eliminating the stimuli that are fear producing.

During this phase in clinical practice the worker should establish a positive atmosphere of warmth and confidence in the client and maintain expectations of success. The progressive relaxation training should be placed in proper perspective with regard to the client's difficulty in the overall treatment plan. Specifically, it should be clarified as to whether the client's tension is seen as a primary difficulty or whether relaxation will be viewed as a means to other therapeutic ends, that is lessening of the fear-producing properties of specific stimuli.

The client is informed that progressive relaxation training consists of learning how to sequentially tense and then relax various muscle groups, and that the state of relaxation is paired with the client attending to items that evoke fear or anxious behavior. Once the client has learned the progressive relaxation technique the importance of regular practice at home is stressed. The worker describes the procedure of systematic de-sensitization and explains how muscle groups will be relaxed. This can be facilitated by the worker modeling the procedures of muscle relaxation. Given no difficulty up to this point, the actual training begins usually with the client's dominant fore-hand. The training procedure was reviewed earlier in the chapter and is the same when used in systematic desensitization.

The Establishment of Subjective Anxiety

Concurrently, while the client is learning the relaxation procedure, the second major component of systematic desensitization is the establishment of the anxiety potential of various stimuli through the use of a scale of subjective anxiety. The client is asked to rate subjective states of anxiety on a scale of 0 to 100, the most anxiety-producing items being rated the highest. This scale is extremely useful to the worker who needs to be aware of the client's assessment of his or her own subjective states of anxiety and for feedback purposes in the systematic desensitzation procedure.

With practice, the clients are generally able to reliably indicate their subjective states of anxiety. The items are labeled according to their subjective units of disturbance, commonly called SUD's. This aids the client in rating the items on the hierarchy before and during the actual imagination of these objects or situations. The difference between the rating of various items should be evenly spaced and should not exceed a difference of 10 between any two consecutive items.

The Construction of Anxiety Hierarchies

An anxiety hierarchy is a rating and sequential listing of anxiety-producing stimuli ranked from the least to the highest with regard to the amount of anxiety they produce. These rankings usually center around a given theme and the difference between items is approximately 10 SUD's. It may be in relation to a particular external stimulus such as dead animals or closed places, or it may be internal such as fear of going insane or a fear of rejection.

For example, aspects of an elaborate theme concerning violent weather may consist of the following items: overcast day; dark, cloudy day; dark, cloudy, and windy day; and dark, cloudy, and windy with lightning, and so forth.

Sometimes a number of physically different external events may function to induce a general internal response. For example, a female with claustrophobia also experienced similar feelings when she wore irremovable nail polish, a tight ring, tightly fitting clothes, and so forth. The common internal response in this case was the fear of a situation in which she lacked control and possibly a generalized fear of confinement (Wolpe, 1973).

Hierarchy construction occurs in the therapeutic process while the client is learning progressive relaxation. It is not seen as a fixed procedure and is always subject to modification as determined by the client and worker. However, the construction of the hierarchy is not done under the influence of relaxation since the scale needs to approximate as closely as possible the client's normal responses. Data for the hierarchy construction are gathered from four main sources. One is the client's past history gathered through interview data; second, the client's responses to the Willoughby questionnaire (Wolpe, 1973), which deals mainly with anxieties associated with certain interpersonal, situational behaviors; third, the client's responses to a fear survey schedule; and finally, the worker's investigation with the client through therapeutic discussions of other stimuli or situations which produce anxiety for the client.

The data are then classified into themes, which requires much skill on the part of the worker who must assess correctly the uniting themes pertaining to fear in several situations with regard to different stimuli. For example, differences in hierarchies of anxiety could be a function of the number of phobic objects (one person versus a crowd), distance from the object (one foot versus a hundred yards), size of the object (small dogs versus big dogs), intensity of the stimulus (soft sound versus loud noise), duration of the stimulus or situation (one minute in an elevator versus ten minutes) or misinformation about a situation or object (a belief that masturbation causes anxiety).

It is not important that the client had a direct experience with each of the items of the hierarchy. However, it is crucial that the client be able to imagine each of the scenes and that they be evenly spaced in a quantifiable format so the client is able to rate them accordingly after having imagined them during the session. The worker needs to be able to discriminate between more normal objective fears and maladaptive ones and additionally to be able to ascertain what an effective degree of fear related to different stimuli should be.

Given differences in individual clients and differences in the number of phobias, the number of scene presentations necessary and so forth varies. Thus, it can be seen that there is no formal timetable for how systematic desensitization should proceed. With regard to specific details of systematic desensitization, the following guidelines may be useful to the practitioner. The more anxiety-producing the scene, the shorter its presentation should be. The average scene presentation lasts from 5 to 7 seconds. Generally, early presentations of scenes are shorter, later ones are longer. The intervals between scenes usually last between 10 to 30 seconds. The more anxious the client, the longer the interval. The spacing of the sessions is usually once or twice a week. Generally, it is the type of phobia and not the person that determines the rate of change. For example, phobias related to the number of fearful objects are generally more rapidly eliminated than are phobias related to proximity to the fearful object. Clients should be provided with copies of the constructed hierarchies and asked by the worker to collect the baseline data on these hierarchies consisting of the frequency and intensity of the anxiety these items produce. This should be done throughout treatment to provide feedback to gauge the progress of treatment.

Systematic Desensitization Procedure: Counteracting Anxiety by Relaxation

After the client has achieved proficiency in deep muscle relaxation and subjective anxiety scaling and the hierarchy has been constructed, the process of systematic desensitization can begin. Basically, the process consists of the imagination of a fear- or anxiety-producing scene in a state of deep muscle relaxation in a controlled environment. It is the imagination that has been postulated to be the essential component for cure (Kazdin & Wilcoxon, 1976). The scenes are imagined in the order of the least anxiety-producing to the most anxiety-producing.

The first scene presented is usually neutral and is called a control scene, that is, it is not expected to be anxiety producing. The purpose of this scene is to evaluate whether the client has any difficulties in forming images. The client is then asked to imagine one scene at a time as described by the worker. Once the image is formed the client signals the worker using a prede-termined cue; usually the raising of the index finger is most visible to the worker. The client is then asked to imagine a scene for approximately 5 to 7 seconds and stop imagining the scene upon instructions from the worker, such as "stop imagining the scene" or simply "stop." The client then rates the scene accord-ing to the Subjective Units Disturbance Scale. Generally 20 to 30 seconds are given between scene presentations to allow the client to again focus on being relaxed. Usually four to seven scene presentations are adequate to lower the anxiety potential of an item. Sometimes as many as 20 to 30 presentations will be necessary.

Prolonged exposure to an aversive scene should be avoided as this may create increased phobic reaction or sensitivity to these items or generate a lack of confidence in the worker.

Problems

The worker needs to be sensitive to two particular problems that can occur when scenes are presented. The first concerns anxiety from the first presentation that is continued or carried over into successive presentations of the same or similar scenes. When this occurs and successive presentations do not reduce the subjective anxiety rating by the client, the worker should present the preceding item on the hierarchy until no anxiety is experienced. Exposure to a very disturbing scene should be avoided since it can increase phobic sensitivity. If a scene pre-sented is extremely disturbing to the client the therapist should stop the presentation of the scene and go through the proper steps to again induce relaxation. The worker might then try to present the scene for shorter intervals of 1 to 2 seconds and build up gradually to the scene on the hierarchy by adding new scenes.

If despite all careful planning and precautions, the client is receiving no benefits from treatment, a number of pitfalls should be looked for. First, if difficulty in relaxation seems to be the main problem the use of CO_2 gas or drugs may be successful in helping to induce relaxation.* Misleading or irrelevant hierarchies can be another difficulty. There are two main problems to be concerned about with hierarchies. The first is when the fear items on the hierarchy are related to the context that involve the setting for the fears but not the sources of the fears. The second concerns constructed fears that are a product of symbolic reactions. This occurs when one stimulus evokes the same internal response as the causal stimulus but is not a part of the stimulus complex that elicits the anxiety. In both these cases the client will proceed through the scene, but there will be no carry over into the client's personal environment. The last difficulty involves inadequacies of image. Some people simply cannot conjure up images, while others can but are not invested with any sense of reality. In these cases the therapist can try adding as much verbal detail as possible to the scenes, asking the client to describe what he imagined until it is adequate, or the therapist should, if possible, resort to the use of real stimuli.

ASSERTIVE TRAINING

Assertive training is a set of procedures composed of feedback, modeling, rehearsal, structured assignments, role playing, coaching, and so forth that is used to increase adaptive responses, that is, standing up for one's rights and developing the ability to express spontaneous emotions where appropriate (Carver & Frazier, 1975; Colter & Guerra, 1976; Heimberg, Montgomery, Madsen & Heimberg, 1977; Hersen, Eisler, & Miller, 1973; Rimm & Masters, 1974). In assertive training, the

---

*Only the experienced worker should attempt to induce relaxation through the use of CO^2 gas. Likewise the use of certain drugs to facilitate relaxation should be executed with a physician. The process should be monitored consistently to ensure desired effects.

role of the worker is to structure interventions to facilitate the acquisition of such behaviors.

The therapeutic objective is to provide the client with direct training in those social skills such as ability to refuse requests, disagreeing both passively and actively, and agreeing with compliments, skills that are lacking in their response repertoires but that could facilitate their acquisition of certain reinforcers (Carver & Frazier, 1975). That is, assertive training deals with behaviors that are primarily concerned with the enhancement or maintenance of personal reinforcement but which risk loss of other reinforcers and even punishment (Rich & Schroeder, 1976).

Such an approach is contrasted with Alberti and Emmons' (1974) definition of assertiveness as "behavior which enables a person to act in his own best interest, stand up for himself without undue anxiety, to express his rights without destroying the rights of others."

Looking at the two approaches one can see how the definition of assertiveness has changed over the last few years. A new definition which is all encompassing is as follows: Assertive behavior is the skill to seek, maintain, or enhance personal reinforcement in an interpersonal situation through an expression of feelings or personal wants when such expression risks loss of other reinforcements or even punishment (Rich & Schroeder, 1976).

The new definition does not specify the content of an assertive response. That is, assertive behavior may express positive or negative feelings or may be directed toward various goals, depending on the values of the individual. The degree of assertiveness may be measured by the effectiveness of an individual's responses in producing, maintaining, or enhancing reinforcement. Strong or mild expressions of desire or feeling may be judged equally assertive if each produces comparable reinforcement in comparable situations. A response may be judged to be more assertive, however, when it elicits reinforcement in a situation unlikely to yield reinforcement or in one involving high risk of losing reinforcement. The magnitude of self-expression depends on the character of the interpersonal situation rather than the degree of assertiveness.

Techniques for Assessment

Many self-inventories are available to the worker for the assessment of assertive behavior. The worker has to choose the inventory that is the most appropriate for his client and the one that has the highest reliability and validity. Behavioral tests are in the primitive stages of development. Lange and Jakubowski (1976) provide four criteria which can help guide the worker in assessing what areas the client's behavior needs to be altered: 1) the ability to say no, 2) the ability to ask for favors or to make requests, 3) the ability to express positive and negative feelings, 4) the ability to initiate, continue, and terminate general conversations.

Development of Assertive Belief System

The development of a cognitive thought system to go along with the assertive behavior is essential. This process focuses on the rights of an individual, illustrating that we have been conditioned in our culture to control and/or not express our feelings, that we have a right to have reasonable needs fulfilled and that we will be happier and so will others if we do so.

Lange and Jakubowski (1976) specify the tenets of an assertive belief system as:

1. By standing up for ourselves and letting ourselves be known to others, we gain self-respect and respect from other people.

2. By trying to live our lives in such a way that we never hurt anyone under any circumstances, we end up hurting ourselves and other people.

3. When we stand up for ourselves and express our honest feelings and thoughts in direct and appropriate ways, everyone usually benefits in the long run. Likewise, when we demean other people, we also demean ourselves and everyone involved usually loses in the process.

4. By sacrificing our integrity and denying our personal feelings, relationships are usually damaged or prevented from developing. Likewise, personal relationships are hurt when we try to control others through hostility, intimidation, or guilt.

5. Personal relationships become more authentic and satisfying when we share our honest reactions with other people and do not block others' sharing their reactions with us.

6. Not letting others know what we think and feel is just as selfish as not attending to other people's thoughts and feelings.

7. When we frequently sacrifice our rights, we teach other people to take advantage of us.

8. By being assertive and telling other people how their behavior affects us, we are giving them an opportunity to change their behavior, and we are showing respect for their right to know where they stand with us.

9. We all have the right to respect from other people.

10. We all have the right to have needs and to have these needs be as important as other people's needs. Moreover, we have the right to ask (not demand) that other people respond to our needs and to decide whether we will take care of other people's needs.

11. We all have the right to have feelings and to express these feelings in ways which do not violate the dignity of other people (e.g., the right to feel tired, happy, depressed, sexy, angry, lonesome, silly).

12. We all have the right to decide whether we will meet other people's expectations or whether we will act in ways that fit us, as long as we act in ways that do not violate other people's rights.

13.   We all have the right to form our own opinions and to express these opinions.

How the worker helps the client develop this belief system is a matter of individual preference. Some aids for the acquisiton of the assertive belief system are reading materials such as Alberti and Emmons' (1974) *Your Perfect Right—A Guide to Assertive Behavior;* Lange and Jakubowski's (1976) *Responsible Assertive Behavior,* Chapter 3; and Smith's (1975) *When I Say No, I Feel Guilty.* Also, therapists' discussions and modeling of assertive behaviors that reflect the system, discussions of cognitive components with individuals who have developed assertive behaviors, and modeling of the behaviors in group contexts will facilitate the acquisition of assertive behaviors.

Techniques That Can Be Used

Once the worker has specified the client behaviors that need to be increased or decreased, the following techniques can be used. Behaviors can be acquired through the use of instructions, modeling, and simulation exercises. In the use of *instructions* the client and therapist discuss various situations and the worker informs the client regarding the appropriate behavior that the client should exhibit such as eye contact, body posture, gestures, distance from another person, facial expression, paralinguistic speech characteristics, socially appropriate content of responses, body language, and composition of verbal statements (Serber, 1972). *Modeling* involves a situation where the therapist or a surrogate takes the place of a client in acting out a particular encounter or interaction while the client observes. Modeling has been used with live models, audio tapes, videotapes, films, and in imagination. Whatever the mode of viewing the model, the client then takes his own place in the interactional situation when he is comfortable in doing so (Eisler, Hersen, & Miller, 1973; Friedman, 1971; Rathus, 1973; Young,

Rimm, & Kennedy, 1973). *Simulation* involves a series of content-related techniques which simulates social processes such as returning of faulty merchandise, initiating a conversation, asking for a raise, and so forth to provide the client the ability to practice being assertive (Galassi, Galassi, & Litz, 1974; Schinke & Rose, 1976).

The first attempt at an assertive response by an individual will probably only approximate the desired form. Techniques under the general class of feedback can help refine the response. Feedback can be provided by the worker, the client himself, peers, and videotape or other medium. Feedback should always contain positive reinforcement for the effort and be structured in such a manner so as to facilitate the client's movement toward the terminal performance criteria. This procedure is analogous to the shaping procedure used in other clinical situations. Many times feedback procedures such as the ones currently discussed are depicted as coaching in the literature (McFall & Lillesand, 1971; McFall & Marston, 1970; McFall & Twentyman, 1973).

Homework

To facilitate the transfer and maintenance of assertive behavior, workers can structure the following homework tasks:

1. Having the client practice the behavior in a situation that as nearly as possible approximates the environment wherein the client desires to exhibit the behavior.

2. Employing cognitive rehearsal procedures involving scenes where the client imagines exhibiting the behavior and securing reinforcement.

3. Programming the client's environment to assure that the assertive responses will be reinforced.

4. Having the client practice the responses in different situations with different individuals to ensure the generalization of behavior.

5.   Reinforcing assertive responses on a variable schedule of reinforcement to ensure maintenance.

Problems

The assessment of the environment to which assertive behaviors are going to be applied is essential. If the responses are going to be applied to close interpersonal interactions such as other family members or fellow workers, the worker must prepare the client to implement the new behavior slowly and to be prepared for these behaviors to be punished initially.

Many theorists posit that the application of assertive techniques in group contexts is more efficacious than on an individual basis (Fensterheim, 1972; Lazarus, 1968; Lomont, 1969; Rathus, 1972). Data are lacking to support these postulates as are the criteria for who will benefit from instructions, modeling, or simulation exercises. It could be argued that group contexts approximate interactional situations more closely where the assertive behaviors are to be exhibited. Therefore the ability to generalize behavior is increased and more feedback can occur which facilitates the acquisition of the behavior. However, much research needs to be executed on what techniques are appropriate with what type of clients and in what type of contexts. It is quite possible that college students can benefit from the application of assertive training through groups with instructions only. However, schizophrenics in psychiatric hospitals may initially benefit the most from an individual approach and gradually be faded into a group approach with modeling and simulation exercises in order to gain the benefits from assertive training (Rose, 1975).

Summary

In this chapter we have reviewed the techniques based on the respondent model. More theoretical development is needed to account for why the techniques work and to provide a rationale for their implementation. These techniques will become more powerful when more stringent criteria are developed regarding when their application is the most appropriate, i.e., what client behaviors benefit the most from what techniques. Moreover, criteria need to be developed in terms of how long the techniques should be implemented, by whom, and where. Finally, most of the treatment techniques reviewed in this chapter are global intervention packages. More research is needed to streamline the packages and evaluate the effective components of each package. When these components are isolated then we can offer clients the most cost-effective procedures.

The techniques were grouped under the respondent model. However, as research has shown, the techniques all have operant and observational modeling learning aspects. Future years will witness the execution of the crucial studies that will provide a more formal theoretical framework that explains the processes operating to account for behavior change.

REFERENCES

Alberti, R. E., & Emmons, M. L. *Your perfect right—A guide to assertive behavior.* (2nd ed.) San Luis Obispo, Ca.: Impact Press, 1974.

Andrews, J. D. Psychotherapy of phobias. *Psychological Bulletin,* 1966, *66,* 455–480.

Bernstein, D. A., & Borkovec, T. *Progressive relaxation training: A manual for the helping professions.* Champaign, Ill.: Research Press; 1973.

Borkovec, T. D. The role of expectancy and physiological feedback in fear research: a review with special reference to subject characteristics. *Behavior Therapy,* 1973, *4,* 449–505.

Brown, H. A. Role of expectancy manipulation in systematic desensitization. *Journal of Consulting Clinical Psychology,* 1973, *41,* 405–11.

Budzynski, T. H. *Relaxation training program.* New York: Biomonitoring Applications, 1977.

Carver, J., & Frazier, J. Some comments on the problem of defining assertive training. *Comprehensive Psychiatry,* 1975, *16,* 269–373.

Cooke, G. Evaluation of the efficacy of the components of reciprocal inhibition psychotherapy. *Journal of Abnormal Psychology,* 1968, *73,* 464–467.

Cotler, S. B., & Guerra, J. J. *Assertion training.* Champaign, Ill.: Research Press, 1976.

Craighead, W. E. The role of muscular relaxation in systematic desensitization. In R. Rubin (Ed.), *Advances in behavior therapy* (Vol. 1), New York: Academic Press, 1973.

Davison, G. C. Systematic desensitization as a counterconditioning process. *Journal of Abnormal Psychology,* 1968, *73,* 91–99.

———— & Valins, S. Maintenance of self-attributed behavior change. *Journal of Personality and Social Psychology,* 1969, *11,* 25–33.

Eisler, M., Hersen, M., & Miller, P. M. Effects of modeling on components of assertive behavior. *Behavior Therapy and Experimental Psychiatry,* 1973, *4,* 1–5.

Farmer, R. G., & Wright, J. M. C. Muscular reactivity and systematic desensitization. *Behavior Therapy 2,* (3), 1971, 1–10.

Fensterheim, H. Behavior therapy: assertive training in groups. In C. J. Sayer, & H. S. Kaplan (Eds.), *Progress in group and family therapy.* New York: Brunner/Mazel, 1972.

Franks, C. M., & Wilson, G. T. (Eds.) *Annual review of behavior therapy, theory and practice.* New York: Brunner/Mazel, 1975.

Friedman, P. H. The effects of modeling and role playing on assertive behavior. In R. D. Rubin, H. Fensterheim, A. A. Lazarus, & C. M. Franks (Eds.), *Advances in behavior therapy.* New York: Academic Press, 1971.

Galassi, J. P., Galassi, M. D., & Litz, M. C. Assertive training in groups using video feedback. *Journal of Counseling Psychology,* 1974, *21*(5), 390–394.

Heimberg, R. G., Montgomery, D., Madsen, C. H., Jr., & Heimberg, J. S. Assertion training: a review of the literature. *Behavior Therapy,* 1977, *8*(5), 953–971.

Hersen, M., Eisler, R. M., & Miller, P. M. Development of assertive responses: clinical measurement and research considerations. *Behavior Research and Therapy,* 1973, *11*(4), 505–521.

Jacobson, E. *Progressive relaxation.* Chicago: University of Chicago Press, 1938.

Kazdin, A., & Wilcoxon, L. Systematic desensitization and nonspecific treatment effects: a methodological evaluation. *Psychological Bulletin,* 1976, *83,* 729–758.

Krapfl, J. E., & Nawas, M. M. Client-therapist relationship factor in systematic desensitization. *Journal of Consulting and Clinical Psychology,* 1969, *33,* 435–439.

Lange, A. J., & Jakubowski, P. *Responsible assertive Behavior. Champaign, Ill.: Research Press, 1976.*

Lazarus, A. A. Behavior therapy in groups. In G. M. Gazda (Ed.), *Basic approaches to group psychotherapy and group counseling.* Springfield Ill.: Charles Thomas, 1968.

Lomont, J. F. Group assertion training and group insight therapies. *Psychological Reports,* 1969, *25,* 463–470.

Lott, D. R., & Murray, E. J. The effect of expectancy manipulation on outcome in systematic desensitization. *Psychotherapy,* 1975, *12,* 28–32.

McFall, R. M., & Lillesand, D. B. Behavior rehearsal with modeling and coaching of assertion training. *Journal of Abnormal Psychology,* 1971, *77,* 313–323.

——— & Marston, A. R. An experiential investigation of behavior rehearsal in assertive training. *Journal of Abnormal Psychology,* 1970, *76,* 295–303.

———, & Twentyman, C. T. Four experiments on the relative contributions of rehearsal, modeling, and coaching to assertion training. *Journal of Abnormal Psychology,* 1973, *81*(3), 199–218.

Morris, R. J., & Sukerman, K. R. The importance of the therapeutic relationship in systematic desensitization. *Journal of Consulting and Clinical Psychology,* 1974, *42,* 148. (a)

———, & Sukerman, K. R. Therapist warmth as a factor in automated systematic desensitization. *Journal of Consulting and Clinical Psychology,* 1974, *42,* 244–250. (b)

Philipp, R., & Wilde, G. Suggestions and relaxation in asthmatics. *Journal of Psychosomatic Research,* 1972, *16,* 193–204.

Rathus, S. An experimental investigation of assertive training in a group setting. *Journal of Behavior Therapy and Experimental Psychiatry,* 1972, *3,* 81–86.

———. Investigation of assertive behavior through video-tape mediated assertive models and directed practice. *Behavior Research and Therapy,* 1973, *11,* 57–65.

Rich, A. R., & Schroeder, H. E. Research issues in assertiveness training. *Psychological Bulletin,* 1976, *83*(6), 1081–1096.

Rimm, O. C., & Masters, J. C. *Behavior therapy: techniques and empirical findings.* New York: Academic Press, 1974.

Rose, S. D. In pursuit of social competence. *Social Work,* 1975, *20,* 33–39.

Rosen, G. M. Subjects initial therapuetic expectancies and subject's awareness of therapeutic goals in systematic desensitization: a review. *Behavior Therapy,* 1976, *7*(1), 14–27.

Russell, R. K., & Sipich, J. F. Cue-controlled relaxation in the treatment of test anxiety. *Journal of Behavior Therapy and Experimental Psychiatry,* 1973, *4*(1), 47–49.

Schinke, S. P., & Rose S. D. Interpersonal skill training in groups. *Journal of Counseling Psychology,* 1976, *23*(5), 442–448.

Serber, M. Teaching the non-verbal components of assertive training. *Journal of Behavior Therapy and Experimental Psychiatry,* 1972, *3*(3), 179–183.

Sirota, D., & Mahoney, J. *Relaxation on cue: the self-regulation of asthma. Journal of Behavior Therapy and Experimental Psychiatry,* 1974, *3*(1), 65–66.

Smith, M. L. *When I say no, I feel guilty.* New York: Dial Press, 1975.

Sue, D. The role of relaxation in systematic desensitization. *Behavior Research and Therapy,* 1972, *10*, 153–158.

Yates, A. J. *Behavior therapy.* New York: John Wiley, 1970.

————. *Theory and practice in behavior therapy.* New York: John Wiley, 1975.

Young, E. R., Rimm, D. C., & Kennedy, T. D. An experimental investigation of modeling and verbal reinforcement in the modification of assertive behavior. *Behavior Research and Therapy,* 1973, *11*(3), 317–319.

Watson, J. B., & Rayner, R. Conditioned emotional reaction. *Journal of Experimental Psychology,* 1920, *3*, 1–14.

Wilkens, W. Desensitization: social and cognitive factors underlying the effectiveness of Wolpe's procedure. *Psychological Bulletin,* 1971, *76*, 311–317.

Woldwitz, H. M. Therapist warmth: necessary or sufficient conditons in behavioral desensitization? *Journal of Consulting and Clinical Psychology,* 1975, *43*, 584–586.

Wolpe, J. *The practice of behavior therapy.* New York: Pergamon, 1973.

Chapter 6

THE APPLICATION OF THE MODELING PARADIGM TO SOCIAL WORK PRACTICE

Thus far has been revealed how the basic principles of operant and respondent learning can be used to explain the acquisition of behaviors, their maintenance, and the modification of behaviors that the client wishes to change. In this chapter, the observational or modeling paradigm of learning, as conceptualized by members of the social learning school of human behavior (e.g., Bandura, 1969, 1971a, b, 1977 a, b; Bandura & Walters, 1963; Bandura, Adams, & Beyer, 1977; Rosenthal, 1976), will be presented.

The modeling paradigm of human learning differs significantly from the respondent and operant models that have been outlined in Chapters 4 and 5 in that it postulates that persons learn not only through direct experience but also through observing the behaviors exhibited by others; that is, learning can take place without an individual exhibiting the desired behavior and being reinforced for it. Social learning theorists have shown that virtually all learning which results from direct experience can occur vicariously through observing the performances of social models, for example: 1) intricate and complex behaviors such as cooperative, moral, assertive, aggressive, and linguistic and emotional reactions in terms of anxiety, fears, and phobias may be acquired by observing the behaviors of others; 2) fearful and avoidance responses may be extinguished, altered, or acquired vicariously through observational processes; 3) behaviors which already exist in a person's repertoire may be inhibited from further expression or disinhibited depending upon the consequences experienced by the model, that is, whether the observer witnesses a model being rewarded or punished for exhibiting a particular behavior or sequence of behavioral responses; and 4) the performance of behaviors that have been acquired previously may be enhanced and altered by the observation of competent models (Bandura, 1969; Bandura & Walters, 1963).

Initially, a summary which traces the historical development of the modeling paradigm is offered, and the theoretical conceptualizations upon which the model is based are presented. Subsequently, the factors which influence the modeling process are discussed and general applications of the modeling paradigm to alter various behaviors are reviewed. Finally, the necessary requisites for the utilization of modeling procedures in social work practice are outlined.

HISTORICAL DEVELOPMENT

Instinctual Explanations

During the early part of this century, the attribution of instinctual forces such as life and death instincts to account for human behavior received both popular and scientific support. Modeling or copying of another's behavior also was attributed to the innate propensities of humans (Morgan, 1896; McDougall, 1908; Trade, 1903). Individuals exhibited a particular behavior since the tendencies were inherited and when the proper cues were given by the environment and the organism's maturation was correct, the behavior would appear. As the value of such explanations came into question, behavioral scientists discarded instinctual theories in favor of respondent and operant learning explanations of modeling.

Respondent Explanations

Learning theorists from the classical school postulated that copying behavior occurs because stimuli that are associated with the modeled performance of behaviors also become cues for observers' subsequent performances, i.e., when original cues are presented to the observer (Allport, 1924; Guthrie, 1952; Holt, 1931; Humphrey, 1921). This associative explanation is seen as incomplete by social learning theorists (Bandura, 1969, 1971a,b), however, because even though it explains how previously learned behaviors might be elicited by the original stimulus cues involved in the learning context, it does not explain 1) why observational learning is controlled by certain social stimuli such as social and physical characteristics of the model, and not by other social stimuli that occurred in the original learning situation, 2) how new responses are learned, 3) how an individual learns a behavior without practice and reinforcement, and 4) does not specify the psychological mechanisms governing the acquisition of novel responses.

Operant Explanations

According to the operant viewpoint, observational learning takes place because modeled behavior is reinforced. The assumption that learning occurs through association is not given up, however, by members of the operant school, but they stress the importance of reinforcement in determining which responses will be copied. The essential elements of the modeling process as conceptualized by operant theorists (e.g., Baer & Sherman, 1964; Gewirtz & Stingle, 1968; Lundin, 1974; Miller & Dollard, 1941; Skinner, 1953) are outlined below:

1. The observer must be motivated to acquire the desired behavior. This motivation is believed to stem from the observer's anticipation of receiving reinforcements for exhibiting modeled responses.

2. Modeling cues for the target behavior must be available, that is, accurate and detailed presentations of the behavior to be acquired. Modeling cues, in this respect, serve as discriminative stimuli to which the observer must attend if he is to copy faithfully the modeled behavior. These cues guide the performance of the observer to facilitate the acquisition of the modeled behavior.

3. Observers must perform matching responses. The observer must attempt to reproduce the modeled behavior by exhibiting differential responses which resemble those exhibited by the model.

4. Matching behaviors must be reinforced. Inaccurate, irrelevant, or inappropriate responses are either not reinforced or are punished.

Bandura (1969, 1971a, b) and Bandura and Walters (1963) are highly critical of the operant explanation of the modeling paradigm. They argue that the outline presented above fails to explain how learning takes place without overt performance of the model's responses during the acquisition phase of learning, and/or without direct reinforcement being received by the model or the observer and why the appearance of the acquired responses may be delayed for long periods of time after initial exposure. Thus, the operant paradigm fails to explain, according to Bandura (1969, 1971a,b), how new behaviors are acquired without the organism practicing the behaviors and receiving reinforcement for it.

The operant procedure of shaping responses through the process of successive approximations is seen by social learning theorists as insufficient to account for the acquisition of all novel responses. That is, in order for the organism to learn a particular behavior, it has to be performed in the course of random behavior which matches accidentally with the modeled behaviors. A positive reinforcement has to occur immediately after the performance for its acquisition to be ensured. They question whether many of the complex behavioral patterns that are exhibited by most members of society would ever be acquired if social training took place solely through this lengthy process of shaping. This is believed to be true especially of those behaviors for which no reliable eliciting stimuli are present apart from the cues, such as verbal statements and physical mannerisms which models provide as they exhibit particular behaviors. Even in cases where other stimulus cues exist, such as physical contexts and thoughts that precede and occur during observational learning, which are known to be capable of eliciting approximations to the desired behavior, social learning theorists have shown that the process of acquiring novel responses can be shortened considerably if the learner is provided with a verbalizing social model who provides detailed instructions on the responses that are to be acquired (Bandura & McDonald, 1963).

Affective Feedback Explanations

Mowrer (1960) posits another explanation of modeling phenomena that argues that when a model exhibits a particular response and rewards the observer for performing the behavior, the observer will imitate the model's behaviors which have become highly valued through their association with positive reinforcements. The repeated association of the modeled response and reward have acquired secondary reinforcing properties. Through stimulus generalization, the observer learns to reproduce self-rewarding experiences by performing the model's behaviors. It also is assumed that the observer experiences vicariously the affective consequences (reinforcing or punishing) which the model enjoys as a result of his performance. The observer, through vicarious conditioning, becomes predisposed to reproduce the modeled behavior in order to gain the attendant pleasurable effects. While the explanation offered by Mowrer (1960) explains the acquisition of emotional responses, it does not adequately account for the acquisition of specific behavioral performances without reinforcement of the model's or observer's behavior. Bandura (1971a) believes that the affective feedback theory of modeling is limited in its ability to account for human behavior. He argues that human functioning would be highly inflexible and unadaptive if acquisition of behavior were controlled by such processes. When one looks at the highly discriminative character of social responsiveness it becomes highly improbable that a substantial proportion of behaviors is controlled by secondary reinforcing properties inherent in the behavior itself. Bandura (1971a) stresses the importance of considering the social context, the target of the behavior and the situational cues for accurately predicting which modeled responses will be exhibited.

Contiguity-Mediation Theory

This final theoretical explanation is the one most accepted today. Its proponent is Albert Bandura who has done extensive research on modeling phenomena (Bandura, 1965, 1969, 1977a). This is a multiprocess theory of observational learning which entails symbolic coding and central organization of modeling stimuli, the representation of stimuli in memory, in verbal (word) and imaginal (picture) codes, and the stimuli's subsequent transformation from symbolic forms to motor equivalents. When a person observes a model's behavior, but otherwise performs no overt responses, he can acquire the modeled responses through coding the behavior in a cognitive, representational form. Any learning under these conditions occurs purely on an observational or covert basis. This mode of response acquisition has been designated as no-trial learning because the observer does not engage in any overt responding trials, although he may require multiple observational trials in order to reproduce accurately modeled stimuli.

A prominent role is assigned to representational mediators that are assumed to be acquired on the basis of a contiguity learning process. After modeling stimuli have been coded into images or words for memory representation, they function as mediators for subsequent acquisition, integration, facilitation, inhibition, and retrieval of response reproduction. Later, reinstatement of these representational mediators, in conjunction with appropriate environmental cues, guide behavioral reproduction of matching responses. Performance of observationally learned responses is regulated largely by reinforcing outcomes that may be externally applied, self-administered, or experienced vicariously.

Modeling phenomena are controlled by several interrelated subprocesses that will be discussed shortly, such as attentional processes, retention processes, motor reproduction processes, and incentive and motivational processes. The absence of modeling effects in any given case may result from either failures in sensory registration due to inadequate attention to relevant social cues, deficient symbolic coding of modeled events into functional mediators of overt behavior, retention decrements, motor deficiencies, or unfavorable conditions of reinforcement.

Main Differences Among Modeling Theories

The major differences between the contiguity-mediation theory (Bandura, 1969, 1971a,b; Bandura & Walters, 1963) and other learning explanations of the modeling process (Allport, 1924; Baer & Sherman, 1964; Gewirtz & Stingle, 1968; Guthrie, 1952; Holt, 1931; Humphrey, 1921; Lundin, 1974; McDougall, 1908; Miller & Dollard, 1941; Morgan, 1896; Mowrer, 1960; Skinner, 1953; Trade, 1903) are:

1.   Learning takes place even though an individual is not *reinforced* for reproducing the model's responses at the time the

behavior is observed. The likelihood of an observer imitating a model's behavior is increased, however, if the learner is rewarded for producing matching responses or observes a model being reinforced for his performance. Even if the behaviors are punished or ignored, the observed behaviors are still learned and become part of the learner's repertoire. These responses may be reproduced later for the first time, long after the observer's initial exposure to the model. According to the contiguity-mediation viewpoint, reinforcement is facilitative rather than essential for observational learning to occur.

2. *Cognitive mediational processes* are given a central role in explaining the learning process. Symbolic coding, organization, storage, and representation of modeling stimuli in both verbal and imaginal forms is believed to take place before they are reproduced motorically (Bandura, 1977a, b; Bandura, Adams, & Beyer, 1977). After modeling stimuli have become coded, they function as mediators for subsequent response retrieval. The performance of observationally acquired response patterns is believed to be regulated by reinforcing outcomes that may take the form of external rewards which may be (1) dispensed by others, (2) obtained instrumentally by the individual himself, (3) self-administered overtly or covertly, and (4) experienced vicariously.

3. Exposure to modeled behavior does not result in *simple mimicry* of specific behavioral responses that had been observed previously. Under conditions where the observer witnesses the performance of a variety of models, novel patterns of behavior are exhibited that represent diverse combinations of the behaviors previously exhibited by various models. Not only are new response patterns created but the effects of modeling also generalize to new and different settings and situational contexts where diverse stimulus cues are present and where the original models are absent (Bandura & Mischel, 1965; Bandura, Ross, & Ross, 1963a).

Factors Influencing Observational Learning

Simple exposure to the behavioral performance of models, however, does not automatically guarantee that the behaviors witnessed by the observer will be learned. A variety of factors are known to influence the extent to which learning will take place by observing the behavior of others. These will be discussed briefly in the subsequent section.

Attentional Processes

The observer will be more likely to acquire response patterns that accurately match those exhibited by a model if he is able to discriminate specific stimulus cues, differentiate relevant features of the model's behavior in terms of appropriate eye contact, body language, conversational characteristics such as sentence construction and voice qualities, and so forth, and follow the sequence of behaviors performed. Individuals will model the behavior of persons who hold their interest, that is, persons to whom they are attracted. Generally, physical, social, educational, and attitudinal attributes affect attractiveness, thus influencing the relevance of a model for any individual.

Retention Process

Contiguity-mediation theorists assert that in order for an individual to reproduce observed behaviors when the modeling cues are no longer present, the observer must be capable of retaining the original observational inputs symbolically in either verbal or imaginal form in terms of symbolic codes such as verbal symbols, vivid images, words, and so forth. Overt practice and covert rehearsal, such as symbolic role playing, can facilitate the retention of observationally learned behaviors because repeated rehearsal enables the learner to code and organize those elements of the model's performance which are essential for competent behavioral reproduction. If the model's behavioral performance is presented in small units and spaced intervals over a period of time, the chance of the observer forgetting what has been learned is reduced.

Motor Reproduction Processes

It is believed that the rate and amount of observational learning, at the motor level, will be governed partially by the availability of essential component responses to the learner. Obviously, learning will proceed more rapidly if the observer can construct new performance patterns by utilizing behavioral responses that he already possesses. If, on the other hand, the observer does not possess the necessary component responses, the modeled behavior may be learned incompletely or reproduced inaccurately. In such cases, a graduated modeling procedure can be introduced whereby the learner is presented with the constituent elements of the behaviors to be acquired in an individually paced and graduated step-wise fashion that begins with simple behavioral units and proceeds to more complex and intricate performance sequences.

Accurate behavioral reproduction may be quite difficult if the model's performance is governed by responses that cannot be observed or by highly coordinated motor skills that are not easily discernible. With such behavior, practice is essential along with the provision of necessary informative feedback to facilitate achievement of desired performances.

Finally, the observer's physical limitations also must be taken into consideration. For example, a short young man of slight frame who weighs 140 pounds will have a difficult time becoming a defensive running back for a professional football team regardless of how well he can master the moves and remember the various signals and plays.

Incentive Processes

Administering rewards to the observer for imitating the behaviors exhibited by a model will increase the probability that the observer will reproduce the modeled responses. The likelihood of an observer reproducing the behavior of a model also is increased if the model is rewarded rather than punished for his performance. Reinforcement influences what models individuals attend to and how accurately they code and rehearse what they have seen. One should not forget, however, that the behavior exhibited by a model who has been punished still may be acquired and stored symbolically by the observer and may be reproduced at a later time when the threat of punishment is no longer present.

Observer's Characteristics

The extent to which modeled behavior is learned and reproduced has been shown to be influenced by a variety of observer characteristics. For example, highly dependent individuals (Jakubczak & Walters, 1959; Kagan & Mussen, 1956; Ross, 1966), persons with low self-esteem (deCharms & Rosenbaum, 1960; Gelfand, 1962; Lesser & Abelson, 1959), low levels of competence (Kanareff & Lanzetta, 1960), and low intelligence (Bandura, 1971a), and individuals who have been frequently rewarded for imitative responses and have an immediate need to learn and exhibit the modeled behavior (Miller & Dollard, 1941; Schein, 1954) are especially prone to adopt the behaviors of successful models.

Model's Characteristics

Models who are highly competent (Gelfand, 1962; Mausner, 1954a, b; Mausner & Bloch, 1957; Rosenbaum & Tucker, 1962), expert (Mausner, 1953), famous (Hovland, Janis, & Kelley, 1953), and can confer symbols of status (Lifkowitz, Blake, & Mouton, 1955) have been shown to be more influential than models who do not possess these qualities. Models who are liked and physically attractive (Bandura & Huston, 1961; Grusec & Mischel, 1966) and who possess prized characteristics such as social power (Bandura, Ross, & Ross, 1963b; Mischel & Grusec, 1966) are more likely to be imitated. Similarities between the models and observers in age (Bandura & Kupers, 1964; Hicks, 1965; Jakubczak & Walters, 1959), sex (Bandura, Ross, & Ross, 1963a; Maccoby & Wilson, 1957; Ofstad, 1967; Rosenblith, 1959, 1961), ethnic status (Epstein, 1966), race and socioeconomic status (Boyer & May, 1968) also influence the degree to which modeled responses are adopted. Individuals who are warm and nurturant have been shown to elicit more spontaneous imitative behavior than models who do not possess these qualities (Bandura & Huston, 1961; Hetherington & Frankie, 1967; Mischel & Grusec, 1966; Mussen & Parker, 1965).

MODELING AS A CLINICAL TOOL

Modeling has been shown to be an extremely powerful clinical technique that can be useful in modifying fears, increasing social skills and assertion, and modifying autistic and sexual behavior (Bandura, 1969, 1971c). In this section, we will describe how modeling procedures have been employed successfully in the treatment of a variety of behavior problems and in a variety of environmental settings. Our purpose is not to review the vast amount of empirical findings that support the effectiveness of modeling practice. Such an endeavor is beyond the scope of this book. The goal, therefore, is to familiarize the reader with some of the ways in which modeling principles may be used to modify behavioral responses in clients.

Personality Formation

Observational learning processes play a central role in personality formation. Numerous studies have shown that modeling cues may facilitate the exhibition of previously learned responses that are not deviant or maladaptive. Behaviors that have been elicited from observers in response to behavioral performances of models have been the performance of a variety of altruistic acts (Blake, Rosenbaum, & Duryea, 1955; Bryan & Test, 1967; Harris, 1968; Rosenhan & White, 1967), that is, volunteering one's services (Rosenbaum, 1956; Rosenbaum & Blake, 1955; Schachter & Hall, 1952), pledging to follow a specific course of action (Blake, Mouton, & Hain, 1956; Helson, Blake, Mouton, & Olmstead, 1956), and assisting persons in distress (Bryan & Test, 1967); information seeking (Krumboltz & Thoresen, 1964; Krumboltz, Varenhorst, & Thoresen, 1967); the choice of specific items from among various selections, such as foods, activities, toys, and so forth (Bandura, Ross, & Ross, 1963b; Barnwell, 1966; Duncker, 1963; Gelfand, 1962; Madsen, 1968); and decisions on moral issues (Bandura & McDonald, 1963). Thus, the modeling process plays a major role in the acquisition of socially relevant behaviors.

Decreasing Undesirable Response Patterns Through Modeling

The reduction of hyperaggressive and domineering behaviors and the increase of socially acceptable behaviors such as sharing and cooperation in schoolchildren has been accomplished by having children observe a series of interaction sequences where puppets modeled prosocial behaviors and cooperative solutions to interpersonal problems (Bandura & Walters, 1963; Chittenden, 1942). Aggressive responses to frustrating situations were reduced substantially in older children who were taught alternative responses through observation of models, behavioral enactment, and role playing (Gittleman, 1965). Filmed models of peers who exhibited approach behaviors to other children were used to reduce social isolation and withdrawal in preschool children (O'Connor, 1969). The work of Lovaas, Freitag, Nelson, & Whalen (1967) in developing procedures to teach complex behavior to autistic children is extremely important. The procedures employ a combination of modeling and operant techniques. Reinforcers are used to draw attention to the teacher, who then models relevant behavior and finally reinforces the child's imitative response. Complex verbal and social behaviors are built from simple behaviors in a series of increasingly complex steps (Lovaas, 1967). If modeling procedures are ineffective in modifying behaviors which are instrumentally rewarded, other behavioral techniques to alter the behavior may be introduced.

Vicarious Extinction of Deviant Behaviors and Emotional Responses

Although many of our emotional responses are acquired by means of direct respondent conditioning reviewed in Chapter 5, the learning of specific emotional responses to certain stimulus cues can also occur through vicarious conditioning. Vicarious conditioning is governed by the same process, i.e., laws of associative learning, as is direct classical conditioning. The main difference, however, is that in direct classical conditioning the learner himself experiences the painful or pleasurable stimulation while in vicarious conditioning the learner observes someone else experiencing the stimulation. The affective behaviors exhibited by the model serve as an arousal stimulus for the observer. The vicarious conditioning process requires vicarious activation of emotional responses in the observer as well as close temporal pairing of these behaviors with environmental stimuli. These environmental stimuli control the subsequent occurrence of such behaviors.

An example of vicarious conditioning is seen in the development of phobic behaviors. Phobias often arise not from direct experience with the feared object, but as a result of observing the actions of others who show fear reactions, exhibit avoidance behaviors, or experience painful physical consequences as a result of their interactions with particular objects such as snakes, dogs, rats, heights, elevators, examinations, and so forth (Bandura & Menlove, 1968; Bandura, Blanchard, & Ritter,

1969). The extinction of fears and deviant behavioral patterns through vicarious conditioning takes place in a similar fashion. Persons are presented with models who perform the fear-provoking behavior without experiencing the adverse consequences that had been anticipated. After gradual and repeated exposure, the capacity of the threatening stimulus to produce fear in the observer is reduced or neutralized. As a result, the fear-producing aspects of these stimuli have been reduced, thus facilitating the extinction of avoidance behavior and enhancing approach behavior. Thus talking about the client's fears and modeling by the worker of normal, nonanxious behavior reduces their fear-producing properties. Likewise, observing the model repeatedly exhibiting fearless behavior without unfavorable consequences, deriving new information about the feared object, and making direct personal contact with the threatening object and experiencing no aversive results are the variables that may account for the changes seen using such observational learning procedures.

Detailed procedures for eliminating phobic behaviors and the accompanying affective responses can be found in the classic studies undertaken to extinguish snake phobias, acrophobia, and fear of water, spiders, darkness, heights, and dogs (Bandura & Menlove, 1968; Bandura, Blanchard, & Ritter, 1969; Bandura, Grusec, & Menlove, 1967; Blanchard, 1969; Leitenberg & Callahan, 1973; Lewis, 1974; Rimm & Mahoney, 1969; Ritter, 1968).

The successful application of covert modeling techniques in the treatment of phobic behaviors, e.g., fear of rats, snakes, dogs, heights, and elevators also has been reported (Cautela, 1971; Kazdin, 1976) and has been shown to be as effective in reducing phobic responses as overt modeling (Cautela, Flannery, & Hanley, 1974). The procedure of covert modeling consists of the therapist presenting a verbal stimulus to the client who is instructed to vividly imagine a model engaged in the behavior suggested by the therapist. This process is similar to systematic desensitization except that deep muscle relaxation is not employed and the model is not the client himself. The assumption that underlies the use of this procedure is that a stimulus that is presented in imagination and accompanied by instructions will affect overt behavior of the client. The utilization of cognitive behavior modification techniques is discussed in detail in Chapter 8.

Development of Assertive Behavior

The use of a variety of behavioral procedures in conjunction with the modeling practices has been successful in helping clients acquire assertive behaviors and other social skills (Eisler, Hersen, & Miller, 1973; Kazdin, 1976; Lazarus, 1966; McFall & Twentyman, 1973; O'Connor, 1972; Rathus, 1973). These published studies show that the effects of modeling can be strengthened when they are used in conjunction with other learning techniques such as behavioral rehearsal, practice, and guided instruction (Hersen, Eisler, & Miller, 1973; Lewis, 1974; Nay, 1975). The training via modeling of social skills, and particularly assertive behaviors, involves the inhibition of a previously learned nonassertive response and the learning of a completely new set of assertive behaviors, such as the ability to say "no," expression of positive and negative feelings, ability to make requests, to initiate and carry on social conversations, and so forth. The process of assertive training was elaborated in Chapter 5.

Vicarious Reinforcement and Punishment, and Their Effects upon Behavioral Performance

Thus far has been described how the acquisition of novel behaviors can be facilitated and the performance of previously acquired behaviors improved through the observation of models. The mechanisms through which emotional reactions are acquired vicariously by observers also have been outlined. In this section will be discussed the role of vicarious punishment and reinforcement and its effect upon the subsequent performance of observationally learned behaviors.

A number of studies have demonstrated that the performance of particular behaviors can be prevented from further expression if the observer witnesses a model who is punished or experiences negative consequences as a result of his behaviors (Bandura, 1965; Bandura & Kupers, 1964; Bandura, Grusec, & Menlove, 1967; Benton, 1967; Parke & Walters, 1967; Porro, 1968; Rosenkrans & Hartup, 1967; Walters, Leat, & Mezei, 1963; Walters, Parke, & Cane, 1965).

The use of negative sanctions may be appealing to some clinicians because it seems to provide a quick and simple means of eliminating deviant behavioral responses in clients. This notion is not altogether accurate, however, and one should be aware that vicarious conditioning through the use of aversive control may result in a variety of undesirable consequences which often occur with the use of punishment in direct conditioning. For example:

1.   The inhibitory effects produced through punishment may only be temporary if the aversive consequences are not of sufficient strength to override the effects of other maintaining conditions or if more effective competing responses for securing the desired outcomes are not developed at the same time.

2.   The effects of punishment may generalize to behaviors other than those that are punished. When this occurs, socially approved responses that are associated with the punished behavior may also be suppressed.

3.   The use of punishment may result in avoidance, escape, and discrimination learning; that is, the client may learn to avoid or flee from those situations in which punishment is received but the behavior may continue to be exhibited in situations where no aversive consequences occur.

4.   The negative emotional responses that inevitably accompany punishment may generalize to both the therapist and the therapeutic relationship.

Since the effects of punishment are incompletely understood and the risks of undesirable side effects are substantial, it is recommended that the therapist refrain from utilizing such aversive techniques to modify deviant behaviors in clients.

Just as behavioral inhibitions can be established through vicarious punishment, so too can previously suppressed or inhibited responses be disinhibited as a result of observing models who are either not punished (Bandura, 1965; Walters, Parke, & Cane, 1965) or who are rewarded for exhibiting antisocial behaviors that previously had been punished (Bandura, Ross, & Ross, 1963b; Epstein, 1966; Walters & Llewellyn-Thomas, 1963; Wheeler, 1966).

Therapeutic Modeling: A Basic Paradigm

From the empirically based material presented in this chapter is derived an outline of the requisites for an effective treatment program that utilizes modeling procedures.

1.   The target behavioral performance or performance sequences that are to be acquired by the client should be specifically identified and delineated. Additionally, the rules that govern the behavior and its essential substeps should be specified.

2.   Whenever possible, high status models similar in age, sex, race, ethnic group, and social class who are physically attractive should be used in order to facilitate imitation.

3.   The client should be directed to 1) focus on the sequence of modeled behaviors, 2) discriminate and identify the relevant cues to which the model attends, and 3) differentiate the appropriate behavioral performances that the model employs in order to achieve the desired goal.

4.   Behavioral performances that are lengthy and complex should be presented in a graded stepwise fashion to facilitate learning.

5.   The client should witness the live or symbolic model being rewarded for his performance.

6. The entire behavior sequence should be explained verbally to the client in order to facilitate verbal and imaginal coding of the behavioral sequence. Restating the instructions in full, giving the rules that govern the behavior and the sequence of sub-steps necessary to reproduce accurately the model's performance ensures the acquisition of the desired behavior.

7. The client should experience repeated exposure in order to facilitate retention of the observationally learned behaviors.

8. If necessary, the client practices the behavior with the verbal guidance of the therapist.

9. Repeated practice is essential if the client is to master the target behaviors, i.e., multiple practice trials with less and less guidance from the therapist until the client performs the behavior to the established criterion. Close supervision of the client's early behavioral performances by the therapist is an important part of the learning process. During such practice trials the therapist should give the client constructive feedback about his performance, use coaching procedures to help the client improve his efforts and reward the client for correct performances and approximations to the desired goal. Covert practice in thought and fantasy are also an integral part of the training process.

10. Once the client is able to perform the desired responses without coaching, he is ready to practice his behaviors in settings outside those in which they had been acquired (e.g., the office, agency, or classroom, etc.). Thus, natural social reinforcers are substituted for therapist reinforcement. At first, the therapist should help the client select those settings that are familiar and least threatening to try out his newly acquired skills. This will maximize the probability of initial success and reinforcement. The client then can proceed at his own pace to tackle more difficult situations and interpersonal encounters and so forth. This practice will facilitate the transfer and generalization of new behaviors and support their maintenance in the real world.

In summary, therapeutic modeling is facilitated by the following conditions: pretherapy instructions, repeated modeling experiences, progressive increases in the complexity and fear-arousing properties of the modeling behaviors, use of multiple models and individuals that resemble the observers, and allowing the model to describe his progress. Modeling is also facilitated by practice by the observer. Practice effects are in turn facilitated by repeated practice; guidance, either verbal or physical; reinforcement, during and after practice; feedback, during and after practice; and favorable, nonthreatening conditions for practice. Finally, to ensure generalization of the newly acquired behavior, there must be some arrangement for sufficient reinforcement of the new behavior to assure performance, and the new behavior should be placed under general social reinforcement or self-reinforcement as soon as possible (Bandura, Adams, & Beyer, 1977).

Summary

In this chapter we have focused our attention on those elements of observational learning that are the most pertinent for clinical practitioners, that is, the role of modeling in acquiring prosocial, nonsocial, and antisocial behavior. After completing this chapter one should see the pervasiveness of modeling and how it can be employed at both micro and macro levels of social work intervention. The clinician also should be aware that in his interactions with clients he serves as a powerful model. Knowing this, each clinician should consider the possible effects that his conduct, personal appearance, behaviors of mastery, competence, openness, warmth, and so forth, have upon the client adopting these behaviors.

The data on the uses of modeling in clinical training suggest that social work educators and practitioners can facilitate the transfer of clinical skills by well-designed videotaped or audiotaped and live presentations by effective practitioners.

Moreover, video modeling can be employed to illustrate to clients what kinds of behaviors they should exhibit in order to facilitate the therapeutic process and what behaviors they can expect from the worker (Goldstein, 1973).

The coming years will witness more research executed on the following issues: Do models who provide verbalized or physical guidance and/or reinforcement facilitate the modeling effect? Are models who are observed in the act of overcoming their own fears and acquiring mastery more effective than those who have already mastered their fear? Is the use of live models more potent than videotaped models? What is the role of repeated practice and repeated exposure to models? How does use of multiple models and multiple fear-producing stimuli affect the modeling process? What is the necessary number of successful exposures to the model and the total time for successful exposure to the model? When these research issues are resolved the applicability of this sophisticated technology to social work practice will be facilitated.

REFERENCES

Allport, F. H. *Social psychology.* Cambridge, Ma.: Riverside Press, 1924.

Baer, D. M., & Sherman, J. A. Reinforcement control of generalized imitation by reinforcing behavioral similarity to a model. *Journal of Experimental Child Psychology,* 1964, *1,* 37–49.

Bandura, A. Influence of models' reinforcement contingencies on the acquisition of imitative responses. *Journal of Personality and Social Psychology,* 1965, *1,* 589–595.

———. *Principles of behavior modification.* New York: Holt, Rinehart and Winston, 1969.

———. *Psychological modeling: Conflicting theories.* New York: Aldine-Atherton, 1971. (a)

———. *Social learning theory.* Morristown, N.J.: General Learning Press, 1971. (b)

———. Psychotherapy based upon modeling principles. In A. E. Bergin, & S. L. Garfield (Eds.), *Handbook of psychotherapy and behavior change: An empirical analysis.* New York: John Wiley, 1971. (c)

————. *Social learning theory.* Englewood Cliffs, N.J.: Prentice Hall, 1977. (a)

————. Self efficacy: toward a unifying theory of behavioral change. *Psychological Review,* 1977, *84,* 191–215. (b)

————, & Huston, A. C. Identification as a process of incidental learning, *Journal of Abnormal and Social Psychology,* 1961, *63,* 311–318.

————, & Kupers, C. J. Transmission of patterns of self-reinforcement through modeling. *Journal of Abnormal and Social Psychology,* 1964, *69,* 1–9.

————, & McDonald, F. J. The influence of social reinforcement and the behavior of models in shaping children's moral judgements. *Journal of Abnormal and Social Psychology,* 1963, *2,* 698–705.

————, & Menlove, F. L. Factors determining vicarious extinction of avoidance behavior through symbolic modeling. *Journal of Personality and Social Psychology,* 1968, *8,* 99–108.

————, & Mischel, W. The influence of models in modifying delay of gratification patterns. *Journal of Personality and Social Psychology,* 1965, *2,* 698–705.

————, & Walters, R. H. *Social learning and personality development.* New York: Holt, Rinehart and Winston, 1963.

————, Adams, N. E., Beyer, J. Cognitive processes mediating behavioral change. *Journal of Personality and Social Psychology,* 1977, *35,* 125–139.

————, Blanchard, E. B., & Ritter, B. The relative efficacy of desensitization and modeling approaches for inducing behavioral, affective, and attitudinal changes. *Journal of Personality and Social Psychology,* 1969, *13,* 173–199.

————, Grusec, J. E., & Menlove, F. L. Vicarious extinction of avoidance behavior. *Journal of Personality and Social Psychology,* 1967, *5,* 16–23.

————, Ross, D., & Ross, S. A. Imitation of film-mediated aggressive models. *Journal of Abnormal and Social Psychology,* 1963, *66,* 3–11. (a)

————, Ross, D., & Ross, S. A. A comparative test of the status envy, social power, and secondary reinforcement theories of identificatory learning. *Journal of Abnormal and Social Psychology,* 1963, *67,* 527–534. (b)

Barnwell, A. K. Potency of modeling cues in imitation and vicarious reinforcement situations. *Dissertation Abstracts.* 1966, *26,* 7444.

Benton, A. A. Effects of the timing of negative response consequences of the observational learning of resistance to temptation in children. *Dissertation Abstracts,* 1967, *27,* 2153–2154.

Blake, R. R., Mouton, J. S., & Hain, J. D. Social forces in petition signing. *Southwestern Social Science Quarterly,* 1956, *36,* 385–390.

————, Rosenbaum, M., & Duryea, R. Gift-giving as a function of group standards. *Human Relations,* 1955, *8,* 61–73.

Blanchard, E. B. The relative contributions of modeling, informational influences, and physical contact in the extinction of phobic behavior. Unpublished doctoral dissertation, Stanford University, 1969.

Boyer, N. L., & May, J. G., Jr. The effects of race and socioeconomic status on imitative behavior in children using white male and female models. Unpublished manuscript, Florida State University, 1968.

Bryan, J. H., & Test, M. A. Models and helping: naturalistic studies in aiding behavior. *Journal of Personality and Social Psychology*, 1967, *6*, 400–407.

Cautela, J. R. Covert extinction. *Behavior Therapy*, 1971, *2*, 192–200.

———, Flannery, R. B., & Hanley, S. Covert modeling: an experimental test. *Behavior Therapy*, 1974, *5*, 494–502.

Chittenden, G. E. An experimental study in measuring and modifying assertive behavior in young children. *Monographs of the Society for Research in Child Development*, 1942, *7* (I., Serial No. 31).

de Charms, R., & Rosenbaum, M. E. Status variables and matching behavior. *Journal of Personality*, 1960, *28*, 492–502.

Duncker, K. Experimental modification of children's food preferences through social suggestion. *Journal of Abnormal and Social Psychology*, 1963, *33*, 489–507.

Eisler, R. M., Hersen, M., & Miller, P. M. Effects of modeling on components of assertive behavior. *Journal of Behavior Therapy and Experimental Psychiatry*, 1973, *4*, 1–6.

Epstein, R. Aggression toward outgroups as a function of authoritarianism and imitation of aggressive models. *Journal of Personality and Social Psychology*, 1966, *3*, 574–579.

Gelfand, D. M. The influence of self-esteem on rate of verbal conditioning and social matching behavior. *Journal of Abnormal and Social Psychology*, 1962, *65*, 259–265.

Gewirtz, J. L., & Stingle, K. C. The learning of generalized imitation as the basis for identification. *Psychological Review*, 1968, *75*, 374–397.

Gittelman, M. Behavior rehearsal as a technique in child treatment. *Journal of Child Psychology and Psychiatry*, 1965, *6*, 251–255.

Goldstein, A. P. *Structured learning therapy.* New York: Academic Press, 1973.

Grusec, J. E., & Mischel, W. The model's characteristics as determinants of social learning. *Journal of Personality and Social Psychology*, 1966, *4*, 211–215.

Guthrie, E. R. *The psychology of learning.* New York: Harper, 1952.

Harris, M. B. Some determinants of sharing in children. Unpublished doctoral dissertation, Stanford University, 1968.

Helson, H., Blake, R. R., Mouton, J. S., & Olmstead, J. A. Attitudes as adjustments to stimulus, background and residual factors. *Journal of Abnormal and Social Psychology*, 1956, *52*, 314–322.

Hersen, M., Eisler, R. M., & Miller, P. M. Effects of modeling on components of assertive behavior. *Journal of Behavior Therapy and Experimental Psychiatry,* 1973, *4,* 1–6.

Hetherington, E. M., & Frankie, G. Effects of parental dominance, warmth and conflict on imitation in children. *Journal of Personality and Social Psychology,* 1967, *6,* 119–125.

Hicks, D. J. Imitation and retention of film mediated aggressive peer and adult models. *Journal of Personality and Social Psychology,* 1965, *2,* 97–100.

Holt, E. B. *Animal drive and the learning process,* Vol. I. New York: Holt, 1931.

Hovland, C. I., Janis, I. L., & Kelly, H. H. *Communication and persuasion.* New Haven: Yale University Press, 1953.

Humphrey, G. Imitation and the conditional reflex. *Pedagogical Seminary,* 1921, *28,* 1–21.

Jakubczak, L. F., & Walters, R. H. Suggestibility as dependency behavior. *Journal of Abnormal and Social Psychology,* 1959, *59,* 102–107.

Kagan, J., & Mussen, P. H. Dependency themes on the TAT and group conformity. *Journal of Consulting Psychology,* 1956, *20,* 29–32.

Kanareff, V. T., & Lanzetta, J. T. Effects of task definition and probability of reinforcement upon the acquisition and extinction of imitative responses. *Journal of Experimental Psychology,* 1960, *60,* 340–348.

Kazdin, A. Effects of covert modeling, multiple models, and model reinforcement on assertive behavior. *Behavior Therapy,* 1976, *7,* 211–222.

Krumboltz, J. D., & Thoresen, C. E. The effects of behavioral counseling in group and individual settings on information seeking behavior. *Journal of Counseling Psychology,* 1964, *11,* 324–333.

————, Varenhorst, B. B., & Thoresen, C. E. Nonverbal factors in the effectiveness of models in counseling. *Journal of Counseling Psychology,* 1967, *14,* 412–418.

Lazarus, A. A. Behavior rehearsal, vs. nondirective therapy, vs. advice in effecting behavior change. *Behavior Research and Therapy,* 1966, *4,* 209–212.

Leitenberg, H., & Callahan, E. J. Reinforced practice and reduction of different kinds of fears in adults and children. *Behavior Research and Therapy,* 1973, *11,* 19–30.

Lesser, G. S., & Abelson, R. P. Personality correlates of persuasibility in children. In C. I. Hovland, & I. L. Janis (Eds.), *Personality and persuasibility.* New Haven: Yale University Press, 1959, pp. 187–206.

Lewis, S. A comparison of behavior therapy techniques in the reduction of fearful avoidance behavior. *Behavior Therapy,* 1974, *5,* 648–655.

Lifkowitz, M. M., Blake, R. R., & Mouton, J. S. Status factors in pedestrian violation of traffic signals. *Journal of Abnormal and Social Psychology,* 1955, *51,* 704–706.

Lovaas, O. I. A behavior therapy approach to the treatment of childhood schizophrenia. In J. P. Hill (Ed.), *Minnesota Symposia on Child Psychology,* Vol. I., Minneapolis: University of Minnesota Press, 1967.

————, Freitag, L., Nelson, K., & Whalen, C. The establishment of imitation and its use for the development of complex behaviors in schizophrenic children. *Behavior Research and Therapy,* 1967, *19,* 171–181.

Lundin, R. W. *Personality: a behavioral analysis* (2nd edition). New York: Macmillan, 1974.

Maccoby, E. E., & Wilson, W. C. Identification and observational learning from films. *Journal of Abnormal and Social Psychology,* 1957, *55,* 76–87.

Madsen, C., Jr. Nurturance and modeling in preschoolers. *Child Development,* 1968, *39,* 221–236.

Mausner, B. Studies in social interaction: III. Effects of variation in one partner's prestige on the interaction of observer pairs. *Journal of Applied Psychology,* 1953, *37,* 391–393.

————. The effects of prior reinforcement of the interaction of observer pairs. *Journal of Abnormal and Social Psychology,* 1954, *49,* 65–68. (a)

————. The effects of one partner's success in a relevant task on the interaction of observer pairs. *Journal of Abnormal and Social Psychology,* 1954, *49,* 557–560. (b)

————, & Bloch, B. L. A study of the additivity of variables affecting social interaction. *Journal of Abnormal and Social Psychology,* 1957, *54,* 250–256.

McDougall, W. *An introduction to social psychology.* London: Methuen, 1908.

McFall, R. M., & Twentyman, C. T. Four experiments on the relative contribution of rehearsal, modeling, and coaching to assertion training. *Journal of Abnormal Psychology,* 1973, *81,* 199–218.

Miller, R. E., & Dollard, J. *Social learning and imitation.* New Haven: Yale University Press, 1941.

Mischel, W., & Grusec, J. Determinants of the rehearsal and transmission of neutral and aversive behaviors. *Journal of Personality and Social Psychology,* 1966, *3,* 197–205.

Morgan, C. L. *Habit and instinct.* London: E. Arnold, 1896.

Mowrer, O. H. *Learning theory and the symbolic processes.* New York: John Wiley, 1960.

Mussen, P. H., & Parker, A. L. Mother nurturance and girls' incidental imitative learning. *Journal of Personality and Social Psychology,* 1965, *2,* 94–97.

Nay, W. R. A systematic comparison of instructional techniques for parents. *Behavior Therapy,* 1975, *6*(1), 14–21.

O'Connor, R. D. Modification of social withdrawal through symbolic modeling. *Journal of Applied Behavioral Analysis,* 1969, *2,* 15–22.

————. Relative efficacy of modeling, shaping and the combined procedure for modification of social withdrawal. *Journal of Abnormal Psychology,* 1972, *79,* 327–334.

Ofstad, N. S. The transmission of self-reinforcement patterns through imitation of sex role appropriate behavior. Unpublished doctoral dissertation, University of Utah, 1967.

Parke, R. D., & Walters, R. H. Some factors influencing the efficacy of punishment training for inducing response inhibition. *Monographs of the Society for Research in Child Development,* 1967, *32,* (I, Serial No. 109)

Porro, C. R. Effects of the observation of a model's affective responses to her own transgression on resistance to temptation in children. *Dissertation Abstracts,* 1968, *28,* 3064.

Rathus, S. A. Instigation of assertive behavior through video-tape mediated assertive models and directed practice. *Behavior Research and Therapy,* 1973, *11,* 57–65.

Rimm, D. C., & Mahoney, M. J. The application of reinforcement and modeling-guidance procedures in the treatment of snake phobic behavior. Unpublished manuscript, Arizona State University, 1969.

Ritter, B. The group treatment of children's snake phobias using vicarious and contact desensitization procedures. *Behavior Research and Therapy,* 1968, *6,* 1–6.

Rosenbaum, M. E. The effects of stimulus and background factors on the volunteering response. *Journal of Abnormal and Social Psychology,* 1956, *53,* 118–121.

————, & Blake, R. R. Volunteering as a function of field structure. *Journal of Abnormal and Social Psychology,* 1955, *50,* 193–196.

————, & Tucker, I. F. The competence of the model and the learning of imitation and nonimitation. *Journal of Experimental Psychology,* 1962, *63,* 183–190.

Rosenblith, J. F. Learning by imitation in kindergarten children. *Child Development,* 1959, *30,* 60–80.

————. Imitative color choices in kindergarten children. *Child Development,* 1961, *32,* 211–223.

Rosenhan, D., & White, G. M. Observation and rehearsal as determinants of prosocial behavior. *Journal of Personality and Social Psychology,* 1967, *5,* 424–431.

Rosenkrans, M. A., & Hartup, W. W. Imitative influences of consistent and inconsistent response consequences to a model on aggressive behavior in children. *Journal of Personality and Social Psychology,* 1967, *7* 429–434.

Rosenthal, T. L. Modeling therapies. In M. Herson, R. M. Eisler, & P. M. Miller (Eds.), *Progress in behavior modification* (Vol. 2) New York: Academic Press, 1976.

Ross, D. Relationship between dependency, intentional learning, and incidental learning in preschool children. *Journal of Personality and Social Psychology,* 1966, *4,* 374–381.

Schachter, S., & Hall, R. Group-derived restraints and audience persuasion. *Human Relations,* 1952, *5,* 397–406.

Schein, E. H. The effect of reward on adult imitative behavior. *Journal of Abnormal and Social Psychology,* 1954, *49,* 389–395.

Skinner, B. F. *Science and human behavior.* New York: Macmillan, 1953.

Trade, G. *The laws of imitation.* New York: Holt, 1903.

Walters, R. H., & Llewellyn-Thomas, E. Enhancement of punitiveness by visual and audiovisual displays. *Canadian Journal of Psychology,* 1963, *17,* 244–255.

———, Leat, M., & Mezei, L. Inhibition and disinhibition of responses through empathetic learning. *Canadian Journal of Psychology,* 1963, *17,* 235–243.

———, Parke, R. D., & Cane, V. A. Timing of punishment and the observation of consequences to others as determinants of response inhibition. *Journal of Experimental Child Psychology,* 1965, *2,* 10–30.

Wheeler, L. Toward a theory of behavioral contagion. *Psychological Review,* 1966, *73,* 179–192.

Chapter 7

MARITAL THERAPY: AN APPLICATION OF BEHAVIORAL TECHNIQUES

Techniques based on the operant, respondent, and modeling paradigms have been reviewed. In this chapter, we review the application of behavioral procedures to the area of conjugal therapy. The incorporation of these techniques into the practicing skill repertoire of the social worker who serves clients through a variety of agencies, for example, child welfare, community mental health settings, family service agencies, and so forth, should enhance the delivery of effective social work services. Moreover, the treatment programs outlined rest on an impressive data base and thus provide a rationale for their use (Jacobson & Martin, 1976).

To aid the clinician's development of a historical perspective and a knowledge base for the procedures employed, four major models of behavioral treatment of marital discord are reviewed. These models have been developed independently and rest on a solid empirical foundation. After reviewing the models, the guidelines that we have developed for their utilization in clinical practice are presented. These guidelines combine positive aspects of all four models.

The focus of this chapter is on changing the behaviors of the marital partners. If one of the presenting problem behaviors centers on the parent-child relationship, then techniques elaborated in the previous chapters, particularly in Chapter 4, may be employed concurrently with procedures to modify each partner's behavior.

BASIC POSTULATES

Behavioral exchange theorists postulate that individuals seek out and continue to participate in relationships only so long as these relationships offer more rewards than are available in alternative ones (Blau, 1964; Homans, 1958, 1961, 1974; Thibaut & Kelley, 1959). Interpersonal transactions are evaluated in terms of whether they produce rewarding, costly, or neutral consequences, and individuals choose one activity over another because it promises greater satisfaction (rewards) for the costs (punishments) involved. Thibaut and Kelley (1959) assume that individuals will continue their marital relationship only if each participant feels that he or she is receiving what he or she deserves based upon what he or she expects (his or her comparison level) for the current interaction and what he or she perceives to be the available alternatives (the comparison level for alternative interactional situations). Thus individuals choose one activity or behavior over another because the action is perceived to offer greater satisfaction for the costs involved (that is, more rewards) than other actions. Marriage is depicted as an interpersonal bargaining endeavor wherein each spouse evaluates continually whether the rewards he or she receives are proportional to his or her investments. Two principles determine an individual's satisfaction with any interpersonal interchange. First, their appraisal that an exchange has been more rewarding for them than costly, and second, an estimation that the profits made by each individual are equivalent and proportional to the investments made, i.e., the exchange principle of reciprocity.

In marital transactions, therefore, each spouse evaluates his own marital rewards and those of his mate. If each spouse feels that the rewards gained by each party to the exchange are justly proportional to each member's investments, both spouses will be satisfied with their marriage. It is important to understand, however, that both spouses must feel that a particular exchange has been justly rewarding for each party in order for marital satisfaction to occur, and exchanges that are profitable for one spouse but costly for the other decrease the probability that marital satisfaction will continue for both participants. The continuation of such an inequitable exchange system would lead ultimately to dissatisfaction and the bargaining process would become no more than a "zero sum situation," a situation in which one spouse constantly profits at the expense and loss of his or her mate. The exchange principle of reciprocity, that is, are my rewards proportional to my investments, has formed the cornerstone for marital therapy as practiced by a number of clinicians (Azrin, Naster, & Jones, 1973; Knox, 1971; Lederer & Jackson, 1968; Patterson & Hops, 1972; Patterson & Reid, 1970; Patterson, Hops, & Weiss, 1975, 1976; Rappaport & Harrell, 1972; Weiss, Birchler, & Vincent, 1974; Weiss, Hops, & Patterson, 1973; Wieman, Shoulders & Farr, 1974; Wills, Weiss, & Patterson, 1974).

A central aspect of all the models reviewed is the use of contracting to reduce marital conflict. The major elements of behavioral contracts are designed to bring about marital satisfaction by helping couples achieve a balance of equitable exchanges that each spouse feels is sufficiently rewarding to warrant continuation of the marital relationship. Four empirically tested programs have reported success in helping distressed couples resolve differences, solve marital problems, and achieve a balance of reciprocal exchanges. The four models are reviewed below: The Behavioral Exchange Program of Rappaport and Harrell, The Operant Interpersonal Program of Richard B. Stuart, Reciprocity Counseling of Azrin, Naster and Jones, and the Oregon Research Group Program.

THE BEHAVIORAL EXCHANGE PROGRAM OF RAPPAPORT AND HARRELL

The behavioral exchange program (Harrell & Guerney, 1976; Rappaport & Harrell, 1972) is conceived of as a program that can be utilized both for marital counseling as well as marital enrichment. Marriage is conceptualized as a mixed motive game wherein each spouse continually attempts to attain the best possible exchanges for himself. When marriage is viewed in this way, conflicts become inevitable. The basic assumption underlying this approach to marital intervention, therefore, is that marital success and satisfaction are achieved by couples who can successfully manage conflict and bargain for exchanges that are mutually satisfying. The behavioral exchange program is designed to teach groups of married couples cooperative negotiation skills so that they will be able to deal more effectively with marital conflict.

The basic paradigm for resolving marital conflict is to teach couples a problem-solving approach to conflict negotiations. The problem solving process includes: (1) identifying problem areas, (2) locating the specific issues, (3) generating and evaluating a variety of solutions, (4) implementing the agreed upon solutions, and (5) evaluating the results. The treatment procedure is outlined below:

1. *Listening carefully.* Initially couples are taught to communicate clearly and openly before actual contracting is attempted. Each spouse is taught to summarize the content of what the other has said before speaking. When a spouse accurately summarizes what his or her mate has said, the speaker knows that the message has gotten through and the partner

really understands what he or she is saying. The spouse who speaks is taught to express his or her feelings and opinions openly and to refrain from accusing, blaming, insulting, or otherwise attacking the mate. In such an atmosphere free from attack, the listening spouse is less likely to feel defensive and can concentrate on what is being communicated. This exercise facilitates mutual understanding. Spouses are instructed to practice the summarizing technique at home and to utilize it throughout the length of treatment.

2. *Locating a relationship issue.* A relationship issue is defined as a behavior or set of behaviors that occur within the relationship that both spouses agree ought to be changed in order for their relationship to be improved. The rationale for concentrating on a relationship issue rather than individual spousal complaints is to help couples understand and pinpoint their reciprocal impact on each other's behavior. Thus, the focus is on a mutual problem and is meant to encourage joint effort toward resolution.

3. *Identifying one's own contribution.* When couples are taught to conceptualize their problem as a mutual one, each spouse is able to look at what he or she is doing that helps to maintain the problem behaviors. Each spouse is encouraged to locate his or her specific behavioral contribution in terms of reinforcement of inappropriate behavior, lack of reinforcement or punishment of appropriate behavior, and so forth. When a spouse hears the other partner accept some responsibility for a problem, he or she becomes more willing to cooperate and negotiate a behavioral contract. Moreover, identifying specific behavioral contributions helps couples isolate those behaviors that need to be changed if a solution is to be reached and a more rewarding relationship achieved.

4. *Identifying alternative solutions.* Once the problematic behaviors are defined, each spouse is encouraged to find appropriate requisite behavior that will resolve the problem. A variety of alternatives are generated so that the likelihood of selecting a behavioral replacement which is acceptable to both

spouses is increased. This process also encourages couples to become more flexible and creative in their problem-solving efforts.

5. *Evaluating alternative solutions.* This is treated as a separate and distinct step in the process because it is posited that alternatives are generated more freely if each one is not evaluated at the time it is introduced. Such a process eliminates the possibility of debating the pros and cons of each alternative as it is presented and decreases the possibility of conflict. Later, evaluation consists of describing the positive and negative aspects of each alternative.

6. *Making an exchange.* Once a behavior is selected by each spouse that both partners agree will help solve the identified issue, a behavioral exchange contract is arranged between the spouses.

7. *Determining the conditions of exchange.* Specific contractual arrangements are made between spouses including what behaviors are expected, where they are to be performed, at what times, and with what frequencies. Both positive and negative contingencies also are agreed upon by both spouses at this time. Spouses are encouraged to identify bonuses and penalties for themselves, being advised to choose bonuses which are not penalties for their partners. The conditions of the exchange are recorded in order to facilitate implementation.

8. *Implementing the exchange contract.* This phase of the program provides the couple with a trial period in which to implement the agreed upon contract. Only informal records are kept during this time. Couples are instructed to note when the contract is particularly successful and when it has failed. These records are reviewed at the next treatment session.

9. *Renegotiation.* At this point, couples identify the positive and negative aspects of the contract and determine whether any changes are necessary. Additional alternatives may be generated and contingencies renegotiated during this phase. Procedures for evaluating progress are determined at this time.

THE OPERANT INTERPERSONAL PROGRAM OF RICHARD B. STUART

Stuart (1969, 1975, 1976) assumes that when couples present themselves for treatment at least one of the spouses has doubts about the wisdom of remaining married. The therapist's task is to help the spouses resolve their indecision by creating the best possible relationship, i.e., experience the highest frequencies of positively reinforcing exchanges possible at that time in their lives. It is assumed, therefore, that if couples feel that this new experience is sufficiently positive to justify further trials, they will continue their relationship together. If, however, they decide that even at its current best, their marriage offers fewer reinforcements than they can expect from other alternatives, they will decide to terminate their association. The therapist's obligation is to help the spouses change their behaviors as an initial and immediate goal. Once these changes are made, the couple can evaluate their reactions to their new experience. A positive evaluation and commitment to maintaining the marriage is the therapist's ultimate goal. The therapist helps to achieve this end by guiding the couple through an orderly sequence of eight steps. Each step includes specific procedures and criteria which must be mastered before a couple can proceed to the next stage of treatment. While the first four stages are utilized with all couples, stages five through eight may be used to a greater or lesser degree depending upon the unique needs of a given couple, e.g., step five may be eliminated for those couples whose communication patterns are functional. The process is as follows:

1. *Completing a pre-counseling inventory.* Both spouses separately complete a Marital Pre-Counseling Inventory (Stuart & Stuart, 1972) that collects data concerning the following areas for both spouses: daily activities, general goals, resources for change, satisfactions, behavioral targets for change

in 12 areas of marital functioning, bases for decision making, and commitment to the relationship. Separate inventories are used when the presenting problem is child management (Stuart & Stuart, 1975) or sexual difficulties (Stuart, Stuart, Maurice, & Szasz, 1975). The data collected in this process provide the therapist the information necessary for planning intervention prior to the first treatment session.

2. *Formalization of the treatment contract.* Upon receiving the Marital Pre-Counseling Inventories, the therapist telephones the couple. At this time, a commitment to joint treatment is secured and the therapist informs the couple that he will treat all information provided by one spouse as though it were common knowledge. Couples also commit themselves to a block of six sessions after which a decision is made whether or not to continue treatment. If, after the initial six sessions, additional goals remain, further interviews are scheduled.

3. *First conjoint session: Logical discussions.* During the first treatment session, the treatment contract is reviewed and may be formalized in writing. Following this, a brief discussion concerning the logic of the intervention strategies to be used is offered. Each couple is presented with the basic theoretical assumptions that underlie the treatment process: (1) thoughts and feelings are antecedents of actions, (2) actions by one spouse lead to reactions by his mate, and (3) the behaviors of an individual lead to changes in his thoughts and feelings. The implications of these assumptions are explained to each spouse (e.g., when spouses are successful in changing their behavior toward each other, positive consequences result that ultimately lead to more favorable evaluations of one's mate and marriage in general). With this in mind, the stage is set for the next procedural assumption: that the best way to initiate change is to help both spouses increase the rate at which they currently exchange positive behaviors. Requests for changes in a spouse's attitudes are translated into specific behavior change objectives and each of these goals must be potentially measurable by an independent observer.

4. *Initiating caring days.* The concept of caring days is introduced by asking each spouse to list those behaviors that he or she would like his mate to perform; the Pre-Counseling Inventory may be used for this purpose. Increasing the rate at which each spouse exhibits these cherished behaviors increases the belief that with increased commitment, marital satisfaction can be achieved. Increasing the frequency of caring behaviors also serves to motivate both partners to continue in treatment. In arranging for caring days, each spouse is asked to exhibit from eight to twenty behaviors daily, and each partner is instructed to emit these behaviors independently of the other's actions in order to demonstrate the commitment to the relationship. Each spouse is also told that although these signs of commitment must be offered initially irrespective of the actions of one's mate, they will ultimately become reciprocal. This process eliminates the problem of "who goes first" since each spouse is expected to initiate behavioral changes. Each spouse is asked to record the number and type of caring behaviors that he or she gives or receives and at the end of each day the total number of behaviors offered becomes a "commitment index" while the total number of behaviors received is termed the "pleasure index." When these show improvement, the couple is ready to move on to the next phase.

5. *Exchanging communication.* From the first session couples are taught to communicate honest, timely, and constructive messages and are trained to censor messages that are distortions or provide barriers to action rather than facilitate it. They are encouraged to use language that (1) deals with how behaviors can be changed as opposed to language that inhibits thinking about change, (2) expresses interest in and respect for one's mate, (3) assumes ownership of all statements and questions by beginning each sentence with the pronoun "I," and (4) clearly states the speaker's position on the issue under discussion.

6. *Contracting for behavior change.* Once both spouses have learned to communicate with one another, they are ready

to begin to change some of the molar behaviors that have been troublesome for them. These molar behaviors comprise three distinct categories in which change will be sought: (1) role responsibilities, (2) conflict management, and (3) interpersonal trust.

In attempting to alter role responsibilities, spouses are encouraged to accept more responsibilities for a behavior that they have exhibited only infrequently in the past or to take responsibility for a behavior that up to this time they had never been expected to perform.

Since conflict is seen as an inevitable by-product of all human relationships, spouses are taught conflict management techniques such as: (1) writing down those changes each would like to see in the other during arguments, (2) planning for the interruption of intense arguments in the hope that stimulus change will break the intensity of the anger, (3) developing mechanisms for respecting the anger of one's mate so that neither person is forced into defensive counterattack, and (4) arranging signals that indicate that a spouse is willing to end an argument.

Trust is increased by helping spouses gain assurance that the behaviors of one's mate will be sufficiently consistent so that future predictions about that mate's behavior can be made with some degree of accuracy. Changes oriented toward producing greater trust between spouses are made, therefore, by having couples make specific commitments to certain classes of molar behaviors which subsequently are honored.

In arranging for these three classes of behavior change, couples are asked to make both explicit and implicit contracts. These contracts are based upon the principle of reciprocity and may include negative sanctions for noncompliance as well as positive consequences for successful completion.

7. *Decision making regarding role responsibilities.* After learning how to make successful contracts, couples are trained in decision making. Each spouse accepts the responsibility for making decisions about specific areas of his or her functioning.

Once the areas of responsibility have been agreed upon, the couple can meet new challenges as they arise. In order to do this properly, couples are trained in problem solving. They are taught how to set goals, assemble facts, plan and carry out strategies, and evaluate the outcomes.

8. *Maintaining behavioral changes.* Once a couple has gone through the above seven steps successfully, they are considered capable of dealing with crises and resolving conflicts over major issues in their marriage. The final task, therefore, is to help couples learn how to maintain those changes that have been brought about by the treatment process. In order to do this, couples are given specific relationship rules that summarize the agreements that they have made for changes in communication, behavior, and decision making. These rules are written down so that couples may refer to them whenever they need. A second maintenance technique involves alerting the couple to the inevitability that either or both will test their new life-style. Spouses are encouraged not to be disheartened by this testing but to understand it and accept it as part of a natural process. Couples are then given a series of exercises aimed at helping them deal constructively with the kinds of testing that they may experience. Each of these exercises requires the person who is the victim to restate the agreement and then for that person to maintain consistent compliance with the rule. Finally, couples are asked to complete the Marital Pre-Counseling Inventory at four-month intervals after the completion of treatment. This self-assessment procedure helps couples to remember the gains they have made and enables them to formulate new objectives for relationship change.

RECIPROCITY COUNSELING OF AZRIN, NASTER, AND JONES

This model of marital intervention also utilizes operant and contractual techniques in the treatment of marital discord and is based on the premise that conjugal happiness results when the reinforcements derived from marriage exceed those which can be derived from nonmarital sources. The best way to assure that reinforcements are obtained from one's spouse, therefore, is to reinforce that spouse for providing the desired reinforcements. Since the nature of the reinforcing interactions is changeable, however, each partner is faced with the task of discovering new reinforcers with which to reward his or her mate. According to this paradigm, the exchange of reinforcements is always contingent upon the behaviors of one's spouse; that is, reinforcements are to be given only when reinforcements are received. The general objectives of therapy are 1) to develop within each spouse the basic goal of striving to please one's mate, and 2) to help spouses maximize the elements of reciprocal reinforcements in their relationship and thereby create a strong motivation to remain married. Spouses, therefore, are helped to:

1. see that many reinforcers are currently being exchanged in spite of the problems being experienced;

2. discover and initiate new reinforcing behaviors and establish mutual contingent agreements that will assure that reinforcements are reciprocated and that failure to reinforce one's spouse will result in nonreinforcement by one's mate;

3. establish this type of reciprocity as a general pattern of interaction and to maintain reciprocity once it has been achieved.

The model of reciprocity counseling to be described below is based on an experimental study conducted with 12 couples (Azrin, Naster, & Jones, 1973) which employed a within-subject comparison procedure. Initially, couples received catharsis counseling for a three-week period which constituted the control phase of the experiment. At the end of this time, couples were trained in reciprocity counseling for four weeks. This constituted the experimental treatment manipulation. A test of marital adjustment was administered each day during the seven-week experiment. Success was assessed by comparing the mean overall marital happiness ratings of the marital adjustment scale for the three weeks of catharsis counseling with the mean ratings of the same measure taken during the final four weeks of reciprocity counseling. Significantly higher scores of marital happiness were recorded for all couples during the reciprocity counseling phase of treatment as compared to the catharsis control phase. A one-month follow-up evaluation showed that marital happiness had continued to increase. The Reciprocity Counseling model of Azrin, Naster, and Jones (1973) consisted of the following:

1. *Catharsis counseling.* During the first session a treatment contract is established between each couple and the therapist. Couples agree to jointly attend two one-hour counseling sessions each week for a period of seven weeks. At this time no distinction between the first three weeks of catharsis counseling and the last four weeks of reciprocity counseling is made by the therapist. The agreed upon goal of treatment is increased marital happiness for both spouses. During the first session each spouse is asked to fill out a Marital Happiness Scale which evaluates nine separate areas of current marital functioning: household responsibilities, child rearing, social activities, money, communication, sex, academic or occupational progress, personal independence, and spousal independence. A 10th category of overall marital happiness is also included. Spouses are told to complete a Marital Happiness Scale every evening before retiring and to mail it to the therapist on the following morning. A reminder is sent to the couple if one day is missed. This process continues for the entire seven-week treatment period. During the catharsis phase couples are encouraged to express their feelings concerning any area of their marriage in which problems exist. Communication between the spouses is interrupted by the therapist only if spouses become physically angry with each other.

2. *Reciprocity awareness procedure.* At the end of the final session of catharsis counseling, a homework assignment is given to the couple. Each spouse is asked to list and enumerate

at least 10 behaviors which his or her mate exhibits toward the other that are experienced as satisfying. At the following session, each list is read and discussed aloud by the therapist and agreement is obtained regarding the specific nature and extent of the reciprocity that already exists. Another home assignment prescribed at the end of the final catharsis session is to have both spouses list the type of interactions that would constitute "a perfect marriage" for each of the nine areas of marital functioning. The desires outlined are used later on in treatment to formulate new interaction patterns.

3. *Reciprocity counseling: 1st week.* During the first session, spouses are asked to exchange their completed Marital Happiness Scales and to discuss their feelings in regard to each of the nine problem areas. Each couple is then told to repeat this exercise each evening and to mail the completed forms to the therapist on the following day. This procedure is used in order to help the spouses discover how successful they had been in pleasing the other spouse that day and, if not successful, to discuss the possible causes.

At the beginning of each session, the therapist asks the spouses to describe the results of their last exchange and discussion session. At this juncture, an Appreciation Reminder Procedure is introduced. Spouses are taught to mention to each other any new or unplanned satisfying behaviors that each has performed in order to please the other. This is done so that one's partner can become aware of, and appreciative of his or her mate's attempts to please the other. Couples are instructed to continue this practice on a daily basis and their progress is routinely discussed with the therapist at each subsequent session. Also during this first Reciprocity Counseling session a Fantasy Fulfillment Procedure is used as a method of discovering, agreeing upon, and listing new satisfactions that would improve the happiness of each spouse. Spouses are asked to fantasize what the other mate could do to increase his or her own happiness in each of the problem areas already outlined in the Perfect Marriage Procedure. After a suggestion is made by a spouse, the mate is asked by the therapist if he or she would agree to perform the act. If an immediate agreement is not secured, a compromise is worked out with which both spouses are comfortable. This procedure is introduced so both spouses can begin to feel that many different types of reinforcement can be provided in the relationship. This is believed to strengthen the marital bond. The frequency of performance, its duration, and the situation in which it is to occur are explicitly agreed upon by the spouses and formally written down.

The final task to be completed in the first session of Reciprocity Counseling is to formalize a Marital Happiness Contract. The purpose of this contract is to obtain formal agreement to the informally agreed upon satisfactions exchanged from the Reciprocity Awareness listing, the new satisfactions negotiated through the Fantasy Fulfillment Procedure, and the negative sanctions and contingencies which a spouse will incur if one fails to fulfill one's part of the agreement. All contracts are written and signed in the presence of the therapist. At the second Reciprocity Counseling Session, the Happiness Contract is reviewed and reevaluated in light of several days of actual implementation. Modifications and changes that are necessary are discussed and incorporated into a new contract.

For homework, couples are given an assignment that requires them to discover new satisfactions that will increase their happiness in those problem areas that have not been dealt with as yet. Couples are also instructed to list suggested improvements in the problem areas that have already been negotiated.

4. *Reciprocity counseling: 2nd week.* When couples return the second week, the homework assignments are discussed and new contracts are written for previously unnegotiated problem areas. During this session, a Positive Statement Procedure is begun with each couple. This process allows each spouse to communicate a negative statement in a less aversive manner. Spouses are instructed to add a positive statement to any negative comment one felt obliged to direct toward one's mate. This

positive statement must always be relevant to the topic being discussed. Spouses are also encouraged not to insult or to attack each other when making negative statements. Each spouse is trained to stop the mate whenever he or she makes a negative statement which does not include a positive note and to refrain from responding until the statement is repeated in a more positive fashion or modified by the inclusion of a positive comment. The therapist also takes part in this process by stopping a spouse from continuing to express oneself negatively if a positive statement is not included. Couples are encouraged to continue using the Positive Statement Procedure during all conversations that occur outside the counseling session. Also during the first Reciprocity Counseling session of the second week, a Sex Feedback Procedure is used that teaches couples a method of communicating, indirectly, as many sexual desires as possible to one's spouse. Each spouse is given a copy of a marriage manual (Ellis, 1966) in which selected passages have been underscored by the therapist that depict a wide variety of sexual acts. Each spouse is encouraged to rate privately on a scale of −5 to +5 the degree to which he or she finds the underscored sexual behavior personally desirable or undesirable. These are discussed with the therapist in the next session. The Sex Feedback Procedure is used to overcome a couple's reluctance to communicate intimate details of their sexual preferences and desires. During the second session, couples also are instructed to devise new satisfactions for the remaining three problem areas, i.e., academic or occupational progress, personal independence, and spousal independence. This is accomplished with minimal therapist assistance. Couples are instructed to negotiate this final contract at home. This contract will be presented to the therapist for discussion at the next session.

5. *Reciprocity counseling: 3rd week.* During the first session, couples present the contractual agreement which they have worked out on their own to the therapist. The contract is discussed with the therapist and modifications are made if re-

quired. The listings of the previous six problem areas are also reviewed and revisions are made if necessary. In the second session of this third week of Reciprocity Counseling, all areas of the Marital Happiness Scale are reviewed and discussed. At this time, changes in any of the nine areas listed on the Marital Happiness Scale are renegotiated.

6. *Reciprocity counseling: Final week.* In the first session of this final segment of Reciprocity Counseling, the therapist reviews the treatment process up to this point and helps the couple work through any unresolved areas of the marital contract. In the final session, the Follow-Up Procedure is outlined. The therapist explains to each couple that once a month they will receive in the mail a self-addressed envelope which includes the Marital Happiness Scale. The couple is asked to complete the scale and return it to the therapist. This constitutes the follow-up component of treatment. Couples are advised that they may contact the therapist at any time in the future if they feel the need of his/her assistance.

The last program for treating distressed couples to be presented in this section is based upon a number of well-designed research projects conducted by a group of clinical researchers at the Oregon Research Institute (Birchler, Weiss, & Vincent, 1975; Patterson & Hops, 1972; Patterson, Hops, & Weiss, 1975, 1976; Patterson, Weiss, & Hops, 1976; Weiss, Hops, & Patterson, 1973; Wills, Weiss, & Patterson, 1974). Both the rationale for the intervention strategies and the treatment process itself are outlined below.

THE OREGON RESEARCH GROUP

For this group, marital conflict is believed to result from faulty behavioral change operations that are utilized by both spouses. Spouses are seen as trying to bring about immediate behavior changes in each other largely through the use of aversive control, i.e., through the use of punishment, negative reinforcement, escape and avoidance conditioning, time out, extinction, and so forth. Each spouse is seen as trying to either accelerate or decelerate the rate of particular behaviors of the mate's through coercive control tactics, and spouses are seen as shaping their mate's behaviors through the singular application of aversive control techniques. Over time the partners learn to terminate the aversive behaviors of the other spouse by changing their own behaviors. This process is based upon the negative reinforcement paradigm, i.e., the probability of a behavior occurring that terminates an aversive stimulus is increased and only serves to strengthen the coercive controlling behaviors of both parties.

The basic assumption of this treatment approach is that couples can be trained to negotiate desired behavior changes in their spouses. The techniques used involve 1) observing, recording, and pinpointing the behaviors to be changed; 2) arranging contingent consequences for fulfillment and noncompliance; and 3) recording all agreements in the form of written contracts. The nine-week therapeutic process is described below:

1. *Phase I.* In the initial intake interview, a history of each couple's marital and premarital interaction is executed. A particular effort is made to elicit information about those events that each spouse experiences as reinforcing or aversive. At this time, a treatment contract is negotiated and couples are informed that daily telephone contact will be made by the therapist for the duration of treatment. The general format of this intervention procedure is that the couple earns the therapist's time by performing tasks each week. Each session begins with each spouse giving a five minute mini-lecture about the reading assignments given for homework at the end of the previous interview. Reading assignments deal with a variety of topics, for example, informational material outlining the general nature of the program and the training procedures, communications exercises, and contingency contracts. These exercises are executed in order to increase the generalization of training results.

2. *Phase II.* During this phase, baseline data are collected. The couple is asked to resolve one of their conflicts. Their interactions and problem-solving attempts are videotaped at this time in the office or at home. After the videotaping, the nonadaptive role of aversive stimuli in the problem-solving process is explained and elaborated upon. A replay of the couple's videotaped problem solving endeavors is then shown and the spouses are asked to tabulate the frequency for each of them of such aversive events as criticism, ridicule, sarcasm, changing the subject, or denial. Following this, two therapists, serving as models, role play a behavioral interchange which focuses on the same problem dealt with by the couple. This interchange, however, is nonaversive; behaviors are carefully pinpointed and trade off negotiations are completed successfully.

The couple is then asked to go through the same performance. They are reinforced for their less aversive problem-solving attempts by both therapists. Usually, however, some training is required to help spouses learn how to specifically pinpoint and identify those behavioral changes he or she would like the other to make. The number of weeks needed to master this process will vary from couple to couple but generally ranges from two to four sessions. It is important that the spouses learn how to be specific in identifying behaviors before going on to the next phase.

3. *Phase III.* When both spouses have learned to pin point behaviors accurately, the couple is taught how to be specific in making complaints and offering one's spouse suggestions for behavior change. Complaints are listed on a blackboard by each spouse without interruption from the partner. Couples are reinforced for their specificity and ambiguous complaints are designated as such at this time and they are concretely specified.

4. *Phase IV.* In the next session, the couple is asked to negotiate changes in each other's behavior from the lists that have been made in the previous session. The couple is informed that compromises are to be made by each spouse and that consequences are to be arranged for both the successful comple-

tion of the contract as well as for failure to comply with the terms of the agreement.

In order to aid in generalization of the successful problem-solving activities from the therapist's office to the couple's home, the couple is asked to negotiate other contracts at home. These attempts at contract negotiations are reviewed at subsequent sessions with the therapist who reinforces their efforts and gives constructive feedback.

UTILIZATION OF MARITAL CONTRACTS: ELEMENTS COMMON TO ALL APPROACHES

In order to profit from a behavioral exchange approach to resolving marital conflict, certain prerequisites must be present. These are

1. Both spouses should express a willingness to bargain, compromise, and modify their problem behaviors for the sake of improving their marriage.
2. Each spouse should possess approximately equal amounts of reward power in the form of personal resources that are valued by the mate and that can be used as exchange commodities in the bargaining process.
3. Both spouses must be willing to record their behaviors and to evaluate their progress periodically by using graphs, charts, diaries, etc.*

If any or all of the above prerequisite conditions are not present, it is unlikely that a behavioral contracting approach will be effective in reducing marital conflict. Even if these prerequisite criteria for successful contracting have been met, however, some precontract negotiation training in communication skills is often required, since successful exchanges can be nego-

*The execution of charts, diaries, and graphs is described elsewhere (Azrin, Naster, & Jones, 1973).

tiated only when both spouses are able to communicate their thoughts, feelings, needs, and expectations freely to each other in an atmosphere of mutual acceptance, trust, and understanding. Guidelines and procedures for establishing open and functional communication between spouses have been outlined by numerous clinicians (Collins, 1971; Ely, Guerney, & Stover, 1973; Lederer & Jackson, 1968; Rappaport & Harrell, 1972; Satir, 1967) and may be utilized for this purpose.

In some instances, however, only one spouse is willing to bargain, compromise, and initiate behavioral changes while the mate refuses to enter treatment. This is likely to occur when the marriage is experienced as a nonvoluntary relationship (Bagarozzi & Wodarski, 1977). In such marriages where contractual bargaining and compromise are not possible, the therapist may choose to work with the more committed spouse. When this alternative is chosen, the therapist can help that spouse change the current exchange system in a number of ways.

First, Knox (1971) has suggested that positive behavioral changes can be brought about in the less committed spouse by having the more committed partner increase the number of pleasurable acts directed toward the mate. Knox (1971) assumes that the less committed member will increase the performance of rewarding behaviors toward the spouse in accordance with the principle of reciprocity.

Second, since the more committed spouse is usually the less powerful partner and possesses fewer personal resources that are valued by the mate (Waller & Hill, 1951), an interventive approach that would enable this spouse to enrich his or her reward power and thereby increase bargaining potential seems to be in order. Through the use of a variety of behavioral techniques (e.g., modeling, positive reinforcement, and so forth), the less powerful spouse can increase power by developing a repertoire of behaviors which the mate finds rewarding. Once a store of resources has been developed, the less powerful spouse can use them as exchange commodities to negotiate a more equitable exchange system.

Third, if neither of these techniques is appropriate, the more committed spouse can be helped to accept the unfortunate situation in which he or she is trapped. The clinician can employ a number of behavioral procedures such as desensitization, cognitive restructuring, "stop think," or covert reinforcement to accomplish this end (Lazarus, 1971, 1972). The less powerful spouse can be helped also to discover other reinforcing activities and interpersonal relationships outside the marriage which may compensate, at least to some degree, for the dissatisfactions of the conjugal relationship.

A PROCEDURE FOR CLINICAL INTERVENTION

Basic Considerations

Based upon the theoretical model of marital interaction outlined above, several aspects of the conjugal relationship must be assessed by the therapist before any planned intervention can be undertaken successfully. Therefore, a therapist must be equipped to help couples pinpoint behaviorally those areas of their relationship in which dissatisfactions are experienced so that the desired behavioral modifications can be negotiated between the spouses. Such an assessment should encompass the following areas of the marital relationship: roles and tasks, finances, sexual relations, communication, in-laws, friendships, religion, recreation, children, and values. In this way, the therapist can begin to ascertain in what areas of the marital relationship a spouse feels that one's outcomes have fallen below one's comparison level for the current interactional situation or one's comparison level for alternative interactional situations.

In addition to locating the sources of felt dissatisfactions, a therapist must be able to help each spouse identify the store of personal resources he or she possesses and which he or she believes to be valued by the partner. Once this has been accomplished, a more objective appraisal can be made and the true reward value of these resources for the spouse can be ascertained. Such a procedure is essential because it offers each spouse the opportunity to discover those personal resources that actually are prized by the mate. These resources can be exchanged subsequently and used as contingent reinforcements for desired behavioral changes once contracting has begun.

Foa (1971) has identified six distinct resource types that can be used as commodities in the social exchange process: love, status, information, money, goods, and services. He proposes that these six classes of resources can be plotted on two coordinates of resource characterization which he refers to as concreteness versus symbolic and particular versus universal. A comprehensive survey of individual resources, therefore, should encompass the entire range of concrete characteristics, behaviors, personal qualities, commodities, and so forth as well as those resources that are symbolic in nature such as smiles, gestures, facial expressions, and nonverbal behaviors. The clinician also should help each spouse identify those resources that are uniquely one's own as opposed to resources that are widely available from a variety of sources outside the marriage.

Recent research findings reported by Wills, Weiss, and Patterson (1974) show the importance of such an assessment. These investigators found that the actual sources of satisfactions for husbands and wives are the opposite of their traditional role prescriptions. Traditionally, husbands are expected to fulfill a primarily instrumental role in a marriage, whereas wives are expected to enact a socioemotional and affectional role vis-à-vis their husbands. These researchers have found, however, that husbands and wives perceive the sources of satisfaction in their relationship as being derived from different areas. Husbands tend to emphasize instrumental behaviors on the part of their wives as the source of pleasurable experiences. Wives, on the other hand, tend to emphasize pleasurable affectional behaviors, on the part of their spouses, from the socioemotional sphere. Taking these findings into consideration, one can see why it is essential for a clinician to help each spouse identify those valued resources possessed by the mate if an exchange approach to marital treatment is to be successful.

Each spouse's commitment to maintaining the relationship and willingness to change problem behaviors also must be evaluated at the outset of treatment. Although questionnaires and precounseling inventories frequently are used for this purpose, they may not be valid predictors of a spouse's actual behavior once treatment has begun. A behavioral assessment of each spouse's motivation and willingness to change can be made, however, by a systematic examination by the clinician of the charts, diaries, graphs, and so forth which routinely are kept by both spouses as part of the contractual treatment process. This behavioral analysis of conjugal interaction is an integral part of contractual approaches to marital intervention and helps the clinician to identify quickly the unmotivated spouse who is unwilling to compromise, bargain, and modify problem behavior. Such an appraisal can be made quite easily in the treatment process, thereby enabling the clinician and both spouses to reassess whether a contractual approach to marital treatment is the most appropriate one for that particular couple.

A final evaluation of two related phenomena must be undertaken by the clinician in order for an assessment to be complete. The therapist must determine 1) the degree to which each spouse experiences the marriage as a nonvoluntary relationship, and 2) the degree to which each spouse perceives rewards and satisfactions as coming from sources which predominantly are external to the marriage. It is essential for these two factors to be evaluated, because they both have direct bearing upon a spouse's willingness to enter into a contractual model of marital intervention and to change problematic behaviors.

As can be seen from the above discussion, a couple's willingness to negotiate is influenced by factors both internal and external to the relationship. We have tried to identify those areas that must be evaluated by the clinician before intervention can be undertaken.* The targets of evaluation are derived from

*The authors have developed a marital inventory based upon the ideas described in this chapter which is in the process of being refined for clinical use.

the theoretical position put forth by the authors and presented in this chapter. The crucial issues that must be determined through such an evaluation process are the motivation for change and the appropriateness of a contractual model for a given couple.

In accordance with the formulations outlined above, clinical intervention can be seen as a conjoint problem-solving process that requires both the couple and the therapist to make a series of collaborative decisions at specific junctures throughout the treatment process. The following decision-making model serves as the authors' outline for the process of intervention and the choice of appropriate techniques for the alteration of behavior.

Procedural Guidelines

PROBLEM IDENTIFICATION, ASSESSMENT, AND DETERMINATION OF TREATMENT PROCEDURES.   In the initial sessions it is essential for the therapist to determine whether the couple's presenting problems are those which he has the expertise to treat. For example, alcoholism, drug abuse, and a variety of sexual dysfunctions in either or both spouses may require referral to agencies that specialize in the treatment of such problem behaviors. In addition to this analysis, the therapist also must assess whether the couple will be able to benefit from a behavioral exchange approach to marital treatment or whether intervention should focus on one member of the dyad. The prerequisites for making such a decision have been outlined previously (see pp. 188–192).

FORMALIZING THE TREATMENT PROCESS.   Once it has been determined that marital intervention is the appropriate course of action, the therapist outlines the entire treatment process for the couple so that both spouses will know precisely what will be required of each of them (e.g., operationalizing behaviors to be changed, keeping charts, graphs and records, practicing newly acquired behaviors in a variety of settings to facilitate transfer, and completing homework assignments) as well as what role the therapist will play in the treatment process (e.g., teacher, model, and/or consultant).

PRELIMINARY TRAINING IN COMMUNICATION.   Training in basic communication skills is often necessary before behavioral contracting can be undertaken successfully. The ability to listen actively and nonjudgmentally and to make open, direct, and nondefensive statements to one's mate that are not hostile personal attacks provides the foundation for the problem-solving process of contingency contracting. Since marital contracting is seen as a structural learning experience that follows a definite sequence, the establishment of a functional communication system is essential if more complex problem-solving behaviors are to be mastered.

LOCATING RELATIONSHIP DISSATISFACTIONS.   Once open communication has been established, spouses are trained to locate specific areas of their relationship where conflicts have developed. Spouses are taught to identify how each contributes to maintaining a particular conflict or set of problem behaviors through the use of reciprocally reinforcing coercive interpersonal strategies. Once this is done, treatment goals for each spouse can be formulated in terms of specific observable behaviors that are to be increased, decreased, and/or acquired.

FORMULATION OF EXCHANGE CONTRACTS.   At this juncture the couple is helped to formulate and implement a contingency contract that both members consider fair. In order to facilitate the couple's learning of the contractual process, a variety of techniques may be utilized, such as assigned readings, observation of live and filmed models, coaching, shaping through successive approximation, supervised practice using feedback, and homework exercises to increase the possibility of transfer and generalization of newly acquired skills to a variety of environmental settings.

In the initial stages of intervention, it is important for the therapist to help couples select and tackle problems that they can resolve without too much difficulty. Such success will reinforce their newly acquired problem-solving skills and will help ensure their continued use in times of conflict. Just as a therapist constructs a stimulus hierarchy with a client in the treatment of phobic behavior through systematic desensitization, the therapist should help couples arrange and resolve marital conflicts in order of their difficulty, beginning with the simple and moving to the more complex, and emotionally charged problem areas. Moreover, the therapist should provide appropriate reinforcement in order to facilitate the progression through the treatment sequence. Similarly, couples should be taught to contract for the modification of specific problematic responses before they attempt to change more complex global behavioral patterns, i.e., spouses should work on changing specific tasks they perform before changing entire role performances.

PHASING OUT AND BUILDING IN.   The final phase of the treatment process is concerned with helping each spouse become less dependent upon tangible reinforcements and to accept social reinforcements in their place. For example, a spouse who was contingently rewarded with a specially prepared meal for time spent previously with his wife or with her husband in after-dinner conversation will continue to spend time with him or her in exchange for praise and appreciation. This can be accomplished by pairing social reinforcements for the performance of desired behavioral responses with tangible reinforcements and withdrawing gradually the concrete reinforcers and increasing the ratios for which a spouse is contingently rewarded with tangible objects. It is important to note, however, that spouses should not discontinue reinforcing one another altogether, because such cessation ultimately would lead to extinction of the desired behaviors. In addition to having spouses dispense social reinforcers, each spouse should be trained to covertly reinforce oneself when one exhibits a behavior that pleases the mate. Such a practice would help to maintain the desired behavior in the absence of external reinforcements.

FOLLOW-UP EVALUATIONS.   Follow-up evaluations can be undertaken periodically by clinicians in order to determine whether reciprocity is being maintained and whether the behaviors which both spouses had learned to perform during the course of treatment still are being utilized. This follow-up may take the form of mailed self-report questionnaires, telephone contacts, or home and office visits where the behavioral skills learned by the spouses can be observed and evaluated according to objective criteria.

Summary

Various models of marital therapy that are based on behavioral principles have been reviewed. It is up to each clinician to select those techniques that one wishes to incorporate into the practicing skills repertory. Undoubtedly, the formulations outlined in this chapter will undergo revisions as additional empirical data become available. At that time the effective components of each model will be combined into an empirically based behavioral model of marital intervention.

REFERENCES

Azrin, N. H., Naster, B. J., & Jones, R. Reciprocity counseling: A rapid learning based procedure for marital counseling. *Behavior Research and Therapy,* 1973, *11,* 365–382.

Bagarozzi, D. A., & Wodarski, J. A social exchange typology of conjugal relationships and conflict development: some implications for assessment and clinical intervention. *Journal of Marriage and Family Counseling,* 1977, *39,* 53–60.

Birchler, G. R., Weiss, R. L., & Vincent, J. P. Multimethod analysis of social reinforcement exchange between maritally distressed and nondistressed spouses and stranger dyads. *Journal of Personality and Social Psychology,* 1975, *31,* 349–360.

Blau, P. *Exchange and power in social life.* New York: John Wiley, 1964.

Collins, J. D. The effects of the conjugal relationship modification method on marital communication and adjustment. Unpublished doctoral dissertation, The Pennsylvania State University, 1971.

Ellis, A. *The art of science and love.* New York: Bantam Books, 1966.

Ely, A. L., Guerney, G. G., & Stover, L. Efficacy of the training phase of conjugal therapy. *Psychotherapy: Theory, Research and Practice,* 1973, *10,* 201–207.

Foa, U. G. Interpersonal and economic resources. *Science,* 1971, *171,* 345–351.

Harrell, J., & Guerney, B. Training married couples in conflict negotiation skills. In D. H. L. Olsen (Ed.), *Treating relationships.* Lake Mills, Iowa: Graphic Publishing, 1976.

Homans, G. Social behavior as exchange. *American Journal of Sociology,* 1958, *62,* 597–606.

―――― *Social behavior: Its elementary forms.* New York: Harcourt, Brace and World, 1961.

―――― *Social behavior: Its elementary forms* (2nd ed.). New York: Harcourt, Brace, Jovanovich, 1974.

Jacobson, N. S., & Martin, B. Behavioral marriage therapy: current status. *Psychological Bulletin,* 1976, *83,* 540–556.

Knox, D. *Marriage happiness.* Champaign, Ill.: Research Press, 1971.

Lazarus, A. A. *Behavior therapy and beyond.* New York: McGraw-Hill, 1971.

―――― (Ed.) *Clinical behavior therapy.* New York: Brunner/Mazel, 1972.

Lederer, W., & Jackson, D. *The mirages of marriage.* New York: Norton, 1968.

Patterson, G. R., & Hops, H. Coercion, a game for two: intervention techniques for marital conflict. In R. C. Ulrich, & P. Mountjoy (Eds.), *The experimental analysis of social behavior.* New York: Appleton-Century-Crofts, 1972.

―――― , & Reid, J. B. Reciprocity and coercion: two facets of social systems. In C. Neuringer & J. L. Michael (Eds.), *Behavior modification in clinical psychology.* New York: Appleton-Century-Crofts, 1970.

―――― , Hops, H., & Weiss, R. L. Interpersonal skills training for couples in the early stages of conflict. *Journal of Marriage and the Family,* 1975, *37,* 295–303.

―――― , Hops, H., & Weiss, R. L. A social learning approach to reducing rates of marital conflict. In R. Stuart, R. Liberman, & S. Wilder (Eds.), *Advances in behavior therapy.* New York: Academic Press, 1976.

————, Weiss, R. L. & Hops, H. Training of marital skills: some problems and concepts. In H. Leitenberg (Ed.), *Handbook of behavior modification.* New York: Prentice-Hall, 1976.

Rappaport, A., & Harrell, J. A behavioral exchange model for marital counseling. *The Family Coordinator,* 1972, *21,* 203–212.

Satir, V. *Conjoint family therapy.* Palo Alto, Ca.: Basic Books, 1967.

Stuart, F., Stuart, R. B., Maurice, W. D., & Szasz, G. *Sexual adjustment inventory.* Champaign, Ill.: Research Press, 1975.

Stuart, R. Token reinforcement in marital treatment. In R. Rubin, & C. M. Franks (Eds.), *Advances in behavior therapy.* New York: Academic Press, 1969.

Stuart, R. B. Behavioral remedies for marital ills: a guide to the use of operant interpersonal techniques. In A. S. Gurman, & D. G. Rice (Eds.), *Couples in conflict.* New York: Jason Aronson, 1975.

———— An operant interpersonal program for couples. In D. H. L. Olson (Ed.), *Treating relationships.* Lake Mills, Iowa: Graphic Publishing, 1976.

————, & Stuart, R. *Marital precounseling inventory.* Champaign: Ill.: Research Press, 1972.

————, & Stuart, R. *Family pretreatment inventory.* Champaign, Ill.: Research Press, 1975.

Thibaut, J., & Kelley, H. H. *The social psychology of groups.* New York: John Wiley, 1959.

Waller, W., & Hill, R. *The family: A dynamic interpretation.* New York: The Dryden Press, 1951.

Weiss, R. L., Birchler, G. R., & Vincent, J. P. Contractual models for negotiation training in marital dyads. *Journal of Marriage and the Family,* 1974, *36,* 321–331.

———— Hops, H., & Patterson, G. R. A framework for conceptualizing marital conflict: a technology for altering it, some data for evaluating it. In L. A. Hammerlynck, L. C. Handy, & E. J. Mash (Eds.), *Behavior change: Methodology, concepts and practice.* Champaign, Ill.: Research Press, 1973.

Wieman, R. J., Shoulders, D. I., & Farr, J. H. Reciprocal reinforcement in marital therapy. *Journal of Behavior Therapy and Experimental Psychiatry,* 1974, *5,* 291–295.

Wills, T. A., Weiss, R. L., & Patterson, G. R. A behavioral analysis of the determinants of marital satisfaction. *Journal of Consulting and Clinical Psychology,* 1974, *42,* 802–811.

Chapter 8

COGNITIVE BEHAVIOR MODIFICATION: SELF-CONTROL PROCEDURES

In the discussion of behavior modification technology one topic often neglected in the social work literature is the area of cognitive behavior modification. This is unfortunate since application of knowledge from this area may help to overcome such problems involved in the maintenance of behavior change as continuance after treatment and generalization of behavior to other contexts. Cognitive techniques may help social workers ensure that the treatment plans discussed in office interviews are actually carried out in the client's environment and furthermore may enable a client to design a modification plan without the aid of a therapist if further problems are encountered after therapy, affording the exciting prospect of helping the client become his own therapist (Cautela, 1969; Goldfried & Merbaum, 1973; Watson & Tharp, 1972). More importantly, however, this body of knowledge focuses on areas of human behavior, i.e., problem solving, self-perception, concept formation, thinking, what clients say to themselves, and so forth that critics of behavior modification practice have indicated will have to be dealt with before behavior modification becomes a viable treatment technology (Chomsky, 1965, 1973; Katz, 1966; Mahoney, 1977; Malcolm, 1964)

This chapter reviews the developing body of knowledge generally defined as cognitive behavior modification. The derived techniques are based on the operant, respondent, and modeling paradigms. These paradigms will not be elaborated here since they have been reviewed in depth in Chapters 4, 5, and 6. The following topics will be reviewed : basic assumptions of the model, techniques based on the operant model, on the respondent model, and on the modeling paradigm, and future research issues to be resolved if the knowledge in this area is to be provided on a more rational and empirical basis.

BASIC ASSUMPTIONS

All models assume that cognitive behaviors comply with the same laws that influence the control of overt behaviors. For example, if a marital partner imagines himself or herself exhibiting a complementary behavior to his or her spouse that is followed by a reinforcing smile the probability of the behavior occurring in reality is increased. Likewise, if a pleasant stimulus is followed by an aversive stimulus the pleasant stimulus decreases its positive value proportionately to the number of pairings with the aversive stimulus (Homme, 1965; Skinner, 1969). Moreover, if a client imagines the behavior in different contexts the ability to generalize the behavior increases. All techniques are applied through imagination; that is, the client forms a number of images of behavioral interactional sequences. He is presented the rationale for each procedure and agrees that he will practice specific procedures a certain number of times in other contexts such as his home and place of employment. The terms "imagining," "cognitive," and "covert" are synonyms for the general process described in this chapter.

As is characteristic of overt behavior modification techniques, behaviors to be increased or decreased have to be specified in terms of observable behaviors. Likewise, where possible, baselines are secured on behaviors and usually behaviors that are to be changed are defined in such a manner that they can be counted. These procedures are employed to enable evaluation of the cognitive procedures, a basic prerequisite of all behavior modification practices. Basic concepts are the probabilities of a behavior occurring and the events controlling the rate of its occurrence. The basic focus is on changing the rates of behavior. The model, therefore, is concerned with gaining knowledge over the antecedent events, i.e., the events in the client's environment occurring just prior to the behavior, and consequences, i.e., events in the client's environment occurring just after the behavior, which control the rate of certain behaviors. Depending upon the situation, either or both of these concepts are utilized in the modification of behavior. As in other behavior modification approaches wherein the client voluntarily comes for therapy, the focus is on helping the client change those behaviors he desires to change. That is, no decisions are made by the therapist as to what other behaviors need to be modified except those behaviors which are directly related to the ones the client wishes changed.

The client's general introduction to therapy using cognitive behavior modification techniques would proceed as follows:

Therapist: Your behavior is controlled by stimuli that precede and follow your behavior. There are many studies to indicate that if you change these stimuli your behavior can change. Many professional therapists believe that if you imagine behavior and the events that control the behavior your analogous overt behaviors will change. I am going to ask you to imagine a sequence of behaviors. [To facilitate the imagination of the scene the process is carried out in a comfortable chair and an office context with minimal external stimuli such as noise from telephones, cars, and airplanes which might distract the client. These factors expedite the client's relaxation since it is believed that clearer images can be more readily formed in such a context.] I want you to have your images correspond as closely as possible to reality and to experience the scene in as many sensory modalities as possible. It is a hot August day and you have been mowing the yard for an hour. Now you decide to have a break with a cold beer. You actually smell the beer, it tantalizes your taste buds, and it is cooling and soothing.

We usually ask the client to raise one of his fingers if the image is clear. Next we ask the client to imagine the scene by himself. The scene is presented alternately by the therapist and by the client until the client has mastered the process. If the client has difficulty imagining a scene the therapist's role is to instruct the client through a vivid description of the scene to help him acquire a clearer image. A week before the commencement of the covert conditioning process the client is requested to practice the scene imagination about five to ten times a day at home.

TECHNIQUES BASED ON THE OPERANT MODEL

Covert Positive Reinforcements

The use of covert reinforcement is analogous to the use of positive reinforcement to increase an overt behavior; however, there is a difference in that the behavior to be increased is imagined by the client and the presentation of a reinforcer is likewise presented in imagination (Cautela, 1970, 1973). The choice of the reinforcer to be presented in imagination is essential to the success of the process just as it is in the overt conditioning of behavior. To determine powerful reinforcers for the client we go through the usual process of asking clients what they like, observing what they do frequently, and administering self-inventories to assess the reinforcing potential of various stimuli (Cautela, 1972; Cautela & Kastenbaum, 1967). It is essential in this process, though, that when the reinforcer is presented in imagination the client has a good image of the various properties of the reinforcer; that is, he experiences it in as many sensory modalities (visual, auditory, and tactual) as possible. It is a good procedure to choose more than one or two reinforcers to have at hand and to use different reinforcers during the conditioning process to prevent the client from becoming satiated on any particular one. We usually ask the client to describe extensively the reinforcing event and thus gain as clear an image and sensation of the reinforcer as possible. For example, when skiing is used as a reinforcer we ask the client to imagine how excited he is over his upcoming trip to Colorado. He packs his bags, arrives at the airport, boards the plane, has cocktails in flight, lands, sees snow-covered mountains, and smells the crisp clean air, the wood burning, and the evergreen of the mountains. He prepares to ski, takes a chair lift, reaches the top of a mountain and says to himself how marvelous it is. As he starts down the slope he feels the exhilaration of the air hitting his face, the scenery whizzing by, and so forth. Now we signal reinforcement.

The following example should enable one to visualize how this process would work. The client is a 21-year-old male who has rarely demonstrated much self-sufficiency and who has been catered to by his parents. He has been generally defined as dependent, unable to make decisions, and lacking initiative. He has recently graduated from a four-year college and is experiencing considerable anxiety over securing his first job. He comes to us and asks for help in securing a job. After the general introduction outlined previously, we ask him to visually construct the many scenes of activities involved in securing a job, such as reading the paper, deciding whether it is a job he wants, making the initial impression, carrying through with the interview process, securing the job, and exhibiting behaviors requisite to keeping the position. All of these steps have to be reinforced sequentially, each one building upon the other. Initially the client is asked to visualize reading the paper and providing himself a reinforcer. After this step is mastered the client would imagine each subsequent behavior until the entire sequence can be visualized and reinforced. Depending on the client's difficulties, other cognitive techniques or noncognitive behavior modification techniques may have to be used before the client can work on the current task. The primary purposes of the office interviews are to construct a modification plan and for the therapist to check the clarity of the scenes. The client is asked to practice the scenes five to ten times a day during the week. The time required for mastery of the behaviors the client desires to change varies.

ITEMS THAT DETERMINE THE RATE OF CONDITIONING. Since it is postulated that covert positive reinforcement complies with the same laws as overt positive reinforcement the following points should be kept in mind. The more times a client practices a trial and is reinforced for it, the higher the probability of his exhibiting the behavior. The time elapsed between the imagination of the behavior to be increased and the presentation of the reinforcer should be less than approximately one-half second and the sequence should be executed consistently. Reinforcers that the client desires should be utilized. In order to increase the client's desire for certain reinforcers we may instruct him to deprive himself of these reinforcers or practice the conditioning trials with specific desirable reinforcers. Toward the end of the conditioning process the client should be utilizing the reinforcers on a somewhat variable schedule (Cautela, 1970).

Covert Extinction

Imagined events that are followed by imaginary nonreinforcing events lead to the decreased probability of the behavior occurring in the future, i.e., covert extinction (Cautela, 1971a, 1973). For example, a 16-year-old youth, who being very anxious about talking to adults, began stuttering in each such interaction. The client was asked to imagine his talking to adults with neutral or no consequences occurring after he stuttered. After this scene he was asked to imagine that he spoke correctly and that the adults were pleased with his verbalizations, smiled at him, nodded their heads, and indicated that the statements he made were very good, and subsequently he experienced a positive feeling and positive self-thoughts about his performance. The use of covert extinction in conjunction with covert positive reinforcement is a common and very effective procedure. The rationale for the combined use of the two procedures is to replace nonadaptive behaviors with adaptive behaviors that will bring positive reinforcement to the client in overt interactions. If only extinction were used with the client who stutters he might increase other maladaptive behaviors rather than prosocial behaviors to secure reinforcers.

ITEMS THAT DETERMINE THE RATE OF CONDITIONING.   The following points should be considered in the use of covert extinction. As the number of extinction trials increases, the probability of the behavior occurring decreases. As is characteristic of overt extinction the client should realize, with the worker's preparation, that after extinction procedures are employed the behavior may increase temporarily above preextinction frequencies through the process of spontaneous recovery. However, the probability of spontaneous recovery of the behavior decreases with an increase in the number of nonreinforced trials. That is, behaviors have a tendency to recur for brief periods of time after extinction procedures have been employed; however, by increasing the number of extinction trials the probability of this phenomenon occurring is reduced.

The extinction process is accelerated with the amount of effort involved in visualizing a scene. Scenes must be kept relatively constant since inconsistency or irregularity of the scenes increases the behavior's resistance to extinction. If more than one reinforcer is maintaining the behavior, scenes should be constructed to cover each reinforcing situation. By merely having the client imagine he is in the behavioral context without exhibiting the behavior the probability of the behavior occurring is reduced. Finally, not every behavior in a sequence has to be extinguished (Cautela, 1971a).

TECHNIQUES BASED ON THE RESPONDENT MODEL

Relaxation

As reviewed in Chapter 5 relaxation training involves the client going through a series of exercises to relax various muscles of the body such as arms, head, legs, shoulders, and back (Wolpe, 1973). After he has had a chance to relax each group of muscles he is asked to say the word "relax." Following mastery of these exercises, he is asked to practice them in his home. After a number of trials the word itself elicits the feeling of relaxation. Next the client is instructed to think, i.e., cognitively say, the word "relax," every time he is in an anxiety- or fear-producing situation. This may be done either in conjunction with the body exercises conducted before or after the anxiety-producing event; by saying or thinking the word "relax" before, during, or after the event; or through imagining the event and saying the word "relax" thereby reducing the anxiety or fear potential of the stimulus. The rationale is that exhibiting such a response elicits behaviors that are incompatible with anxiety. As mentioned in Chapter 5 there are various good descriptions of the relaxation process that can be used by therapists and/or clients to help them become proficient in the exercises. Also, recordings are available which provide clients with assistance in practicing relaxation in contexts other than the therapist's office (Bernstein & Borkovec, 1973; Budzynski, 1977).

In many clinical situations the imagination of certain scenes, coming to therapy, and other events cause the client to become anxious. Cognitive relaxation can be used effectively by the therapist to reduce the client's anxiety in order that the client and he can proceed to structure other modification plans.

Systematic Desensitization

After a client has mastered the complete process of relaxation, another self-control procedure that can be utilized is "systematic desensitization." First the client is presented the rationale; that is, the general purpose of relaxation is to reduce the overall level of anxiety, and the specific intention of systematic desensitization is to reduce anxiety or fear produced by specific stimuli. The client is asked to construct scenes of anxiety- or fear-producing stimuli that he can present to himself. With the help of a therapist he is asked to construct a hierarchy of items consisting of the least to the most fearful or anxiety-producing. The client places himself in a relaxed state and then is asked to imagine the least fearful or anxiety-producing object first and then to imagine the next most fearful or anxious scene. If the client becomes anxious with any one scene he imagines a relaxed state. If this does not reduce the anxiety he engages in a series of thoughts to reproduce the relaxed state. If relaxation does not follow, exercises are introduced to produce a satisfactory state of relaxation. The therapist monitors the entire process and the client is asked to practice the process at home.

In the use of systematic desensitization the client may construct irrelevant scenes and/or have inadequate images. The therapist's role here is to clarify the anxiety- or fear-producing scene or scenes and help the client form more vivid images. The actual criteria to determine when relaxation or systematic desensitization is appropriate were reviewed in Chapter 5. Until additional research is executed, the pace at which the client can go through the anxiety- or fear-producing scenes, how many scenes, and how many presentations should be made remain open to conjecture (Cooke, 1968; Davison & Wilson, 1972; Kazdin & Wilcoxon, 1976; Morgan, 1973; Wilkins, 1971, 1972, 1973).

Covert Sensitization

These techniques have been used primarily with people who exhibit excessive alcoholic, smoking, drug, eating, and deviant sexual behavior (Cautela, 1966, 1967, 1973; Flannery, 1972; Kendrick & McCullough, 1972; Wisocki, 1973). The client is asked to imagine the excessive or deviant behavior such as the intake of alcohol. After this image is formed he is asked to imagine an undesirable stimulus such as vomiting, the assumption being that as in overt conditioning of behavior, when a positive stimulus is paired with a negative stimulus the value of the positive stimulus decreases, thus decreasing the client's desire for the positively valued stimulus. As in the use of covert positive reinforcement the key to the success of the techniques is for the therapist and client to isolate an adequate adversive stimulus and for the client to be able to imagine this stimulus in as many sensory modalities as possible.* Usually the covert sensitization technique is paired with the use of covert positive reinforcement to increase desirable behaviors. For example, one of the authors once treated an extremely obese person with covert sensitization in conjunction with covert positive reinforcement and a series of other behavioral techniques. The client was asked to imagine having a tremendous appetite and sitting down to dinner. The next scene to be imagined was one in which he took in food, and as soon as the food reached his mouth he began to feel a deep churning in his stomach which rose up through his throat and suddenly culminated in his vomiting all over his food. He continued to throw up and the green mess mixed with food particles was everywhere, on his mouth, clothes, dish, floor, and persons next to him. At this time, everyone was looking at him; he felt he had to get up and leave, and in the process of leaving he imagines he begins to feel better. The farther he gets away from the food the more relaxed he becomes. As in preceding examples the client was required to practice this scene many times at home.

Likewise, a 30-year old pot smoker was treated by having him imagine smoking which resulted not in a euphoric feeling but in development of a nauseous feeling that caused him to

---

*To facilitate isolation of appropriate adversive stimuli, see J. R. Cautela, The adversive scene survey schedule. *Behavior analysis forms for clinical intervention.* Champaign, Ill.: Research Press, 1977.

vomit and experience hot and cold sensations. As he stopped smoking he began to feel better and the feeling increased as more time passed. Covert positive reinforcement and other behavioral techniques were used also to help the individual improve his study skills, heterosexual interaction skills, and so forth.

Covert Modeling

Covert modeling is utilized many times when clients cannot involve themselves in the imagination scene (Cautela, 1971b). The client is asked to imagine someone else performing the behaviors since imagining himself in the situation produces too much anxiety for him to participate in the process. Before using the modeling procedure we would explain the rationale of the modeling phenomenon; that is, that a person's behavior can be increased or decreased by watching other persons exhibiting the behavior and viewing the ensuing consequences. Therefore, if one imagines another individual performing a behavior and the consequences that follow the behavior it should either increase or decrease the probability that the person who is imagining the behavior will actually exhibit the behavior.

Next, the client is asked to visualize someone else performing the desired behavior and the clarity of the scene is checked by the therapist. If the image is clear the therapist constructs scenes to facilitate the desired behavior change. The total situation is presented in imagination via instructions. For instance, a female client who is very anxious and concerned about her low frequency of sexual behavior with her husband and who cannot form an image of herself performing various behaviors is asked to imagine that another person whom she admires is performing the behaviors of undressing, lying in bed nude, fondling her partner, and so forth. When the person feels comfortable with these scenes the therapist gradually introduces the client as the person performing the behaviors. Concurrently, the therapist has the client imagine that she is experiencing extreme pleasure. The modeling process increases the probability of the client exhibiting the behavior in reality since the empirical literature indicates that we tend to more readily model those behaviors that are exhibited by individuals held in high esteem and who secure reinforcers for their behavior (Bandura, 1969, 1971).

One difficulty that might arise is when a client changes the imagined scenes without consulting the therapist. When adversive stimuli are being used the client might change the scene to decrease its adversity thus hindering the conditioning process. Therefore the therapist must check the composition of the scenes the client is presenting to him or herself.

ISSUES

Cognitive behavior modification is a relatively new field and the research upon which many of the techniques are based is limited. Comparatively, however, the research on overt techniques is extensive. Even so, one must not jump to the conclusion that overt and covert behaviors function analogously. Further research is indicated in this area such as the studies being executed on covert modeling to isolate the essential components of the process (Cautela, Flannery, & Hanley, 1974, Kazdin, 1974;) and to provide empirical support for many of the techniques being implemented. Moreover, additional research should isolate what technique or combination of techniques works best for various behaviors. What characteristics such as self-motivation, verbal ability, and so forth are possessed by therapists and clients who can apply these procedures, and what proportion of the techniques should be implemented by the client himself and what proportion by the therapist (Schallow, 1975)? Until these issues are resolved the successful application of the techniques continues to depend largely on the artistic ability of the therapist, that is, his ability to choose appropriate techniques to change behavior without empirical data to guide these decisions.

Having the client practice the techniques in other contexts increases the maintenance of the behavior and the ability to generalize to other contexts. Likewise, increasing the number of learning trials increases the rate of acquisition of certain behaviors and the rate of elimination of others. Cognitive procedures seem to obviate one of the evident problems in conducting mere 55-minute interviews once a week to discuss the client's problems (Murray & Jacobson, 1971). That is, structuring a client's environment to facilitate the learning of new behaviors and elimination of others increases the probability of generalization and maintenance of behavior to other contexts. Actually, the maintenance of behavior will also be greater because the client can practice or be his own therapist after the termination of treatment. Thus, if the previous maladaptive behavior recurs or new maladaptive behaviors occur, the client, by himself or with minimal assistance from his therapist, might be able to structure his own modification plan. However, it is of obvious necessity that clients who engage in this type of therapeutic practice must possess good imaginations.

One of the overriding problems that will be encountered is the lack of practice by clients. This might be dealt with by having clients reinforce themselves for practicing their sessions through structuring an overt reinforcement procedure. An excellent procedure is for the therapist to have the client imagine his practicing the sessions at home and using covert positive reinforcement of the practice sessions.

Many of the techniques are readily accepted by clients. They like being their own therapists and having partial control over the implementation of therapeutic techniques. This increases their positive self-images, i.e., self-confidence and self-worth since it leads to their believing that they can help themselves (Murray & Jacobson, 1971; Rehm & Marston, 1968). Also, research from social psychology indicates that a certain amount of commitment to change is necessary before clients can change. Thus, these procedures which involve the client more in treatment increase the probability that his behavior will change in the desired direction (Feldman & Wodarski, 1975; Secord & Backman, 1964).

Covert techniques seem to open up many new vistas for the behavioral social worker. Various adversive techniques that currently involve the use of expensive equipment now can be implemented without the additional cost. Moreover, the problem of client dropout related to the use of such adversive physical stimuli as electrical shock and chemical treatments to induce nausea can be eliminated. This undesirable side effect does not seem to occur in the use of adversive imagery. We have always wondered how to get out into the client's environment. Now we are not limited to what the client says about his environment, we can bring his environment as he experiences it into our clinical context and help him structure behavior modification techniques to deal with his problems.

Summary

In this chapter we reviewed the techniques based upon cognitive conditioning, a rapidly expanding area of behavior modification. The discussion emphasizes that what clients are thinking about and saying to themselves are crucial variables in the modification process. In the years to come this area of behavior modification will definitely increase in its sophistication thus enhancing the potential of behavioral techniques in the alteration of behavior.

REFERENCES

Bandura, A. *Principles of behavior modification.* New York: Holt, Rinehart and Winston, 1969.
———. (Ed.) *Psychological modeling.* Chicago: Aldine-Atherton, 1971.
Bernstein, D. A., & Borkovec, T. D. *Progressive relaxation training.* Champaign, Ill.: Research Press, 1973.

Budzynski, T. H. *Relaxation training programs.* New York: Bio Monitoring Applications, 1977.

Cautela, J. R. Treatment of compulsive behavior by covert sensitization. *Psychological Record,* 1966, *16,* 33–41.

———. Covert sensitization. *Psychological Record,* 1967, *20,* 459–468.

———. Behavior therapy and self-control: techniques and implications. In C. M. Franks (Ed.), *Behavior therapy: appraisal and status.* New York: McGraw-Hill, 1969.

———. Covert reinforcement. *Behavior Therapy,* 1970, *1,* 33–50.

———. Covert extinction. *Behavior Therapy,* 1971, *2,* 192–200. (a)

———. Covert modeling. Paper presented at the Fifth Annual Meeting of the Association for Advancement of Behavior Therapy, Washington, D.C. September, 1971. (b)

———. Reinforcement survey schedule: evaluation and current applications. *Psychological Reports,* 1972, *30,* 683–690.

———. Covert processes and behavior modification. *Journal of Nervous and Mental Disease,* 1973, *157,* 27–36.

———, & Kastenbaum, R. A reinforcement survey schedule for use in therapy, training and research. *Psychological Reports,* 1967, *20,* 1115–1130.

———. Flannery, R. B., & Hanley, S. Covert modeling: an experimental test. *Behavior Therapy,* 1974, *5,* 494–502.

Chomsky, N. *Aspects of the theory of syntax.* Cambridge, Ma.: MIT Press, 1965.

———. Psychology and ideology. In N. Chomsky, *For reasons of state.* New York: Vintage, 1973.

Cooke, G. Evaluation of the efficacy of the components of reciprocal inhibition psychotherapy. *Journal of Abnormal Psychology,* 1968, *75,* 464–467.

Davison, G. C., & Wilson, G. T. Critique of "Desensitization: social and cognitive factors underlying the effectiveness of Wolpe's procedure." *Psychological Bulletin,* 1972, *78,* 28–31.

Flannery, R. B., Use of covert conditioning in the behavioral treatment of a drug dependent college dropout. *Journal of Counseling Psychology,* 1972, *19,* 547–550

Feldman, R. A., & Wodarski, J. S. *Contemporary approaches to group treatment.* San Francisco: Jossey-Bass, 1975.

Goldfried, M. R., & Merbaum M. (Eds.). *Behavior change through self control.* New York: Holt, Rinehart and Winston, 1973.

Homme, L. E. Control of coverants: the operants of the mind. *Psychological Record,* 1965, *15,* 501–511.

Katz, J. A. *Philosophy of language.* New York: Harper & Row, 1966.

Kazdin, A. E. The effect of model identity and fear relevant similarity on covert modeling. *Behavior Therapy,* 1974, *5,* 624–635.

———, & Wilcoxon, L. A. Systematic desensitization and nonspecific treatment effects: a methodological evaluation. *Psychological Bulletin,* 1976, *83,* 729–758.

Kendrick, S. R., & McCullough, J. P. Sequential phases of covert reinforcement and covert sensitization in the treatment of homosexuality. *Journal of Behavior Therapy and Experimental Psychiatry,* 1972, *3,* 229–231.

Mahoney, M. M. Reflection on the cognitive-learning trend in psychotherapy. *American Psychologist,* 1977, *32* (1), 5–13.

Malcolm, N. Behaviorism as a philosophy of psychology. In T. W. Wann (Ed.), *Behaviorism and phenomenology.* Chicago: University of Chicago Press, 1964.

Morgan, W. G. Non necessary conditions or useful procedures in desensitization: a reply to Wilkins. *Psychological Bulletin,* 1973, *79,* 373–375.

Murray, E. J., & Jacobson, L. T. The nature of learning in traditional psychotherapy. In A. E. Bergin, & S. L. Garfield (Eds.), *Handbook of psychotherapy and behavior change.* New York: John Wiley, 1971.

Rehm, L. P., & Marston, A. R. Reduction of social anxiety through modification of self-reinforcement: an instigation therapy technique. *Journal of Consulting and Clinical Psychology,* 1968, *32,* 565–574.

Schallow, J. R. Locus of control and success at self-modification. *Behavior Therapy,* 1975, *6,* 667–671.

Secord, P. F., & Backman, C. W. *Social psychology.* New York: McGraw-Hill, 1964.

Skinner, B. F. *Contingencies of reinforcement.* New York: Appleton-Century-Crofts, 1969.

Watson, D. L., & Tharp, R. G. *Self-directed behavior: self-modification for personal adjustment.* Belmont, Ca.: Brooks/Cole Publishing, 1972.

Wilkins, W. Desensitization: social and cognitive factors underlying the effectiveness of Wolpe's procedure. *Psychological Bulletin,* 1971, *76,* 311–317.

———. Desensitization: getting it together with Davison and Wilson. *Psychological Bulletin,* 1972, *78,* 32–36.

———. Desensitization: a rejoinder to Morgan. *Psychological Bulletin,* 1973, *79,* 376–377

Wisocki, P. A. The successful treatment of a heroin addict by covert conditioning techniques. *Journal of Behavior Therapy and Experimental Psychiatry,* 1973, *4,* 55–62.

Wolpe, J. *The practice of behavior therapy* (2nd ed.) New York: Pergamon Press, 1973.

Chapter 9

TECHNIQUES FOR GROUP LEVEL
INTERVENTION

Traditional social group work methods have been in use for over three decades (Coyle, 1947, 1948). Initially the focus of social group work was to help individuals develop skills in democratic living (Klein, 1953) and to promote social development among group members (Phillips, 1957; Schwartz, 1961, 1962, 1963; Trecker, 1955; Tropp, 1965; Wilson & Ryland, 1949). The post-World War II era, however, saw a shift in the direction taken by social group work practitioners, and small groups began to be used for therapeutic, corrective, and rehabilitative purposes (Konopka, 1954, 1963; Redl & Wineman, 1951). This trend has continued steadily over the years and social group work practices increasingly are being directed toward remedial treatment of clients in small groups (Bernstein, 1970; Feldman, 1968, 1969; Glasser and Garvin, 1971; Maier, 1965; Northern, 1969; Papell & Rothman, 1966; Rose, 1969, 1977; Spergel, 1966; Vinter, 1967).

Unfortunately, the practice of social group work, like other fields of interpersonal helping, is not a unified field of service and what constitutes social group work treatment varies according to the agency in which group work is practiced, the specific theoretical orientation of the group work practitioner, and the needs of the client groups served. The diversity of these agencies in terms of their traditions, goals, and objectives; the populations they serve; and the treatment procedures they employ, i.e., recreational, educational, or rehabilitative, has made qualitative evaluation of social group practices difficult at best. With very few exceptions social group work theoretical frameworks have been descriptive, that is, about group processes, and have lacked specification as to what behaviors social workers exhibit in order to deliver services to clients. While empirical examination of the clinical casework process has just begun (Fischer, 1973), few outcome investigations have been executed within the field of social group work (Feldman & Wodarski, 1975; Schwartz, 1966, 1971; Wodarski, Feldman, & Pedi, 1976c). The major reviews of change induction within a small group context have come from disciplines outside the social work profession. The results of these reviews are encouraging in terms of supporting the use of groups to deliver services to clients (Bednar & Lawles, 1971; Hartley, Roback, & Abramowitz, 1976; Lieberman, 1976; Lieberman, Yalom & Miles, 1973).

A substantial number of the clients seen by social work practitioners lack interpersonal skills, such as how to start and maintain conversations, giving and receiving compliments, making and refusing reasonable requests, and using appropriate nonverbal behavior, as well as problem-solving skills. The group can facilitate the acquisition of these skills in the following ways. The presence of other individuals in a group setting can provide an arena for the observation of appropriate behavior through the various models group members present, and for the acquisition and practice of appropriate behaviors to help the client become more competent in his interpersonal functioning and more effective in handling those problems for which professional assistance initially was sought. Moreover, group contexts provide the realistic feedback necessary to acquire requisite behavior and consensual validation of decisions and future problem-solving plans. Additionally, when a behavior is learned in a group context, it is likely to come under the control of a greater number of discriminative stimuli; therefore, greater generalization of the behavior can occur to a broader variety of interactional contexts. The group interactional situation more frequently typifies many kinds of daily interactions. Services which facilitate the development of behaviors that enable clients to interact in groups are likely to better prepare them for participation in society, that is with the social skills necessary to secure reinforcement (Feldman & Wodarski, 1975). These factors provide the rationale for the larger use of groups in social work practice (Meyer & Smith, 1977; Wodarski, Feldman, & Pedi, 1976c).

In this chapter the authors review general considerations involved in starting a group which empirical data show are related to successful behavioral change, group level techniques derived from the behavioral model which can be used as a means of producing behavioral change in groups, and how token economies can be implemented in social work practice.

The application of basic concepts of behavioral theory to group practice will not be reviewed. For a discussion of these concepts and examples of their application, the reader may consult Chapter 5 of "Contemporary Approaches to Group Treatment" by Ronald A. Feldman and John S. Wodarski (San Francisco: Jossey-Bass, 1975). This chapter is an elaboration of the initial knowledge developed. The items covered in the aforementioned volume include historical development, theoretical framework, interventions to decrease undesirable behaviors, stimulus generalization and stimulus discrimination, interventions to increase desirable behaviors, behavioral diagnosis, establishing relationships, verbal communication, reward and punishment, and techniques for prosocial behavioral change.

GENERAL CONSIDERATIONS

Homogeneity and Heterogeneity of Group Composition

Successful behavioral treatment in groups most often has been reported for adult clients who are similar in educational and social background (Lazarus, 1968). Even though Rose (1974a, 1977) reported that differences in educational and socioeconomic status were not barriers to successful treatment outcome, the majority of the empirical studies reviewed by the authors have reported success with groups of adults alike in social attributes and exhibiting similar presenting problems.

The most frequently reported method of group treatment for individuals who manifest similar behavioral problems is group desensitization. This procedure has been used to treat specific fears and phobias and behaviors such as *test anxiety* (Donner & Guerney, 1969; Geer & Hurst, 1976; Holroyd, 1976; Ihli & Garlington, 1969; Russell, Wise, & Stratoudakis, 1976; Snider & Oetting, 1966; Spielberger & Weitz, 1964), *general anxiety* (Paul, 1965; Paul & Shannon, 1966), *public speaking* (Paul, 1965; Russell & Wise, 1976), *smoking* (Marrone, Merksamer & Salzberg, 1970), *overeating* (Hagen, 1974; Harmatz and Lapuc, 1968; Penick, Filion, Fox, and Stunkard, 1971; Wollersheim, 1970), *excessive drinking* (Miller & Nawas, 1970), *depression* (Lewinsohn, Weinstein, & Alper, 1970; Killian, 1971), and *hysteria* (Kass, Silvers, & Abroms, 1972).

Successful group treatment also has been reported for clients who have such similar social and interpersonal problems as the following: *lack of appropriate assertiveness* (Brockway, Brown, McCormick, & Resneck, 1972; Hedquist & Weinhold, 1970; Rathus, 1972, 1973; Rose, 1977), *inadequate child management skills* (Aragona, Cassady, & Drabman, 1975; Becker, 1971; Hirsch & Walder, 1969; McPherson & Samuels, 1971; Mira, 1970; O'Dell, 1974; Patterson, 1971; Patterson & Reid, 1973; Rose, 1974b; Walder, Cohen, Breiter, Daston, Hirsch, & Liebowitz, 1969; Walter & Gilmore, 1973; Whaler, Winkel,

Peterson, & Morrison, 1965; Williams, 1959), *weight control* (Abrahms & Allen, 1974; Stuart & Davis, 1972; Wollersheim, 1970), and *sexual dysfunctions* (McGovern, Kirkpatrick, & LoPiccolo, 1976).

Although grouping adults who exhibit similar fears, present related interpersonal difficulties, and lack specific social skills has substantial empirical support to warrant the continuation of such practices, evidence is accumulating that seriously challenges the time-honored practice of treating antisocial and delinquent children in homogeneous small groups. This traditional grouping of delinquent children is seen as perpetuating the dehumanizing practice of diagnostic labeling and stigmatization. Such segregation also prevents this client population from interacting with a variety of prosocial peer models who can exert group pressure to conform to more socially acceptable behaviors and group norms, and in many instances, increases the chance for acquisition of deviant behavior exhibited by models (Feldman, Wodarski, Flax, & Goodman, 1972; Feldman, Wodarski, Goodman, & Flax, 1973; Wodarski, Feldman, & Pedi, 1976a, 1976b).

The inconsistent data on homogeneity and heterogeneity of group composition indicate the need for more research to isolate how such variables interact to produce behavioral change, that is, under what conditions is it appropriate to match clients on relevant variables. The literature suggests that treating individuals who exhibit similar difficulties in groups may be beneficial if powerful behavioral change techniques such as progressive relaxation, systematic desensitization, assertive training, and so forth are employed. Likewise, data on matching client and worker characteristics also are inconclusive (Gurman & Razin, 1977).

Client Goals and Leader Activity

The role taken by the social group worker with any group of clients will depend upon the purpose for which the group was formed. The amount of direction offered by the group worker also will depend upon the needs of the group members in terms of skills to be acquired and the behaviors to be modified. The treatment techniques utilized by the worker to bring about the desired behavioral changes will depend upon a variety of factors, such as the ages of the clients, the clients' physical and intellectual limitations, and the agency setting in which treatment is to take place.

For example, the treatment of institutionalized psychotic adults or autistic children who must acquire socially relevant behaviors and self-care skills in order to be able to function outside of the institutional setting will require an extended period of monitoring and treatment and a highly active and directive role on the part of the therapist. Group treatment contracts with such populations would have to be short, concise, and uncomplicated. A greater reliance upon group contingencies and group sanctions over individual incentives may be required in order to build group cohesion and cooperation, and to maintain newly acquired behavioral patterns, such as group cooperation, task mastery, and goal attainment. Such groups may require extended periods of practice, shaping, and repeated exposure to models before new behavioral skills are adopted. Primary reinforcers paired with social reinforcers may have to be used initially before tokens can be introduced as a means of altering behavior. Such groups may have difficulty utilizing various behavioral techniques, such as self-control methods and cognitive behavioral approaches that require symbolic modeling, patience, vivid imagination of scenes, concentration, and a certain degree of abstract reasoning ability.

On the other hand, a group of middle-class adults who have come to a neighborhood center or to a church affiliated agency in order to learn self-control procedures and techniques of behavioral management, or a group of married couples who desire to learn more effective problem-solving skills and conflict negotiation strategies, will require a somewhat different role from the social worker. For example, such groups may be expected to deposit an initial fee with the social worker who contracts to refund a specific amount of money to each individual or couple for attendance; punctuality; completion of homework assignments such as practicing newly acquired behaviors in order to increase the probability of transfer and generalization; reading specified books, pamphlets, and articles; charting and monitoring behavior; and correctly using contingencies and stimulus control procedures. The creation of a cohesive group bond may be less important in such groups, especially when the focus of treatment is on building each member's self-sufficiency or on strengthening a marital bond between spouses. The role of the social worker in such groups, therefore, would be that of a consultant or an advisor who functions more as an educator than as an active group director. Groups such as these may be able to employ filmed and videotaped models in order to achieve the desired skill level, and cognitive behavioral approaches may be used more effectively with such clientele. Such clients also can be expected to cognitively rehearse alternative behaviors while they are observing other group members practicing or role playing specific behavioral assignments.

In summary, preliminary data on the type of leadership role and characteristics the worker should take on indicate that the worker should be attractive and possess good interpersonal communication skills; be similar to the client on relevant variables such as age, sex, educational level, and expectations for behavioral change; exhibit empathy, genuineness, and nonpossessive warmth; be able to provide initial structure necessary to motivate clients to change; and possess behaviors that facilitate bargaining and negotiations between himself and other clients (Lieberman, 1976). Moreover, the worker chosen should be an exemplar of the behaviors the clients wish to acquire. Thus variables affecting the process of modeling the worker behavior such as age, sex, social attributes, and so forth (Bandura, 1977) should be taken into account before a worker is assigned to a group.

Assessment, Monitoring, and Evaluation in Groups

Just as the leadership role enacted by the group worker must change in order to meet the unique needs of the particular group with which he is engaged, so too should the procedures employed for monitoring the treatment process, assessing behavior change, and evaluating goal attainment vary in accordance with the group members' abilities and skills.

The central issue which the clinician must consider is whether the group members can carry the major responsibility for behavioral assessment, self-monitoring, and the objective evaluation of goal attainment and behavior change, which are essential aspects of behavioral treatment, or whether these tasks will have to be undertaken by the social worker himself. The social worker must be able to assess, therefore, the group members' abilities to:

1.   Complete pretreatment assessment questionnaires, checklists, interview schedules, etc., which provide the data necessary to delineate the antecedents and consequences that are controlling the behaviors they desire to be altered.

2.   Specifically identify problematic behaviors in concise behavioral terms.

3.   Observe and record baseline data in the form of frequency counts, diaries, and other record keeping forms, and make person-in-situation analyses.

4.   Make accurate behavioral assessments of the conditions that precede, parallel, follow, and maintain problematic behaviors.

5.   Make use of friends, relatives, and other individuals to help monitor behavior in order to provide reliability checks and serve as potent change agents.

6.   Identify reinforcers and punishments and utilize them appropriately in devising contingency contracts that can be negotiated with members of the group or with oneself.

7.   Complete homework assignments such as reading specific material, practicing newly acquired behaviors, and following prescribed programs.

For example, a group of public assistance recipients who have limited educational backgrounds but who wish to learn more effective child management techniques and parenting skills may find it difficult to complete pretreatment assessment inventories and to utilize behavioral checklists and observational rating scales. These clients may require a number of individual pregroup meetings where such schedules and inventories can be completed with the help of the social worker. Preparation for treatment is extremely important for such client populations since research has shown that pretreatment sessions in which clients learn what will be expected of them, how they can expect the therapist to behave, and what goals can be achieved realistically through the treatment process is an extremely important factor in determining treatment outcome and whether the clients will prematurely terminate therapeutic contracts (Goldstein, Heller, & Sechrest, 1966). Research suggests that the more congruent the clients' expectations are with what actually takes place in therapy, the better the chances for successful treatment outcome (Frank, 1974; Hoehn-Saric, Frank, Imber, Nash, Stone, & Battle, 1964). Similarly, these clients may require several group sessions that are devoted to learning how to make accurate behavioral assessments. Such clients also may find it hard to refrain from attempting to modify their children's behavior while observing them during the baseline period. In such instances, the social worker may arrange to make home visits during which he can model the self-control behaviors for the clients, offer constructive feedback, coach them in the use of specific techniques, and supervise their performances through providing guided practice instructions so that they can develop the skills necessary for making accurate behavioral assessments.

If it is determined by the clients and the social worker that the group should continue intact and serve as a support system for the members once formal treatment is completed, a buddy system may be built into the formal structure of group operations. Under such an arrangement, group members are taught to work in subgroups of two or three as part of the group process and as part of their homework assignments. Buddies may serve as monitors who track each other's behavior, as models for effective performance, and as companions who provide important feedback and reinforcement in the absence of a professional therapist. Such procedures increase the probability that the relevant behaviors will be maintained and generalized to appropriate contexts. Reorganizing buddy subgroups throughout the duration of the treatment process can help the group become cohesive, especially if each member has the opportunity to work intimately with all other members of the group since this process increases the number of ties between the members.

If these parents find it difficult to locate sources of reinforcement that can later be used to reward their children, the social worker may have to make another series of home visits to help them overcome this difficulty. If another group member is skilled in behavioral observation and assessment, however, he may serve as a buddy who can help other group members identify those satisfying behaviors which frequently are engaged in by their children, such as watching particular television programs, eating certain types of foods and treats, and playing certain games. Once these reinforcing behaviors have been identified, their use as incentives can be discussed and evaluated with the other group members at the next session.

It is quite possible that clients who have limited educational backgrounds would not be well accustomed to completing homework assignments that are of an academic nature, such as reading assignments, keeping diaries, and periodically filling out self-evaluation reports. Much of the group's time in the beginning stages of treatment, therefore, might have to be devoted to in-group discussions of homework assignments and in-group practice sessions where members can receive immediate feedback and reinforcement for their initial attempts at performing these tasks, and where members who are competent in such behaviors can model them for other group members to facilitate their acquisition of the behavior.

The major responsibility for evaluating goal attainment in such a group will rest with the individual members, and the social worker's last requisite task may be to help the members devise programs to increase the probability of transfer and generalization of their newly acquired parenting skills and to institute programs and routines that will encourage their maintenance.

Different procedures for assessing, monitoring, and evaluating behavior change will have to be used, however, for a group composed of young children in their middle childhood years who have been referred to a child guidance clinic for the modification of their antisocial behaviors. In such cases pretreatment questionnaires and behavioral checklists will have to be completed by parents or other professionals who have referred the children for treatment. Trained behavioral raters will have to be employed to identify problem behaviors, their antecedents, and consequences, and to make person-in-situation analyses. This will require extensive naturalistic observations of the children in a variety of settings and environments, such as schools, homes, neighborhoods, and peer groups. Similarly, behavioral observations for the purpose of collecting baseline data in the beginning phases of treatment will be the responsibility of family members, friends, and professionals. Later, as treatment progresses, the clients themselves can begin to take some responsibility for monitoring their own behavior.

When children who exhibit antisocial behaviors are assigned to groups of prosocial youngsters for treatment, group contingencies can be used to build group pressure for shaping prosocial behaviors and reducing antisocial responses in the target children (Feldman et al., 1972, 1973; Wodarski, Feldman, & Pedi, 1976a, 1976b). Homework assignments may be impractical for such children and extended group discussions that focus on problem behaviors of group members may become boring or perceived as punishment. These discussions also may take valued time away from group activities that have been programmed to achieve specific behavioral goals and that are designed to increase the group's attractiveness (Rose, 1972).

The generalization of newly acquired behaviors to other environments through the selection of those situations where these children can experience success and reinforcement for their prosocial responses will have to be considered by the social worker. One cannot assume that transfer will occur automatically or that the children will be able to select situations that will provide them with initial success and offer immediate reinforcement for successful performance. Finally, the evaluation of goal attainment for these youngsters will most probably be made by professionals, parents, and school personnel, rather than by the children themselves.

Termination and Maintenance of Achieved Behavioral Changes

Two basic considerations must be dealt with at the close of therapy: (1) the transfer and generalization of newly acquired behaviors to settings that differ from those in which these skills originally were learned, and (2) the maintenance of newly acquired responses once formal treatment procedures have been terminated.

The social worker's role at this juncture of treatment is to help facilitate transfer and maintenance. A variety of techniques can be used toward this end:

1. Repeating in-group practice of newly acquired skills so that they are overlearned and become more resistant to extinction.

2. Holding group meetings in a variety of environmental settings, finding different relevant locations where newly ac-

quired behaviors can be practiced, and using a variety of workers to increase the number of discriminative stimuli to which the behaviors are connected.

3. Using role plays that present unpredictable, stressful, and novel situations to group members which they may encounter once they leave the group.

4. Helping members join already existing community groups that will foster the maintenance of new behaviors, e.g., joining Alcoholics Anonymous, Weight Watchers, and other such natural groups that provide a social system that reinforces the behavior.

5. Using variable schedules of reinforcement.

6. Using multiple models who exhibit the desired terminal behavior not only facilitates the acquisition of the behavior but also increases the number of discriminative stimuli that control the behavior, thus increasing the potential for the generalization of the behavior to desired contexts.

Once the group has terminated, follow-up interviews, telephone calls, and mailed questionnaires should be used by the therapist in order to assess whether changes are being maintained or whether new difficulties have cropped up. Follow-up procedures of this type also serve as additional supports for maintaining behavioral gains. This is especially true if follow-up group meetings are held and group members know that maintenance of behavioral gains will be reinforced by other group members.

GROUP LEVEL TECHNIQUES

While most social group work practitioners conceptualize treatment as taking place within the context of a group setting, few social workers have utilized the group itself as the means for producing behavior change (Feldman & Wodarski, 1975; Vinter, 1967). In order to utilize the group for the purpose of modifying the behavior of one or more of the group members, the clinician must be skilled in the application of group contingencies.

Group Contingencies

Group contingencies are one of the unique and powerful techniques group workers and clients can use to secure desired behavioral changes. Group contingencies are reinforcements that are awarded to all or most group members following the accomplishment of certain objectives by the entire group or by selected members of the group. Although research has not determined whether they can be applied in a prolonged sequence of behavioral exchanges, they are nonetheless characterized by relatively high predictive potency when certain designated behaviors are clearly outlined by the social worker or the group members themselves (Buckholdt & Wodarski, 1978; Hamblin, Hathaway, & Wodarski, 1971; Slavin & Wodarski, 1978; Wodarski, Hamblin, Buckholdt, & Ferritor, 1972, 1973).

When group contingencies are conceptualized, they can vary along at least two major dimensions (Feldman & Wodarski, 1975). These dimensions are represented by the proportion of members who must *enact* a given set of behaviors in order to receive reinforcement (enactors) and the proportion of members who are to *receive* reinforcement for the enacted behavior (recipients). When viewed as ratios according to the number of group members, these two dimensions respectively may be denoted as the enactor ratio and the recipient ratio. It is posited that varying group contingencies composed of different enactor or recipient ratios will result in differential conformity pressures exerted upon those group members who are expected to enact a certain behavioral response. The conformity pressures that are produced by different group contingencies will result in differing degrees of conformity proneness for the enactors in a group to exhibit desired behaviors. Conformity proneness is considered to be a function of the relationship between a group's enactor ratio and the recipient ratio (Feldman & Wodarski, 1975). The following formula has been proposed by Feldman and Wodarski (1975) for determining an enactor's conformity proneness: $C_E = [(E) - (N - E)^2/N] - (R/N)$, where N = number of members in a group, E = number of enactors in a group who must perform a particular behavior in order to receive reinforcement, R = number of recipients in the group who will receive reinforcement once the particular behavior is enacted, and C_E = conformity proneness for each enactor.

It should be understood that C_E is only an estimated probability ranging from 0.00 to 1.00, which represents each enactor's likelihood of yielding to conformity pressure that can result from the interaction between enactor ratios and recipient ratios. Also, C_E is considered to be a function of both the extent to which conformity expectations are shared among peers (enactor ratio) and the extent to which reinforcements for enactor behavior are distributed among group members (recipient ratio).

Based upon this hypothetical formulation, conformity proneness is expected to be its highest when group contingencies are applied to all members of the group since all members have to exhibit a given behavior form. Similarly, group contingencies are likely to be very effective when they are unanimously directed toward a single individual, that is, as the number of group members who are to receive reinforcement (recipients) within the group begins to decrease, the corresponding conformity pressures and conformity proneness for each individual is expected to decrease.

It is important to emphasize that this model of group treatment assumes the possibility for certain members to obtain reinforcement when members other than themselves are the enactors within the group. Thus, for example, it is possible to structure a group contingency wherein all members will receive reinforcement, such as the opportunity to attend a professional sports event, if just one group member substantially improves his antisocial behavior during a given time period. Such a contingency is extremely potent for the lone enactor since all the group members will direct strong conformity pressures toward him in order to assure their own reinforcements. In contrast, if fewer members are promised reinforcements for progress made by a single member, the corresponding conformity pressures are likely to be much weaker.

For example, assume that a social worker has managed to make contact and develop a working relationship with a group of antisocial inner city adolescents who have been causing disturbances within the neighborhood. His goal in working with these youngsters may be to help them reduce their aggressive behaviors and to teach them more socially acceptable ways of problem solving and conflict management. In order to accomplish this, the social worker will have to possess valued resources which the group members desire but are unable to obtain without his assistance. These reinforcements may be, for example, the social worker's ability to have the group members gain access to a neighborhood swimming pool from which the youngsters previously had been barred because of their behavior, or the social worker's ability to secure a club room in the local community center for the group to use for meetings. In either case, the continued use of these facilities by all group members may be made contingent upon the enactment of specified prosocial behaviors by one or two of the group members or all group members.

Likewise, group contingencies can be employed to alter the behavior of a group of depressed middle-aged professional males. Group contingencies can be structured to help set up behavioral goals, such as increasing positive statements about themselves, increasing the frequency of participation in reinforcing activities, and so forth, and designing appropriate change strategies and monitoring their implementation.

UNIQUE FEATURES OF GROUP CONTINGENCIES.   It is important to emphasize that behavior change can be promoted through group experiences where either individual reinforcement contingencies or varying group reinforcement contingencies are structured by the social worker or the group members themselves. Implementing behavior modification programs on an individual basis has been characteristic of the behavioral change programs implemented in groups. By employing only individual reinforcement contingencies, however, the social worker severely limits the range of treatment strategies that he might employ in a group context and effectively denies himself the opportunity for utilizing an extremely powerful treatment tool to secure behavior change—that is the influence the individual peers have for behavior change.

By employing only individual reinforcement contingencies within the group context, the reinforcements that can be provided by the social worker alone are limited in comparison to those available from the group as a whole. It also is important to realize that individual contingencies make reinforcement dependent upon individual performance that, when viewed in the context of the entire group, may be at variance with the particular needs of given members or the group as a whole. Since such contingencies place special emphasis upon discrete individual performances, overall group cohesion and integration may be diminished, especially if varying individual performances tend to countervail one another, or if they lead to the monopolization of available reinforcements by certain group members. Through the systematic application of group reinforcement contingencies, on the other hand, the social worker can structure exchanges and interactional sequences that will lead to group integration and to more frequent interpersonal helping. This is more likely to occur when each member's reinforcements are contingent upon the performance of the entire group rather than upon the isolated and uncoordinated efforts of one individual (Staats & Staats, 1964).

A number of empirical investigations have shown that a variety of behaviors, including prosocial and cooperative as well as antisocial behaviors, can be produced in group contexts by structuring differential group reinforcement contingencies (Azrin & Lindsley, 1965; Bachrach, Candland, & Gibson, 1961; Cohen, 1962; Dinoff, Horner, Kurpiewski, Rickard, & Timmons, 1960; Hart, Reynolds, Baer, Brawley, & Hollis, 1968; Hastorf, 1967; Hinztger, Sanders, & DeMeyer, 1965; Lindsley, 1966; 1967; Shapiro, 1963; Sherif, 1956). Group contingencies have an advantage in that they enable group members to acquire prosocial reinforcement value for one another. If an entire group is offered reinforcement for improved behavior by certain members, two obvious consequences can be posited: (1) greater peer group pressure toward the enactment of prosocial behavior, and (2) greater interpersonal attraction among the group members as they share the reward. These outcomes are mutually reinforcing. Greater attraction leads to stronger conformity pressures, increased susceptibility to such pressure, greater group cohesion, more effective goal attainment, greater normative integration, more frequent reward sharing and, in turn, increased sense of belongingness, greater interpersonal attraction among members, and greater commitment to prosocial norms (Cartwright & Zander, 1968; Johnson & Johnson, 1974).

On the other hand, individual contingencies frequently may lead to dysfunctional or unanticipated outcomes. For example, in a group of children structuring competitive activities among group members may result in failure, embarrassment, and rejection for some members, exclusion from power positions in the group, lower goal attainment for the group as a whole, factionalism and dysfunctional subgrouping and allegiances, and possibly, an increase in antisocial behavior on the part of some members, distrust of others, and less empathy and altruism toward others. Reinforcing only selected members of the group in the presence of others, moreover, may be perceived by the nonrewarded members as punishment, and the effect of this perception upon the behavior of the nonreinforced members can increase dislike of students receiving reinforcement, decrease nonreinforced members' self-esteem, and decrease their ability to relate to other group members (Buckholdt & Wodarski, 1978).

Hence, the utilization of individual reinforcement contingencies within the group inadvertently may produce a number of undesired outcomes. It not only may produce adverse consequences for the nonreinforced group members, but, in addition, it may result in the lowering of the members' attraction to one another, inhibit group sharing, cooperation and cohesiveness, and diminish the group's overall effectiveness as a treatment vehicle. Moreover, the few members who are singled out as the recipients of reinforcements may acquire aversive stimulus and/or discriminative properties for the other group members. This may suggest to the latter that further interpersonal exchange with the "successful" members will be likely to result in continued failure to receive desired reinforcements. The nonrewarded individuals may resent those more fortunate than themselves, avoid contact with them, or become hostile or antagonistic toward them. A more severe consequence may be their avoidance or withdrawal from the group as the number of nonreinforcing exchanges increases.

By employing group reinforcement contingencies in work with clients, the worker can eliminate the likelihood that only a limited number of clients will receive reinforcements within the group, and it becomes unnecessary to induce competition for available reinforcers. Instead, members can be encouraged to exhibit prosocial behaviors that will contribute to the procurement of reinforcers for all. Moreover, they may be more likely to exert strong pressure upon their peers to exhibit such behaviors. Increased prosocial behaviors can lead to the acquisition of additional reinforcers and, therefore, to the group members' acquisition of secondary reinforcing properties for each other, thus increasing their influence potential for each other (Staats & Staats, 1964). As the group develops valuable reinforcing properties, its effectiveness as a treatment vehicle is likely to be enhanced. As a result, through the use of selected group contingencies, the group no longer will serve solely as a context for behavioral change. It also will constitute an active agent for behavioral change.

THE TOKEN ECONOMY

A powerful treatment approach that can be applied successfully within the context of a group setting is the token economy. The token economy is conceptualized as a motivational environment which is based primarily upon principles derived from the operant model (Ayllon & Azrin, 1968; Kazdin, 1977b), but aspects of both the classical and modeling paradigms also play significant roles in token systems. The central feature of the token economy is the programming of environments so that predictable consequences always follow certain selected behaviors.

When viewed within this framework, the token economy may be seen as a simple system of contingent rewards. When one examines the variables involved, for example, the range of behaviors that can be modified, the number and variety of tokens that can be earned, utilized, and exchanged for reinforcers, and the various schedules of reinforcement that can be applied within a given program, this seemingly simple paradigm becomes rich and complex (Mumford, Lodge-Patch, Andrews, & Wyner, 1975).

Token economies are sophisticated programs which involve the behaviors of all individuals in a given group (Atthowe & Krasner, 1968) and as such they truly exemplify the group level application of behavioral technology (Hall & Baker, 1973). While all token systems need not be applied at the group level, the major use of token economies has been with groups of institutionalized individuals typically classified as antisocial, psychotic, and retarded (Atthowe & Krasner, 1968; Ayllon & Azrin, 1965, 1968; Cohen, Florin, Grusche, Meyer-Osterkamp, & Sell, 1972; Milby, 1975; Mumford, et al., 1975; Phillips, 1968, Phillips, Phillips, Fixsen, & Wolf, 1971; Rybolt, 1975).

The major components that distinguish token systems from other operant reinforcement procedures are the use of tokens and the economic and exchange features of token economies that have practical implications for use in everyday life situations. A token is a tangible conditioned reinforcer. Its use is based on research that shows that a response is strengthened when reinforcement is delivered immediately after its occurrence (Ayllon & Azrin, 1968). The major advantages of using conditioned reinforcers (tokens) are that they (1) permit reinforcement at any time, (2) allow sequences of responses to be reinforced without interruption, (3) maintain reinforcing properties because of their relative independence of deprivation states, (4) allow for the use of the same reinforcers for individuals who may have different preferences in back-up reinforcers, and (5) may take on greater incentives than a single primary reinforcer since the effects that result from association with each primary reinforcer may summate (Kazdin & Bootzin, 1972). Typically used tokens include plastic discs, stars, and play money.

Implementation of Token Economies

Several general areas must be considered in the planning and execution of token systems. These are:

1. The selection, defining, and delimiting of those target behaviors that are to be increased, decreased, or acquired.
2. Locating those reinforcers that will provide the incentive for clients to make modifications in their behavior.
3. Maximizing the effects of these reinforcements once they have been determined.
4. Making sure that contingent reinforcements follow immediately after the performance of the targeted behaviors.
5. Clearly specifying the contingent arrangements between various behaviors and tokens.
6. Shaping the desired responses.

It is important to note that to properly conduct a token economy system there must be a large investment of time, money, and training. Staff must be trained in behavioral methods to ensure coordination of interventive attempts, records and monitoring must be maintained, and reinforcers chosen, and in some instances, purchased by the institution. A token economy cannot run by itself. Workers implementing the system require constant feedback in order to make the adjustments necessary to produce the desired behavioral changes.

Some basic procedural rules for implementing token economies have been outlined by Ayllon and Azrin (1968). These will be discussed briefly to elucidate for the reader the basic requisites of a token economy.

SELECTION OF BEHAVIORS TO BE MODIFIED. Behaviors that are chosen for modification should be described in specific behavioral terms that require a minimum of interpretation and personal evaluation on the part of the observer. The use of two or more behavioral raters to ensure interrater agreement may be used for this purpose.* Behaviors that are selected for intervention should be those that have utilitarian value for the client. If a variety of new skills or related behaviors can be learned by the client that will help him develop a general ability that he can use in a variety of settings, these skills should be the focus of training (Kazdin, 1977a). Typical categories of behavior chosen for alteration have been related to social, vocational, and academic skills. Once such skills are acquired, they are likely to be maintained by the reinforcements they secure for the client in his everyday life.

DELINEATION OF REINFORCERS. Recording those behaviors which clients frequently exhibit when the opportunity arises can give the clinician a good indication of what high probability behavioral performances can be used contingently to reinforce

---

*For a full discussion of how to make accurate and concise behavioral assessments and observations and how to collect baseline data for the purpose of planned intervention, the reader is referred to Chapter 3 of this book.

those behaviors that have a low probability of occurrence. Similarly, by administering the Incentive Preference Survey discussed in Chapter 3 and by asking the client which items he desires, observing the frequency of activities freely engaged in by the client, noting the objects frequently utilized by him, and observing the individuals with whom he often associates in terms of their likes and dislikes important clues can be found as to what a particular individual finds reinforcing.

MAXIMIZING THE EFFECTS OF REINFORCERS.   A distinct, palatable and easily identifiable stimulus item such as a plastic disc, stars on charts or in books, play money, and so forth may be utilized to bridge the delay between the desired behavioral performance and the presentation of the reinforcer. For this purpose, conditioned reinforcers in the form of tokens are utilized. Tokens are practical since they can be dispensed with relative ease and frequency without the normal routine being disrupted.

Ayllon and Azrin (1968) point out the positive features that tokens have as conditioned reinforcers. These are:

1.   The number of tokens can bear a simple quantitative relationship to the amount of reinforcement that is directly proportionally related to the accomplishment of various behavioral goals.

2.   Tokens are portable and can be retained by the client even when he is in situations that are far removed from that in which they were earned.

3.   No limit is placed on the number of tokens a client can earn or possess and ultimately use.

4.   Tokens can be used to barter and operate devices for the automatic delivery of reinforcers whenever the client so desires.

5.   The physical characteristics of tokens can be easily standardized.

6.   Tokens can be made fairly indestructible so that they will not deteriorate during the delay, i.e., the time between

when the client exhibits the behavior which secures tokens and when the tokens are redeemed for rewards.

7. Tokens can be made unique and nonduplicable so that the social worker can be sure that they are received only in the prescribed manner.

To avoid the possibility of the client becoming satiated with the reinforcements that are awarded for specific behavioral performances, it is wise to have a variety of back-up reinforcers that can be made available to the client in exchange for the tokens he has acquired. The scheduling of reinforcers also is an important tactical and strategic issue that must be considered. The social worker should avoid scheduling reinforcing activities jointly or simultaneously because this practice weakens the effect of any one given reinforcer. In order to circumvent this possibility, the clinician should plan not to dispense more than one reinforcer at a time, and should avoid programming reinforcing activities concurrently during the same time period.

Before using any event or stimulus as a reinforcer, it is extremely important to test the potency of that reinforcer in all those new situations in which it will be used. This is done in order to determine its effectiveness and to evaluate whether any unanticipated emotional reactions will result from the presentation of an unfamiliar stimulus in the client's environment.

ASSURING THAT CONTINGENT REINFORCEMENTS FOLLOW IMMEDIATELY UPON BEHAVIORAL ENACTMENT.   Since it is impossible for observers always to be on hand to evaluate whether target behaviors have been performed, a means for measuring their successful completion in the absence of direct supervision must be devised. One way of arranging for such evaluation is to structure situations so that the performance of target behaviors will produce enduring and observable changes in clients and their physical environments. For example, in a residential setting clients can learn to request tokens from staff members once they have completed specific task assignments, such as shaving, dressing in street clothes rather than pajamas, making their own beds, and cleaning their own rooms.

The time and place for the performance of the desired response as well as the time when reinforcements are to be delivered to the client must be specifically outlined, preferably in written form. In addition to where and when, it also is essential to specify which individual or individuals will be responsible for administering back-up reinforcers. In order to reduce the possibility of making errors in the dispensing of reinforcers, automated reinforcement delivery devices can be utilized, such as machines that dispense cigarettes, candy, and gum and coin-operated televisions, radios, and phonographs. Such devices can be monitored easily for the purpose of gathering data and evaluating the treatment program. Once these data are collected it can be made available to the clients. They in turn can check the data against their own records and notify program administrators of any discrepancies in reinforcement procedures.

SHAPING DESIRED RESPONSES.   In helping clients acquire responses that were not initially in their behavioral repertoires, the social worker should begin by identifying and reinforcing any existing responses which have component relations to the target behavior. Next, the clinician should reinforce variations of the component relations that are closer to the target behavior. Finally, the worker should reinforce the components which approximate the target response. This procedure is particularly useful in working with nonverbal clients. When clients are verbal, however, verbal prompting in conjunction with shaping procedures can shorten the acquisition process. Shaping procedures also can be shortened considerably by reinforcing clients for the imitation of behaviors exhibited by models. The use of corrective feedback also can speed up behavioral acquisition.*

Critical Issues in the Application of Token Systems

A major issue that must be considered in utilizing token systems with clients who are being cared for in institutions or residential treatment settings is that of client's rights. In order to safeguard each client's individual rights, it is essential that he be permitted to choose freely whether or not to participate in this type of treatment approach. Any person who elects to participate, therefore, must have full knowledge of the procedures to be used and must give written consent before participating. Signing a consent form and committing oneself to a particular treatment modality, however, should not deprive the client of his right to discontinue treatment, to return to his previous mode of therapy or to sign himself out of the institution if he so desires. In the case of severely retarded individuals, chronically disabled psychiatric patients or institutionalized children, special committees should be set up to assure that the rights of any clients assigned to this mode of treatment be strictly upheld.

The issue of client's rights is intimately bound to the selection and utilization of reinforcers which can be used to back up token systems. For example, a comfortable bed, clean clothes and linen, a personal closet or locker, nutritionally adequate and appropriately prepared meals, and ample outdoor exercise are an individual's right and cannot be made available to a client conditionally. Making these rights contingent upon the performance of prescribed behaviors not only has ethical and moral implications, but legal ramifications as well. Every environment, however, has items which can be made contingent upon certain behavior with-

*For a full discussion of modeling as a clinical tool the reader is referred to Chapter 6 of this book.

out depriving the client of his rights (Braun, 1975; Wexler, 1973).

The issue of generalization also must be explored in greater depth if token systems are to be used to their fullest advantage. When considering generalization, the major concerns are whether the behavioral gains made within the token supported environment can be maintained once the client returns to the community where a similar system of reinforcements is not in effect, and to what extent the behaviors modified by token economies will generalize to responses other than those that were the original target of the treatment program.

A variety of proposals for ensuring response generalization and stimulus generalization have been offered by Kazdin and Bootzin (1972). These are:

1. Selecting target behaviors that are most likely to be reinforced in the natural environment once training is completed.

2. Pairing token reinforcers with social reinforcers such as approval, smiles, praise, and recognition of accomplishments. Once social reinforcers gain value in their own right, the token reinforcers gradually are removed. In this way social approval can take over the reinforcement function once the client leaves the institutional setting.

3. Requiring institutionalized clients to spend increasingly greater amounts of time in the community before their release. Such a procedure affords the possibility of clients exhibiting the behavior in socially relevant contexts and receiving subsequent reinforcement.

4. Training relatives, friends, and significant others to use social approval and to continue the contingencies on a variable schedule of reinforcement once the client returns to the home.

5. Training clients in the use of self-reinforcement, self-management, and self-control techniques.

6.   Using variable schedules of reinforcement once behaviors are acquired.

7.   Having clients return periodically to the institution or to after care facilities for follow-up evaluations and implementation of appropriate maintenance programs that involve reinforcements provided by the professional staff or the client's peers meeting in groups.

The final issue to be examined is nonresponsiveness of certain patients to token programs. This was not recognized as a problem for a long time because of the enthusiasm for token programs and was often explained away rather than investigated. A recent review of this problem area, however, indicates that a consistent 10 to 20 percent of participants in token economies do not respond to the procedure (Gripp & Magaro, 1974; Kazdin, 1973, 1977b; O'Leary & Drabman, 1971). Especially interesting are several studies reviewed that indicate that severely impaired persons may not respond well to reinforcement. Such impaired persons include psychotics, retardates, and autistic children, common targets of token economies. Two types of explanations are usually offered to account for this phenomenon. Some investigators assert that the design of the token economy is inadequate. They point to inadequate reinforcers or the lack of the response in the patient's repertoire, i.e., the token program requires the client to exhibit too complex responses. Other researchers argue that the operant model may not be applicable to such clients.

As in other areas of behavior modification, we must be able to match problem behavior to interventive strategy. Several innovations in token programs design have been proposed (Kazdin, 1973). Effectiveness of contingencies can be improved by reinforcer sampling and the manipulation of back-up reinforcers to include items that have more motivation inducing properties. In instances where clients do not initially respond to the reinforcers available, a worker may want to provide the tokens noncontingently to the client enabling him to sample the items or activities that are available, which may increase their attractiveness, particularly if others enjoy the rewards. Moreover, patients can be motivated by including them in the development and administration of the program. Finally, response priming can be employed through the provision of instructions to patients as to how to perform desired responses to secure reinforcement.

Summary

In this chapter has been provided a brief overview of behavior therapy in groups. While some issues such as group composition and the selection of reinforcers for a particular client group are not resolved and await further empirical investigation, the efficacy of behavioral approaches within the context of the group has substantial empirical support. The authors stress the importance of the social worker's ability to perform a variety of roles in working with groups. The type of role enacted, e.g., active, directive, consultative, or advisory, however, will depend upon the unique needs of a particular group. Assessment, monitoring, and evaluation, essential components of successful intervention in groups, will vary widely depending upon the type of clients being trained. Here again the resourcefulness and sound judgment of the clinician come into play.

The issues of transfer, generalization, and maintenance of newly acquired behaviors are discussed and a variety of suggestions to minimize these difficulties are outlined.

While most behavioral approaches have utilized the group as a context for treating the individual, little work has been done concerning the use of group contingencies which employ the entire group as a means for treatment. The implications of such group level methods of intervention are discussed.

Finally, the use of token economies is reviewed, guidelines for their implementation are offered, and the legal and moral implications involved in the use of token systems and issues related to increasing their efficacy are discussed.

REFERENCES

Abrahms, J. L., & Allen, G. J. Comparative effectiveness of situational programming, financial payoffs, and group pressure in weight reduction. *Behavior Therapy,* 1974, *5,* 391–400.

Aragona, J., Cassady, J., & Drabman, R. S. Treating overweight children through parental training and contingency contracting. *Journal of Applied Behavior Analysis,* 1975, *8,* 269–278.

Atthowe, J. M., & Krasner, L. (Eds.) Preliminary report on the application of contingent reinforcement procedures on a chronic psychiatric ward. *Journal of Abnormal Psychology,* 1968, *73,* 37–43.

Ayllon, T., & Azrin, N. H. The measurement and reinforcement of the behavior of psychotics. *Journal of Experimental Analysis of Behavior,* 1965, *8,* 357–383.

————. *The token economy: A motivational system for therapy and rehabilitation.* New York: Appleton-Century-Crofts, 1968.

Azrin, N. H., & Lindsley, O. R. The reinforcement of cooperation between children. In L. P. Ullmann, & L. Krasner (Eds.), *Case studies in behavior modification.* New York: Holt, Rinehart and Winston, 1965.

Bachrach, A. J., Candland, D. K., & Gibson, J. T. Group reinforcement of individual response experiments in verbal behavior. In I. A. Berg, & B. N. Bass (Eds.), *Conformity and deviation.* New York: Harper and Row, 1961.

Bandura, A. *Social learning theory.* Englewood Cliffs, N.J.: Prentice-Hall, 1977.

Becker, W. C. *Parents as teachers: A child management program.* Champaign, Ill.; Research Press, 1971.

Bednar, R. L., & Lawles, F. Empirical research in group psychotherapy. In A. E. Bergin, & S. L. Garfield (Eds.), *Handbook of psychotherapy and behavior change.* New York: John Wiley, 1971.

Bernstein, S. (Ed.) *Further explorations in group work.* Boston: Milford House, 1970.

Braun, S. H. Ethical issues in behavior modification. *Behavior Therapy,* 1975, *6,* 61–62.

Brockway, B. S., Brown, F. W., McCormick, D. J., & Resneck, H. Assertive training in the group context. Unpublished manuscript, Madison, Wisc.: University of Wisconsin, 1972.

Buckholdt, D. R., & Wodarski, J. S. The effects of different reinforcement systems on cooperative behaviors exhibited by children in classroom contexts. *Journal of Research and Development in Education,* 1978, in press.

Cartwright, D., & Zander, A. (Eds.) *Group dynamics: Research and theory,* *(3rd. ed.)* New York: Harper and Row, 1968.

Cohen, D. J. Justin and his peers: an experimental analysis of a child's social world. *Child Development,* 1962, *33,* 697–717.

Cohen, R., Florin, I., Grusche, A., Meyer-Osterkamp, S., & Sell, M. The introduction of a token economy in a psychiatric ward with extremely withdrawn chronic schizophrenics. *Behavior Research and Therapy,* 1972, *10,* 73–82.

Coyle, G. L. *Group experience and democratic values.* New York: Association Press, 1947.

————. *Group work with American youth.* New York: Harper and Row, 1948.

Dinoff, M. R., Horner, F., Kurpiewski, B. S., Rickard, H. C., & Timmons, E. O. Conditioning verbal behavior of schizophrenics in a group therapy-like situation. *Journal of Clinical Psychology,* 1960, *16,* 371–372.

Donner, L., & Guerney, B. G., Jr. Automated group desensitization for test anxiety. *Behavior Research and Therapy,* 1969, *7,* 1–13.

Feldman, R. A. Interrelationships among three bases of group integration. *Sociometry,* 1968, *31,* 30–46.

————. Group service programs in public welfare: patterns and perspectives. *Public Welfare,* 1969, *27,* 266–271.

————, Wodarski, J. S. *Contemporary approaches to group treatment.* San Francisco: Jossey-Bass, 1975.

————, Wodarski, J. S., Flax, N., & Goodman, M. Treating delinquents in traditional agencies. *Social Work,* 1972, *17,* 72–78.

————, Wodarski, J. S., Goodman, M., & Flax, N. Pro-social and anti-social boys together. *Social Work,* 1973, *18,* 26–37.

Fischer, J. Is casework effective? a review. *Social Work,* 1973, *18,* 5–22.

Frank, J. D. Therapeutic components of psychotherapy. *The Journal of Nervous and Mental Diseases,* 1974, *159,* 325–342.

Geer, C. A., & Hurst, J. C. Counselor-subject sex variables in systematic desensitization. *Journal of Counseling Psychology,* 1976, *23,* 296–301.

Glasser, P. H., & Garvin, C. Social group work. *Encyclopedia of social work.* New York: National Association of Social Workers, 1971.

Goldstein, A. P., Heller, K., & Sechrest, L. B. *Psychotherapy and the psychology of behavior change.* New York: John Wiley, 1966.

Gripp, R., & Magaro, P. The token economy program in the psychiatric hospital: a review and analysis. *Behavior Research and Therapy,* 1974, *12,* 205–28.

Gurman, A. S., & Razin, A. M. (Eds.) *Effective psychotherapy.* New York: Plenum, 1977.

Hagen, R. L. Group therapy versus bibliotherapy in weight reduction. *Behavior Therapy,* 1974, *5,* 222–234.

Hall, J., & Baker, R. Token economy systems: breakdown and control. *Behavior Research and Therapy,* 1973, *11,* 253–258.

Hamblin, R. L., Hathaway, C., & Wodarski, J. S. Group contingencies, peer tutoring, and accelerating academic achievement. In E. A. Ramp, & B. L. Hopkins (Eds.), *A new direction for education: Behavior analysis.* Lawrence, Kansas: The University of Kansas Press, 1971.

Harmatz, M. G., & Lapuc, P. Behavior modification of overeating in a psychiatric population. *Journal of Consulting and Clinical Psychology,* 1968, *32,* 583–587.

Hart, B. M., Reynolds, N. J., Baer, D. M., Brawley, E. R., & Hollis, F. R. Effects of contingent and non-contingent social reinforcement on the cooperative play of the pre-school child. *Journal of Applied Behavior Analysis,* 1968, *1,* 73–76.

Hartley, D., Roback, H. B., & Abramowitz, S. I. Deterioration effects in encounter groups. *American Psychologist,* 1976, *31,* 247–255.

Hastorf, A. H. The reinforcement of individual actions in a group setting. In L. Krasner, & L. P. Ullmann (Eds.), *Research in behavior modification.* New York: Holt, Rinehart and Winston, 1967.

Hedquist, F. J., & Weinhold, B. K. Behavioral group counseling with socially anxious and unassertive college students. *Counseling Psychologist,* 1970, *17,* 237–242.

Hinztger, J. N., Sanders, B. J., & DeMeyer, M. K. Shaping cooperative responses in early childhood schizophrenia. In L. P. Ullmann, & L. Krasner (Eds.), *Case studies in behavior modification.* New York: Holt, Rinehart, and Winston, 1965.

Hirsch, I., & Walder, L. Training mothers in groups as reinforcement therapists for their own children. *Proceedings of the 77th Annual Convention of the American Psychological Association,* 1969, *4,* 561–562.

Hoehn-Saric, R., Frank, J. D., Imber, S. D., Nash, E. H., Stone, A. R., & Battle, C. C. Systematic preparation of patients for psychotherapy. I. Effects on therapy behavior and outcome. *Journal of Psychiatric Research,* 1964, *2,* 252–259.

Holroyd, K. A. Cognition and desensitization in the group treatment of test anxiety. *Journal of Consulting and Clinical Psychology,* 1976, *44,* 991–1002.

Ihli, K. L., & Garlington, W. K. A comparison of groups versus individual desensitization of test anxiety. *Behavior Research and Therapy,* 1969, *7,* 207–210.

Johnson, D. W., & Johnson, R. T. Instructional structure: cooperative, competitive, or individualistic. *Review of Educational Research,* 1974, *44,* 213–240.

Kass, D. J., Silvers, F. M., and Abroms, G. M. Behavioral group treatment of hysteria. *Archives of General Psychiatry*, 1972, *26*, 42–50.

Kazdin, A. E. The failure of some patients to respond to the token programs. *Journal of Behavior Therapy and Experimental Psychiatry*, 1973, *4*, 7–14.

————. Assessing the clinical or applied importance of behavior change through social validation. *Behavior Modification*, 1977, *1*, (4), 429–452.(a)

————. *The token economy*. New York: Plenum, 1977. (b)

————, & Bootzin, R. R. The token economy: an evaluative review. *Journal of Applied Behavior Analysis*, 1972, *5*, 343–372.

Killian, D. H. The effects of instruction and social reinforcement on selected categories of behavior emitted by depressed persons in a small group setting. *Dissertation Abstracts International*, 1971, *36*(6-B), 3640.

Klein, A. F. *Society, democracy, and the group*. New York: Women's Press, 1953.

Konopka, G. *Group work in the institution*. New York: Association Press, 1954.

————. *Social group work: A helping process*. Englewood Cliffs, N.J.: Prentice-Hall, 1963.

Lazarus, A. A. Behavior therapy in groups. In G. M. Gazda (Ed.), *Basic approaches to group psychotherapy and group counseling*. Springfield, Ill.: Charles C Thomas, 1968.

Lewinsohn, P. M., Weinstein, M. S., & Alper, T. A behavioral approach to the group treatment of depressed persons: a methodological contribution. *Journal of Clinical Psychology*, 1970, *26*, 525–532.

Lieberman, M. A. Change induction in small groups. In M. R. Rosenzweig, & L. W. Porter (Eds.), *Annual review of psychology* (Vol. 27). Palo Alto, Ca : Annual Reviews, 1976.

————, Yalom, I. D., & Miles, M. B. *Encounter groups: First facts*. New York: Basic Books, 1973.

Lindsley, O. R. Experimental analysis of cooperation and competition. In T. Verhave (Ed.), *The experimental analysis of behavior: Selected readings*. New York: Appleton-Century-Crofts, 1966.

McGovern, K., Kirkpatrick, C., & LoPiccolo, J. A behavioral group treatment program for sexually dysfunctional couples. *Journal of Marriage and Family Counseling*, 1976, *2*, 397–404.

McPherson, S. B., & Samuels, C. R. Teaching behavioral methods to parents. *Social Casework*, 1971, *52*, 148–153.

Maier, H. W. (Ed.) *Group work as part of residential treatment*. New York: National Association of Social Workers, 1965.

Marrone, R. L., Merksamer, M. A., & Salzberg, P. M. A short duration group treatment of smoking behavior by stimulus saturation. *Behavior Research and Therapy,* 1970, *8,* 347–352.

Meyer, R. B., & Smith, S. S. A crisis in group therapy. *American Psychologist,* 1977, *32,* 638–643.

Milby, J. B. A review of token economy treatment programs for psychiatric inpatients. *Hospitals and Community Psychiatry,* 1975, *26,* 651–658.

Miller, H. R., & Nawas, M. M. Control of aversive stimulus termination in systematic desensitization. *Behavior Research and Therapy,* 1970, *8,* 57–61.

Mira, M. Results of a behavior modification training program for parents and teachers. *Behavior Research and Therapy,* 1970, *8,* 309–311.

Mumford, S. J., Lodge-Patch, I. C., Andrews, N., & Wyner, L. A token economy ward program with chronic schizophrenic patients. *British Journal of Psychiatry,* 1975, *61,* 126–134.

Northern, H. *Social work with groups.* New York: Columbia University Press, 1969.

O'Dell, S. Training parents in behavior modification: a review. *Psychological Bulletin,* 1974, *82,* 418–433.

O'Leary, K., & Drabman, R. Token reinforcement programs in the classroom: a review. *Psychological Bulletin,* 1971, *75,* 379–98.

Papell, C. P., & Rothman, B. Social group work models: possession and heritage. *Journal of Education for Social Work,* 1966, *2,* 66–67.

Patterson, G. R. Behavioral intervention procedures in the classroom and the home. In A. E. Bergin, & S. L. Garfield (Eds.), *Handbook of psychotherapy and behavior change: An empirical analysis.* New York: John Wiley, 1971.

———, & Reid, J. B. Intervention for families of aggressive boys: a replication study. *Behavior Research and Therapy,* 1973, *11,* 383–394.

Paul, G. L. *Insight versus desensitization in psychotherapy: An experiment in anxiety reduction.* Stanford: Stanford University Press, 1965.

———, & Shannon, D. T. Treatment of anxiety through systematic desensitization in therapy groups. *Journal of Abnormal Psychology,* 1966, *71,* 124–135.

Penick, S. B., Filion, R., Fox, S., & Stunkard, A. J. Behavior modification in the treatment of obesity. *Psychosomatic Medicine,* 1971, *33,* 49–55.

Phillips, E. L. Achievement Place: Token reinforcement procedures in a home-style rehabilitation setting for predelinquent boys. *Journal of Applied Behavior Analysis,* 1968, *1,* 213–223.

———, Phillips, E. A., & Fixsen, D. L., Wolf, M. M. Achievement Place: modification of the behavior of pre-delinquent boys within a token economy. *Journal of Applied Behavior Analysis,* 1971, *4,* 45–59.

Phillips, H. V. *Essentials of social group work skills.* New York: Association Press, 1957.

Rathus, S. A. An experimental investigation of assertive training in a group setting. *Journal of Behavior Therapy and Experimental Psychiatry,* 1972, *3,* 81–86.

———. Instigation of assertive behavior through video tape-mediated assertive models and direct practice. *Behavior Research and Therapy,* 1973, *11,* 57–65.

Redl, F., & Wineman, D. *Children who hate - Controls from within.* New York: Free Press, 1951.

Rose, S. D. A behavioral approach to the group treatment of parents. *Social Work,* 1969, *14,* 21–29.

———. *Treating children in groups.* San Francisco: Jossey-Bass, 1972.

———. Group training of parents as behavior modifiers. *Social Work,* 1974, *19,* 156–162.(a)

———. Training parents in groups as behavior modifiers of their mentally retarded children. *Journal of Behavior Therapy and Experimental Psychiatry,* 1974, *5,* 135–140. (b)

———. *Group therapy: A behavioral approach.* Englewood Cliffs, N.J.: Prentice-Hall, 1977.

Russell, R. K., & Wise, F. Treatment of speech anxiety by cue controlled relaxation and desensitization with professional and paraprofessional counselors. *Journal of Counseling Psychology,* 1976, *23,* 583–586.

———, Wise, F., & Stratoudakis, J. P. Treatment of test anxiety by cue-controlled relaxation and systematic desensitization. *Journal of Counseling Psychology,* 1976, *23,* 563–566.

Rybolt, G. A. Token reinforcement therapy with chronic psychiatric patients: A three-year evaluation. *Journal of Behavior Therapy and Experimental Psychiatry,* 1975, *6,* 188–191.

Schwartz, W. The social worker in the group. In *New perspectives on services to groups.* New York: National Association of Social Workers, 1961.

———. Toward a strategy of group work practice. *Social Service Review,* 1962, *36,* 268–279.

———. Small group science and group work practice. *Social Work,* 1963, *8,* 39–46.

———. Neighborhood centers. In H. S. Maas (Ed.), *Five fields of social service: Review of research.* New York: National Association of Social Workers, 1966.

———. Neighborhood centers and group work. In H. S. Maas (Ed.), *Research in the social services: A five-year review.* New York: National Association of Social Workers, 1971.

Shapiro, D. The reinforcement of disagreement in a small group. *Behavior Research and Therapy,* 1963, *1,* 267–272.

Sherif, M. Experiments in group conflict. *Scientific American,* 1956, *195,* 54–58.

Slavin, R. E., & Wodarski, J. S. Peer tutoring and student teams. Center for Social Organization of Schools, Johns Hopkins University, 1978, (report forthcoming).

Snider, J. G., & Oetting, E. R. Autogenic training and the treatment of examination anxiety in students. *Journal of Clinical Psychology,* 1966, *22,* 111–114.

Spielberger, C. D., & Weitz, H. Improving the academic performance of anxious college freshmen: a group counseling approach to the prevention of underachievement. *Psychological Monographs,* 1964, *78,* (3, Whole No. 590).

Spergel, I. *Street gang work: Theory and practice.* Reading, Ma.: Addison-Wesley, 1966.

Staats, A. W., & Staats, C. K. *Complex human behavior.* New York: Holt, Rinehart and Winston, 1964.

Stuart, R. B., & Davis, B. *Slim Chance in a fat world: Behavioral control of obesity.* Champaign, Ill.: Research Press, 1972.

Trecker, H. B. *Social group work: Principles and practice.* New York: Association Press, 1955.

Tropp, E. Group intent and group structure: Essential criteria for group work practice. *Journal of Jewish Communal Service,* 1965, *61,* 229–250.

Vinter, R. D. (Ed.). *Readings in group work practice.* Ann Arbor, Mich.: Campus Publishers, 1967.

Walder, L. O., Cohen, S. I., Breiter, D. E., Daston, P. G., Hirsch, I. S., & Liebowitz, J. M. Teaching behavioral principles to parents of disturbed children. In B. G. Guerney, Jr., (Ed.), *Psychotherapeutic agents: New roles for non-professionals, parents, and teachers.* New York: Holt, Rinehart and Winston, 1969.

Walter, H. I., & Gilmore, S. K. Placebo versus social learning effects in parent training procedures designed to alter the behavior of aggressive boys. *Behavior Therapy,* 1973, *4,* 361–377.

Wexler, D. B. Token and taboo: behavior modification, token economies, and the law. *Behaviorism,* 1973, *1,* 1–5.

Whaler, R. G., Winkel, G. H., Peterson, R. F., & Morrison, D. C. Mothers as behavior therapists for their own children. *Behavior Research and Therapy,* 1965, *3,* 113–124.

Williams, C. D. The elimination of tantrum behavior by extinction procedures. *Journal of Abnormal and Social Psychology,* 1959, *59,* 269.

Wilson, G., & Ryland, G. *Social group work practice: The creative use of group process.* Boston: Houghton-Mifflin, 1949.

Wodarski, J. S., Feldman, R. A., & Pedi, S. J. Integrating anti-social children into pro-social groups at summer camp: a three year study. *Social Service Review,* 1976, *86,* 257–272 (a)

————. The reduction of anti-social behavior in ten-, eleven-, and twelve-year-old boys participating in a recreation center. *Small Group Behavior,* 1976, *7,* 183–196.(b)

————. Reduction of anti-social behavior in an open community setting through the use of behavior modification. *Child Care Quarterly,* 1976, *5*(3), 198–210.(c)

Wodarski, J. S., Hamblin, R. L., Buckholdt, D. R., & Ferritor, D. E. The effects of low performance group and individual contingencies on cooperative behaviors exhibited by fifth graders. *Psychological Record,* 1972, *22,* 359–368.

————. Individual contingencies versus different shared consequences contingent on the performance of low achieving group members. *Journal of Applied Social Psychology,* 1973, *3,* 276–290.

Wollersheim, J. P. Effectiveness of group therapy based upon learning principles in the treatment of overweight women. *Journal of Abnormal Psychology,* 1970, *76,* 462–474.

Chapter 10

THE APPLICATION OF BEHAVIOR MODIFICATION TO THE ALLEVIATION OF SOCIAL PROBLEMS

As can be seen from the previous chapters, under the rather general label of behavior modification a highly potent behavior change technology is being developed (Bergin & Suinn, 1975; Feldman & Wodarski, 1975; Kazdin, 1975; Thomas, 1974). Technological development in behavior modification has focused largely on changing behavior on the individual level of analysis and to a lesser extent on the group level of analysis, which has been characterized by individual programs carried out in group contexts to remedy problem behaviors, rather than through the use of the group as a vehicle of change. Moreover, only a few applications of this technology have focused on macrolevel intervention, that is, organizational, institutional, and societal levels (Arkava, 1974; Fellin, Rothman, & Meyer, 1967; Lind, 1967; Luthans & Kreitner, 1975). It appears obvious that in order to change behavior and to ensure its maintenance such macrolevel applications are necessary since our laws, norms, and customs specify contingencies for the society as a whole as well as for each of the reference groups to which we belong. These contingencies substantially influence and determine the behaviors we exhibit in specific social contexts. Focus on these levels in terms of their effects on behavior, therefore, should ensure the maintenance and the generalization of behavioral change exhibited by individuals in individual or group interactional situations (Kazdin, 1975). Furthermore, the inclusion of this level of analysis will enable specification of the distribution of reinforcers and punishments by various societal units as well as determine how these units control behavior.

Behavior modification theory applied at the macrolevel should expedite the solution of such various societal problems as excessive energy consumption, pollution control, economic systems dysfunctions, welfare reform, worker performance, social action, illegal behavior, and social integration, all of which this chapter will address in a review of many of the pilot efforts made in these areas of research. The upcoming years will witness a greater sophistication of applications and inclusion of variables in the behavioral approach that will make the control of these behaviors more feasible and facilitate the maintenance of behaviors changed through interpersonal approaches.

BASIC ASSUMPTIONS OF THE SOCIAL BEHAVIORAL MODEL

The assumption is made that laws of social behavior can be formulated. The desire is to isolate those variables that control behavior and formulate descriptive statements about the operation of those events which control it. It is postulated that once these variables are isolated the worker can modify the behavior. Behavior is controlled by the events that occur before the behavior (antecedents) and consequences that occur after the behavior. Depending upon the situation, either or both of these concepts are utilized in the modification of behavior.

Behavior is defined in terms of observable events in such a manner that two individuals can agree the behavior has occurred. Likewise, behavior is defined in such a manner that it may be counted in terms of rates per unit of time, and the interest is on changing probabilities of behavior (rates) occurring in the future. Baselines are secured on all behaviors in order to enable evaluation of whether the influence strategy has been effective. The one characteristic of behavior modification technology which differentiates this approach to changing behavior from traditional methodologies is the emphasis placed on the provision of data to facilitate the evaluation of whether worker interventions produced the desired behavioral change.

For the purposes of this chapter, social entities such as groups, complex organizations, and social institutions are defined as social units that can be characterized as being composed of a series of interconnected reinforcers and punishers and which consist of a plurality of individuals who can control reinforcers, both positive and negative, for each other regardless of the size of the unit and in many instances for other constituencies (Arkava, 1974). The social entities communicate the conditions of reinforcement and punishment, that is, consequences, through the provision of discriminative stimuli to individuals. Formal discriminative stimuli of social entities are contracts signed, informational memos communicating policy, manuals of rules and regulations, informal norms and folkways of the entities, and so forth. For example, through taxation governments secure a generalized reinforcer from individuals' money and then welfare departments and other agencies redistribute these reinforcers through guidelines (contingencies) set forth by Congress. There is no desire to deemphasize the complexity of this process, but for the purposes of this chapter this definition suffices. In the future a more sophisticated model will include other essential variables.

ENERGY CONSUMPTION

One area in which behavioral analysis will be indicated in the next decade is energy consumption. In a pilot study conducted by Wodarski (1978) a four-member household provided the site for the experimental study. The experimental group went through a standard A,B,A,B, design with a follow-up baseline period. A unique measurement system was employed to monitor the amount of time that the television, stereo, radio, oven, and heat were used. A point system was devised which consisted of various contingencies and utilized such reinforcers as food; savings, i.e., money deposited in the bank; nights out on the town, including steak dinners and movies; and enjoyable activities such as camping and hiking and was used to modify consumption of electrical energy. A significant reduction in the use of electrical power was noted during all the periods in which the reinforcement system was utilized. Unfortunately, however, the behaviors were not maintained during the follow-up period. These preliminary data and additional data provided by other investigators indicate that behavior modification techniques can be utilized to temporarily reduce electrical, natural gas, and fuel-oil energy consumption in a typical household and large buildings where people work and live (Hayes & Cone, 1975; Kagel, Battalio, Winkler, & Winett, 1975; Kohlenberg & Phillips, 1973; Kohlenberg, Phillips, & Proctor, 1976; Seaver & Patterson, 1976; Slavin & Wodarski, 1977; Slavin, Wodarski, & Blackburn, 1978; Winett & Nietzel, 1975).

In the Wodarski (1978) study, the implementation of behavior modification techniques was fairly easy and accepted by all members. However, results of the study point to two problems, the need to employ a maintenance procedure once behavior change is achieved and consideration of larger social variables in controlling behavior. While at the same time the family significantly reduced their electrical consumption, the power company increased the general rates by 20 percent. A societal contingency was imposed on the family which served to punish their attempts to conserve energy. It seems that if indeed there is an energy crisis, then power companies should utilize incentives for people to reduce their electrical consumption rather than penalize them for reducing consumption. However, one could also argue from a behavior modification perspective that as the cost of energy use increases the utilization will decrease accordingly (Ehrlich & Ehrlich, 1974; Winett, 1976).

POLLUTION CONTROL

In the last few years there has been an increasing interest in the use of behavioral analysis to help solve environmental problems such as littering, the lack of citizen participation in mass transit, and the use of nonreturnable bottles (Robinson, 1976). Clark, Burgess, and Hendee (1972) and Burgess, Clark, and Hendee (1971) were able to modify littering behavior both in a forest campground and a movie theater. In both instances positive reinforcement, i.e., money, comic books, gum, and Smokey Bear shoulder patches, were utilized to increase the number of bags of litter that children turned in to a specific area. Likewise, Powers, Osborne, and Anderson (1973) were successful in increasing litter removal in a national forest through the use of a small monetary reward, and Kohlenberg and Phillips (1973) increased the deposit of litter in urban parks through the use of a ticket that could be exchanged at the concession stand for a soft drink. The ticket was provided after a litter deposit occurred. As they entered the park individuals were made aware of the contingencies through a sign which read, "At times persons depositing litter in containers will be rewarded." Chapman and Risley (1974) were moderately successful in reducing the litter in a high-density urban neighborhood and found the most effective contingency in increasing antilitter responses was a monetary payment for clean yards. Baltes and Hayward (1976) reduced littering at two college football games through the use of monetary incentives and visual prompts. The provision of litter bags with an appeal not to litter had little effect on the behavior, however.

Geller, Farris, and Post (1973) increased the use of return-able bottles through passing out handbills designed to prompt the purchase of soft drinks in returnable rather than throw-away containers. The handbills provided a rationale in terms of environmental benefits for encouraging purchase of returna-bles. Likewise, paper recycling was increased through the use of incentives. For every pound of paper they recycled, individu-als were given a ticket which enabled them to increase their chances of winning a prize. Contests where groups of dormitory students could win 15 dollars for the most paper saved also were successful (Witmer & Geller, 1976). Subsequent research has continued to show littering behavior can be decreased and recycling increased by providing explicit instructions on how to dispose of the litter, monetary payments, and conveniently placed disposal and recycling containers (Geller, Witmer, & Orebaugh, 1976; Reid, Luyben, Rawers, & Bailey, 1976).

In regard to increasing the use of ecologically focused modes of transportation, Everett, Hayward, and Meyers (1974) used token reinforcement procedures to increase the ridership of buses on a college campus. Utilizing a token system in which individuals could exchange tokens for ice cream, beer, pizza, coffee, cigarettes, movies, flowers, and records at various desig-nated business establishments resulted in a 150 percent increase in ridership. Likewise, Foxx and Hake (1977), through the use of various incentives such as cash, tours of a mental health facility, car servicing, and a university parking sticker, reduced the miles driven by college students by an average of 20 percent.

With the exception of these few research projects, the use of behavior modification in the environmental movement re-mains a relatively unexplored area of research. However, these preliminary data do indicate that specific reinforcement contin-gencies can be utilized to effectively control pollution behavior of individuals. Future research endeavors should isolate what combination of techniques yields the best results in terms of reducing pollution. Questions to be answered through future investigations will pertain to whether punishment of undesirable behavior is adequate, whether positive reinforcement for antipollution behavior is adequate, or whether a combination of these two techniques is more efficacious. Additionally, the role played by significant models in either producing or reducing pollution behavior will have to be determined as well as what type of observational procedures are necessary to ensure the conservation and improvement of our environment (Christophersen, Doke, Messmer, & Risley, 1975; Willens, 1974).

TOKEN ECONOMIES

Present monetary policies of world governments represent a hit and miss approach. It is unfortunate that policy makers in certain countries make economic policy without use of a reliable data base. For affluent individuals, this approach may be of minor consequence. However, for the populations dealt with in social work practice the consequences are more serious. Token economies utilized in mental hospitals, correctional institutions, schools, and other agencies represent miniature economic systems and present the behavior modifier with the opportunity to control a variety of variables to determine how they affect the behavior of individuals. We therefore are able to contribute to the development of a technology of economic behavior. Such an empirical opportunity has rarely been available in economic analysis. The components of the token system correspond with various aspects of our economic systems, e.g., tokens may be considered as currency, amounts of reinforcement as wages, exchange rates as prices, and pay periods as schedules of reinforcement.

Recent experiments utilizing token economies to test various economic principles such as consumption schedules, Engel curves, elasticity of a demand curve, and so forth are enabling behavioral scientists to make beginning propositions concerning how certain economic variables affect behaviors. For example, high savings lead to poor performance rates in various behaviors, low savings lead to improved performance rates. Individuals tend to spend more on leisure items as earnings go up and less on basic necessities. Thus, if an individual wants to increase performance behaviors more incentives will have to be provided. One means of increasing incentives is to increase prices. Thus, if a social worker is employing a token economy in a mental hospital to increase such behaviors as work, self-care, and academic, an increase in prices should produce a general corresponding increase in desired behaviors. As this knowledge base develops, it would be in the best interest of the social work profession to utilize such data and to communicate the findings to monetary policy makers in order to benefit the individuals we serve. Token economies viewed as miniature economic systems present numerous possibilities for investigating such things as the effects of guaranteed income, negative income tax, and the various other welfare programs on a scale model. Recommendations therefore can be based on empirical data rather than on faith (Ayllon & Azrin, 1968; Fethke, 1972, 1973; Kagel & Winkler, 1972; Kazdin, 1977; Winkler, 1971a, b; 1972, 1973a, b).

Thus, token economies and simulations have made beginning contributions to the understanding of microeconomics and have the possibility of providing a preliminary data base for present monetary policies. More experimentation will be needed to determine how generalizable the results are to large economic systems. No doubt this process will involve the specification of large numbers of variables and how they affect economic behavior.

ARCHITECTURAL CONTROL OF BEHAVIOR

Recent research indicates that we can architecturally structure environments to control many behaviors. In the area of crime control, a recent development has been the utilization of bucket seats rather than benches in various terminal facilities where derelicts formerly slept. Also, buildings are now being constructed with corridors and passageways which are open to public observation since recent research evidence indicates that more crime takes place in corridors and passageways that are hidden from public view (Jeffery, 1971, 1976; Reppetto, 1976).

New research is being conducted to isolate those variables that are crucial in offering adequate services to children in day care center environments (Twardosz, Cataldo, & Risley, 1974). Preliminary research seems to indicate that open environments where children are continuously visible to staff, and the staff are almost continuously visible to supervisors, facilitate interaction among the children and staff (Doke & Risley, 1972; LeLaurin & Risley, 1972). Certain toys that require at least two individuals to participate such as cards, checkers, "pick-up stixs," "Don't Cook Your Goose," "Don't Break the Ice," and "Don't Spill the Beans" lead to more interaction whereas materials such as crayons, gyroscopes, tinker toys, puzzles, books, and "Play-Doh" decrease the interactional levels among children (Quilitch & Risley, 1973).

Hospital wards are being remodeled to make use of light-colored paint, brightly painted doors, attractive and modern furniture, and brightly colored bedspreads. These items seem to increase positive behaviors exhibited by the patient; that is, patients' attitudes become more positive and they socialize more (Holahan & Saegert, 1973; Price & Moos, 1975). Moreover, in hospital settings therapists are learning that seating patterns that place individuals at right angles and closer together increase the interaction among the professional staff and patients and among the patients themselves (Holahan, 1972).

Results of other studies suggest that seating arrangements in waiting rooms and workers' offices either increase or decrease interaction among clients and/or workers. Again, furniture placed so that individuals sat at right angles increased interaction. Likewise, a seating arrangement in a group context either facilitates or deters the interaction among group members with more interaction occurring when individuals are seated in a circle (Dinges & Oetting, 1972; Lauver, Kelley, & Froehle, 1971; Seabury, 1971; Widgery. & Stackpole, 1972). Also, through providing verbal and nonverbal prompts to individuals in a nursing home such as placing materials in their hands and discussing materials with them, McClannahan (1973a,b) and McClannahan and Risley (1975) significantly increased such verbal and nonverbal behaviors as talking to one another, nodding, smiling, or visually attending to one another, eating or drinking together, using recreational equipment such as puzzles and participating together in games.

WELFARE

In a study conducted by Miller and Miller (1973) wherein positive reinforcers were utilized to increase welfare clients' attendance at self-help group meetings it was demonstrated that the following reinforcers are very practical: toys, stoves, refrigerators, furniture, clothing, rugs, kitchen utensils, and information about social services. The authors suggest that these might also be used to increase attendance at adult education programs, in projects that create income for self-help groups, and in neighborhood rehabilitation projects. Briscoe, Hoffman, and Bailey (1975) helped lower income adults learn appropriate behaviors for participation on a policy board of a federally funded rural community project through behavioral modification techniques such as social praise and videotape feedback of behavior acquisition. Behavior analysis helped these individuals acquire the ability to define a problem, define and evaluate solutions according to their merits, formulate action plans, and implement the solutions. Both of these studies were aimed at changing individual welfare clients' behaviors. It would seem that a feasible solution to the welfare problem in various countries might be found in first specifying what types of behavioral changes are desirable in welfare clients such as increased self-sufficiency and decreased dependency and then in structuring the appropriate institutions to implement the contingencies for exhibition of these behaviors. Currently, most welfare systems structure reinforcement contingencies that do not reinforce self-sufficiency (Maclean, 1977; Piven & Cloward, 1971).

WORKER PERFORMANCE

Two problems certain to be encountered by employers are absenteeism and decreased worker productivity. Pedalino and Gamboa (1974) executed an interesting study in which they utilized monetary reinforcement contingencies in order to decrease employee absenteeism at an industrial plant. Likewise, Hermann, de Montes, Dominguez, Montes, and Hopkins (1973) utilized monetary reinforcement contingencies with industrial workers to increase punctuality on the job. Another strategy was employed by Lind (1967) to reduce tardiness in workers. The primary contingency for tardiness was punishment; whenever the employee was late the employer would call him to his office and make him wait 5 to 10 minutes in the waiting room before confronting him about his behavior. Punishment was chosen because other positive reinforcers such as monetary incentives, promotion, and bonuses were out of the question due to administrative constraints.

Evidence from behavioral analysis is beginning to accrue to indicate that monetary reinforcers should be made contingent upon specific job performances. Research indicates that this can improve accurate changemaking in a family style restaurant (Marholin & Gray, 1976), job performance of workers in neighborhood youth corps (Pierce & Risley, 1974), professional and nonprofessional workers' performances in an institution for the mentally retarded (Iwata, Bailey, Brown, Foshee, & Alpern, 1976; Quilitch, 1974; Patterson, Griffin, & Panyan, 1976) and on psychiatric wards (Loeber, 1971; Pomerleau, Bobrove, & Smith, 1973), and teachers' behaviors with students

(Harris, Bushell, Sherman, & Kane, 1975). Moreover, research seems to indicate that incentives are necessary for good therapeutic practice; that is, in order for professionals to change their behaviors feedback must occur and incentives be provided for the changes (Rinn & Vernon, 1975). It has been observed furthermore that workers are more highly productive when they are satisfied with what they are doing, administrators or executives show interest in them and consideration for their concerns, and channels of communication are open, when they have autonomy in accomplishing tasks and are reinforced for good work, when administrators set an example in terms of working productively, and when they have a chance to complete a whole task. Such work environments are characterized as being very reinforcing (Katz & Kahn, 1966; Weick, 1969).

Rinn and Vernon (1975) reported the use of monetary incentives in a community health center to facilitate workers' acquisition of knowledge and treatment skills and their implementation in terms of record keeping competencies, such as specifying a written contract between the worker and client concerning therapy goals, collecting and graphing data, keeping current dictation on behavior to be modified and techniques to be employed, and entering process and termination notes. Worker salary increments were then based on how well they executed these functions. The use of concrete standards reduced subjective biases involved in delivering increments, and worker response to the procedures was very favorable (Bolin & Kivens, 1974).

Lind (1967) applied social behavior theory to factors linked to individuals' malperformance during committee meetings. The following committee behaviors were chosen for modification: interruption rate, inattentiveness, cross talk, and inappropriate comments for the topic under discussion. Reinforcement contingencies were implemented to end cross talking and interruptions, to link hand raising and requests for recognition, and to limit the length of the discussion. The following positive reinforcers (smiles, recognition through note taking, and turning on tape recorders) and negative reinforcers (looking away, turning off the tape recorder, and temporary termination of note taking) were utilized by the change agent to either decrease inappropriate or increase appropriate committee behaviors. Moreover, the change agent raised his hand to obtain recognition to speak and spoke only when called upon thereby modeling the appropriate behaviors and facilitating their acquisition by committee members.

SOCIAL ACTION

An increasing call for social workers to engage in social action with their clients has been noted in recent years. However, the technology for social action has not been available. Behavior analysis now presents us with a beginning methodology for social action. We can ask and determine what reinforcers social workers and their clients possess that can be utilized to manipulate other individuals who distribute such reinforcers as housing, jobs, medical care, and other social services. Our collective reinforcers such as knowledge, money, and so forth, and our ability to effectively organize could be used to exert considerable force on politicians. Once organized, for example, our social action strategies should begin by asking an official to secure more adequate social conditions for certain disadvantaged groups in return for our political support. If this strategy did not work, a subsequent strategy might be to utilize a punishing contingency such as a demonstration in front of the politician's office or indications to the general public that he does not care about people through such various media as newspapers, radio, and T.V. Finally, the ultimate strategy would be some type of economic boycott in order to secure necessary items.

Caution should be used while applying such change strategies since empirical guidelines are yet to be developed that will indicate appropriate choices. The approach is applicable to the extent that targets of social action consist of recurrent and habituating behaviors on the part of accessible agency officials. However, some of the most intolerable situations involve relatively inaccessible decision makers engaging in ad hoc behaviors. How to influence such targets needs additional theoretical and empirical development.

CRIME

Society has always tried to control behaviors that we have variously labeled as criminal. However, attempts to control these behaviors have met with little success. New research from behavior analysis proposes that at least three avenues are open to control criminal behavior: eliminate those stimuli that cue criminal behavior, i.e., do not provide the conditions for it to occur; make the consequences for criminal behavior severe; and/or provide everybody with the opportunity to enjoy positive reinforcers through the provision of adequate employment thus making it unnecessary to engage in criminal behaviors to secure positive reinforcements. The last item is based on the recent applications of the conceptual formulation of the tenets of economic theory to the causation of criminal behaviors. These data are preliminary and indicate that certain crimes clearly do have an economic base, as demonstrated by fluctuation in their rates with changes in economic conditions of the society; that is, there is a direct relationship between unemployment rates and certain criminal behaviors (Hann, 1972; Rottenberg, 1973; Sullivan, 1973).

The highjacking of airplanes has been handled through a behavioral approach involving developing devices to detect weapons and firm consequences for the behavior (Boltwood, Cooper, Fein, & Washburn, 1972). The behavioral approach was used also by Azrin and Wesolowski (1974) who did an interesting experiment that may be very applicable to controlling stealing behavior. They found that requiring children who stole items from each other in one experimental condition to return them did not reduce the rate of stealing behavior. It was only when they implemented a procedure they titled "over correction" that stealing behaviors were reduced drastically. In this procedure not only did the individual have to return the item that was stolen, but he had to add an item of comparable value. Such preliminary research is an example of what is needed to place the control of criminal behavior on an empirical basis.

SOCIAL INTEGRATION

Societies have always struggled with how to implement procedures to help people interact positively with one another. Historically, people of different faiths, races, and nationalities have not been able to live harmoniously. Behavior analysis offers a way of structuring reinforcement contingencies to facilitate social integration among individuals. A recent study in which children were reinforced with tokens and social praise to choose interracial teams indicates that liking for other races increased (Hauserman, Walen, & Behling, 1973). Likewise, research suggests that structuring classroom situations where reinforcement of a group of individuals is dependent upon the whole group's performance increases liking for all of the group members. Thus, one strategy for increasing the liking among individuals is to place them in contexts where the reinforcers each individual secures is dependent on other group members' performances (Aronson, Blaney, Sikes, Stephan, & Snapp, 1975; Harris, 1975; Lucker, Rosenfield, Sikes, & Aronson, 1976). These procedures increase the attractiveness each group member has for others since each member's rewards are dependent on other individuals' performances. Likewise, sharing and enjoying positive reinforcers increase the frequency of positive behavior exchanges among individuals (Berscheid & Walster, 1969; DeVries & Slavin, 1975; Feldman & Wodarski, 1975).

Summary

Historically, most attempts at intervention in social work practice have focused on the individual. Analogously, as behavior modification technology developed, it also focused on modifying the individual's behaviors to fit the environment. We have now seen evidence to support the application of behavioral analysis to the solution of selected social problems (Tuso & Geller, 1976). Even though this is, at this point, a very futuristic approach, it is believed that in the coming years we will witness more developments in the area in terms of theory development to isolate how macrolevel variables affect behavior and interact with microlevel variables to produce, maintain, and alter behavior. Moreover, behavior analysis will be applied increasingly to the solution of many other social problems such as increasing participation of low-income children in dental care programs (Reiss, Piotrowski, & Bailey, 1976), decreasing shoplifting (McNees, Egli, Marshall, Schnelle, & Risley, 1976), improving job finding performance (Jones & Azrin, 1973), population control (Zifferblatt & Hendricks, 1974), and food consumption (Madsen, Madsen, & Thompson, 1974); to the study of politician's behaviors (Weisberg & Waldrop, 1972); to the study of different police patrolling strategies and their effects on crime rates (Schnelle, Kirchner, McNees, & Lawler, 1975); to the study of the effects of various changes in institutional policy on clients (Schnelle & Lee, 1974); and to train people to be their own therapists (Mahoney, 1977; Thoreson & Mahoney, 1974; Watson & Tharp, 1972; Wodarski, 1975).

Perhaps the greatest issue for behavior modification in the next decade will be the structuring of an individual's environment to ensure the maintenance and generalization of behavior change. The process of generalization and maintenance has been greatly neglected, or left up to chance. More structure hopefully will characterize future sophisticated behavior modification systems that will include the alteration of reinforcement patterns of significant social entities that affect the client's behavior.

It has been emphasized that behavior can be controlled through intervention at the various levels: individual, group, organizational, institutional, and societal. However, adequate control will be achieved only through coordination of these components and the social work professional should become equipped to provide such coordination.

Implementation of behavior modification interventions through large social systems poses the same ethical and political dilemmas that implementation on the individual level does. However, the inclusion of this level of intervention will increase the probability that the behavior will be modified and maintained. If one can entertain the notion that we already have a social system that modifies and controls our behavior, the question is should we ourselves make the system as humane as possible through our control or permit it to act on us in a laissez-faire manner?

REFERENCES

Arkava, M. L. *Behavior modification: a procedural guide for social workers.* Missoula, Montana: Department of Social Work, University of Montana, 1974.

Aronson, E., Blaney, N., Sikes, J., Stephan, C., & Snapp, M. Bussing and racial tension: the jigsaw route to learning and liking. *Psychology Today,* 1975, *8,* 43–44, 47–50.

Azrin, N. H., & Wesolowski, M. D. Theft reversal: an overcorrection procedure for eliminating stealing by retarded persons. *Journal of Applied Behavior Analysis,* 1974, *7*(4), 577–581.

Ayllon, T., & Azrin, N. *The token economy: a motivational system for therapy and rehabilitation.* New York: Appleton-Century-Crofts, 1968.

Baltes, M. M., & Hayward, S. C. Application and evaluation of strategies to reduce pollution: behavioral control of littering in a football stadium. *Journal of Applied Psychology,* 1976, *61*(4), 501–506.

Bergin, A. E., & Suinn, R. M. Individual psychotherapy and behavior therapy. In M. R. Rosenzweig, & L. W. Porter (Eds.), *Annual review of psychology.* Palo Alto, Ca.: Annual Reviews, 1975.

Berscheid, A., & Walster, E. H. *Interpersonal attraction.* Reading, Ma.: Addison-Wesley, 1969.

Boltwood, C. E., Cooper, M. R., Fein, V. E., & Washburn, P. V. Skyjacking, airline security, and passenger reactions: toward a complex model for prediction. *American Psychologist,* 1972, *27*(6), 539–545.

Bolin, D. C., & Kivens, L. Evaluation in a community mental health center: Huntsville, Alabama. *Evaluation,* 1974, *2*(1), 26–35.

Briscoe, R. V., Hoffman, D. B., & Bailey, J. S. Behavior community psychology: training a community board to problem solve. *Journal of Applied Behavior Analysis,* 1975, *8*(2), 157–168.

Burgess, R. L., Clark, R. N. & Hendee, J. C. An experimental analysis of anti-litter procedures. *Journal of Applied Behavior Analysis,* 1971, *4*(2), 71–75.

Chapman, C., & Risley, T. R. Anti-litter procedures in an urban high-density area. *Journal of Applied Behavior Analysis,* 1974, *7*(3), 377–383.

Christophersen, E. R., Doke, L. A., Messmer, D. O., & Risley, T. B. Measuring urban problems: a brief report on rating grass coverage. *Journal of Applied Behavior Analysis,* 1975, *8*(2), 230.

Clark, R. N., Burgess, R. L., & Hendee, J. C. The development of anti-litter behavior in a forest campground. *Journal of Applied Behavior Analysis,* 1972, *5*(1), 1–5.

DeVries, D. L., & Slavin, R. E. Effect of team competition on race relations in the classroom: further supportive evidence. Paper presented at the American Psychological Association's 83rd Annual Convention. Chicago, September, 1975.

Dinges, N. G., & Oetting, E. R. Interaction distance anxiety in the counseling dyad. *Journal of Counseling Psychology,* 1972, *19*, 146–149.

Doke, L. A., & Risley, T. R. The organization of day-care environments: required versus optional activities. *Journal of Applied Behavior Analysis,* 1972, *5*(1), 405–420.

Ehrlich, P. R., & Ehrlich, A. H. *The end of affluence.* New York: Ballantine Books, 1974.

Everett, P. B., Hayward, C., & Meyers, A. W. The effects of a token reinforcement procedure on busridership. *Journal of Applied Behavior Analysis,* 1974, *7*(1), 1–9.

Feldman, R. A., & Wodarski, J. S. *Contemporary approaches to group treatment.* San Francisco: Jossey-Bass, 1975.

Fellin, P., Rothman, J., & Meyer, H. J. Implications of the social-behavioral approach for community organization practice. In E. J. Thomas (Ed.), *The socio-behavioral approach and application to social work.* New York: Council on Social Work Education, 1967.

Fethke, G. C. The relevance of economic theory and technology to token reinforcement systems: a comment. *Behavior Research and Therapy,* 1972, *10*(2), 191–192.

———— Token economies: a further comment. *Behavior Research and Therapy,* 1973, *11*(2), 225–226.

Foxx, R. M., & Hake, D. F. Gasoline conservation: a procedure for measuring and reducing the driving of college students. *Journal of Applied Behavior Analysis,* 1977, *10*(1), 61–74.

Geller, E. S., Farris, J. C., & Post, D. S. Prompting a consumer behavior for pollution control. *Journal of Applied Behavior Analysis,* 1973, *6*(3), 367–376.

————, Witmer, J. F., & Orebaugh, A. L. Instructions as a determinant of paper disposal behaviors. *Environment and Behavior,* 1976, *8*(3), 417–439.

Hann, R. G. Crime and the cost of crime: an economic approach. *Journal of Research in Crime and Delinquency,* 1972, *9*(1), 12–30.

Harris, G. T. Jigsaw teaching: out of racial strife, a better way to learn. *Psychology Today,* February 1975, 44.

Harris, V. W., Bushell, O., Jr., Sherman, J. A., & Kane, J. F. Instructions, feedback, praise, bonus payments, and teachers' behavior. *Journal of Applied Behavior Analysis,* 1975, *8,* 462.

Hauserman, N., Walen, S. R. & Behling, M. Reinforced racial integration in the first grade: a study in generalization. *Journal of Applied Behavior Analysis,* 1973, *6*(2), 193–200.

Hayes, S. C., & Cone, J. D. Reducing residential electrical energy use: payment, information and feedback. Unpublished manuscript, West Virginia University, 1975.

Hermann, J. A., de Montes, A. I., Dominguez, B., Montes, F., & Hopkins, B. L. Effects of bonuses for punctuality on the tardiness of industrial workers. *Journal of Applied Behavior Analysis,* 1973, *6*(4), 563–567.

Holahan, C. Seating patterns and patient behavior in an experimental day room. *Journal of Abnormal Psychology,* 1972, *80,* 115–124.

————, & Saegert, S. Behavioral and attitudinal effects of large-scale variation in the physical environment of psychiatric wards. *Journal of Abnormal Psychology,* 1973, *82*(3), 454–462.

Iwata, B. A., Bailey, J. S., Brown, K. M., Foshee, T. J., & Alpern, M. A performance-based lottery to improve residential care and training by institutional staff. *Journal of Applied Behavior Analysis,* 1976, *9,* 417–431.

Jeffery, C. R. *Crime prevention through environment design.* Beverly Hills: Sage, 1971.

———— Criminal behavior and the physical environment. *American Behavioral Scientist,* 1976, *20*(2), 149–174.

Jones, R. J., & Azrin, N. H. An experimental application of a social reinforcement approach to the problem of job-finding. *Journal of Applied Behavior Analysis,* 1973, *6*(3), 345–353.

Kagel, J. H., Battalio, R., Winkler, R. C., & Winett, R. A. Energy conservation strategies: an evaluation of the effectiveness of price changes and information on household demand for electricity. Manuscript in preparation, Texas A. & M. University, 1975.

———, & Winkler, R. C. Behavioral economics: areas of cooperative research between economics and applied behavioral analysis. *Journal of Applied Behavior Analysis,* 1972, *5*(3), 335–342.

Katz, D., & Kahn, R. L. *The social psychology of organizations.* New York: John Wiley, 1966.

Kazdin, A. E. *Behavior modification in applied settings.* Homewood, Ill.: Dorsey, 1975.

——— *The token economy.* New York: Plenum Press, 1977.

Kohlenberg, R., & Phillips, T. Reinforcement and rate of litter depositing. *Journal of Applied Behavior Analysis,* 1973, *6*(3), 391–396.

———, Phillips, T., & Proctor, W. A behavioral analysis of peaking in residential electrical-energy consumers. *Journal of Applied Behavior Analysis,* 1976, *9,* 13–18.

Lauver, P. J., Kelley, S. P., & Froehle, T. C. Client reaction time and counselor verbal behavior in an interview setting. *Journal of Counseling Psychology,* 1971, *18,* 26–30.

LeLaurin, K., & Risley, T. R. The organization of day-care environments; "zone" versus "man-to-man" staff assignments. *Journal of Applied Behavior Analysis,* 1972, *5*(3), 225–232.

Lind, R. M. Applications of socio-behavioral therapy to administrative practice. In E. J. Thomas (Ed.), *The socio-behavioral approach and application to social work.* New York: Council on Social Work Education, 1967.

Loeber, R. Engineering the behavioral engineer. *Journal of Applied Behavior Analysis,* 1971, *4*(4), 321–326.

Lucker, G. W., Rosenfield, D., Sikes, J., & Aronson, E. Performance in the interdependent classroom: a field study. *American Educational Research Journal,* 1976, *13*(2), 115–123.

Luthans, F., & Kreitner, R. *Organizational behavior modification.* Glenview, Ill.: Scott Foresman and Company, 1975.

Maclean, M. E. Learning theory and chronic welfare dependency: a hypothesis of etiological and contingency relationships. *Journal of Behavior Therapy and Experimental Psychiatry,* 1977, *8*(3), 255–259.

Madsen, C. H., Madsen, C. K., & Thompson, F. Increasing rural head start children's consumption of middle-class meals. *Journal of Applied Behavior Analysis,* 1974, *7*(2), 251–262.

Mahoney, M. J. Reflections on the cognitive-learning trend in psychotherapy. *American Psychologist,* 1977, *32*(1), 5–13.

Marholin, D., & Gray, D. Effects of group response-cost procedures on cash shortages in a small business. *Journal of Applied Behavior Analysis,* 1976, *9,* 25–30.

McClannahan, L. E. Therapeutic and prosthetic living environments for nursing home residents. *The Gerontologist,* 1973, *13,* 424–429.(a)

———— Recreation programs for nursing home residents: the importance of patient characteristics and environmental arrangements. *Therapeutic Recreation Journal,* 1973, *7,* 26–31.(b)

————, & Risley, T. R. Design of living environments for nursing home residents: increasing participation in recreation activities. *Journal of Applied Behavior Analysis,* 1975, *8,* 261–268.

McNees, M. P., Egli, D. S., Marshall, R. S., Schnelle, J. F., & Risley, T. R. Shoplifting prevention: providing information through signs. *Journal of Applied Behavior Analysis,* 1976, *9,* 399–405.

Miller, L. K., & Miller, O. L. Reinforcing self-help group activities of welfare recipients. *Journal of Applied Behavior Analysis,* 1973, *3*(1), 57–64.

Patterson, E. T., Griffin, J. C., & Panyan, M. C. Incentive maintenance of self-help skill training programs for non-professional personnel. *Journal of Behavior Therapy and Experimental Psychiatry,* 1976, *7*(3), 249–253.

Pedalino, E., & Gamboa, V. N. Bahavior modification and absenteeism: intervention in one industrial setting. *Journal of Applied Psychology,* 1974, *59*(6), 694–698.

Pierce, C. H., & Risley, T. R. Improving job performance of neighborhood youth corps aides in an urban recreation program. *Journal of Applied Behavior Analysis,* 1974, *7*(2), 207–215.

Piven, F. F., & Cloward, R. A. *Regulating the poor.* New York: Pantheon, 1971.

Pomerleau, O. F., Bobrove, P. H., & Smith, R. H. Rewarding psychiatric aides for the behavioral improvement of assigned patients. *Journal of Applied Behavior Analysis,* 1973, *6*(3), 383–390.

Powers, R. B., Osborne, J. G., & Anderson, D. G. Positive reinforcement of litter removal in the natural environment. *Journal of Applied Behavior Analysis,* 1973, *6*(4), 579–586.

Price, R., & Moos, R. H. Toward a taxonomy of inpatient treatment environments. *Journal of Abnormal Psychology,* 1975, *84*(3), 181–188.

Quilitch, R. H. A comparison of three staff-management procedures. *Journal of Applied Behavior Analysis,* 1974, *8*(1), 59–66.

————, & Risley, T. R. The effects of play materials on social play. *Journal of Applied Behavior Analysis,* 1973, *6*(4), 573–578.

Reid, D. H., Luyben, P. D., Rawers, R. J., & Bailey, J. S. Newspaper recycling behavior: the effects of prompting and proximity of containers. *Environment and Behavior,* 1976, *5*(3), 471–482.

Reiss, M. L., Piotrowski, W. D., & Bailey, J. S. Behavioral community psychology: encouraging low-income parents to seek dental care for their children. *Journal of Applied Behavior Analysis,* 1976, *9*(4), 387–397.

Reppetto, T. A. Crime prevention through environmental policy. *American Behavioral Scientist,* 1976, *20*(2), 275–288.

Rinn, R. C., & Vernon, J. C. Process evaluation of out-patient treatment in a community mental health center. *Journal of Behavior Therapy and Experimental Psychiatry,* 1975, *6*(1), 5–11.

Robinson, S. N. Littering behavior in public places. *Environment and Behavior,* 1976, *8*(3), 363–384.

Rottenberg, S. (Ed.) The economics of crime and punishment. Washington, D.C.: American Enterprise Institute for Public Policy Research, 1973.

Schnelle, J. F., & Lee, J. F. A quasi-experimental retrospective evaluation of a prison policy change. *Journal of Applied Behavior Analysis,* 1974, *7*(3), 483–494.

———, Kirchner, R. E., McNees, M. P., & Lawler, J. M. Social evaluation research: the evaluation of two police patrolling strategies. *Journal of Applied Behavior Analysis,* 1975, *8*(4), 353–365.

Seabury, B. A. Arrangement of physical space in social work settings. *Social Work,* 1971, *16*(3), 43–49.

Seaver, B. W., & Patterson, A. N. Decreasing fuel-oil consumption through feedback and social commendation. *Journal of Applied Behavior Analysis,* 1976, *9,* 147–152.

Slavin, R. E., & Wodarski, J. S. Using group contingencies to reduce natural gas consumption in master-metered apartments. Center for Social Organization of Schools, Johns Hopkins University, 1977, Report No. 232.

———, Wodarski, J. S., & Blackburn, B. L. A group contingency for electricity conservation in master-metered apartments. Center for Social Organization of Schools, Johns Hopkins University, 1978, Report No. 242.

Sullivan, R. F. The economics of crime: an introduction to the literature. *Crime and Delinquency,* 1973, *19*(2), 138–149.

Thomas, E. J. (Ed.) *Behavior modification procedure.* Chicago: Aldine, 1974.

Thoresen, C. E., & Mahoney, M. J. *Behavioral self-control.* New York: Holt, Rinehart and Winston, 1974.

Tuso, M. A., & Geller, E. S. Behavior analysis applied to environmental/ecological problems: a review. *Journal of Applied Behavior Analysis,* 1976, *9*(4), 526.

Twardosz, S., Cataldo, M. F., & Risley, T. R. An open environment design for infant and toddler day care. *Journal of Applied Behavior Analysis,* 1974, *7*(4), 529–546.

Watson, D. L., & Tharp, R. G. *Self-directed behavior: self-modification for personal adjustment.* Belmont, Ca.: Brooks/Cole, 1972.

Weick, K. E. *The social psychology of organizing.* Reading, Ma.: Addison-Wesley, 1969.

Weisberg, P., & Waldrop, P. B. Fixed-interval work habits of Congress. *Journal of Applied Behavior Analysis,* 1972, *5*(1), 93–97.

Widgery, R., & Stackpole, G. Desk position, interviewee anxiety and interviewer credibility: an example of cognitive balance in a dyad. *Journal of Counseling Psychology,* 1972, *19,* 173–177.

Willens, E. P. Behavioral technology and behavioral ecology. *Journal of Applied Behavior Analysis,* 1974, *7*(1), 151–165.

Winett, R. A. Disseminating a behavioral approach to energy conservation. *Professional Psychology,* 1976, *7*(2), 222–228.

———, & Nietzel, M. T. Behavioral ecology: contingency management of residential energy use. *American Journal of Community Psychology,* 1975, *3,* 123–133.

Winkler, R. C. Reinforcement schedules for individual patients in a token economy. *Behavior Therapy,* 1971, *2*(4), 534–537.(a)

——— The relevance of economic theory and technology to token reinforcement systems. *Behavior Research and Therapy,* 1971, *9*(2), 81–88.(b)

——— A theory of equilibrium in token economies. *Journal of Abnormal Psychology,* 1972, *79*(2), 169–173.

——— An experimental analysis of economic balance savings and wages in a token economy. *Behavior Therapy,* 1973, *4*(1), 32–40.(a)

——— A reply to Fethke's comment on "The relevance of economic theory and technology to token reinforcement systems." *Behavior Research and Therapy,* 1973, *11*(2), 223–224.(b)

Witmer, J. F., & Geller, S. E. Facilitating paper recycling: effects of prompts, raffles, contests. *Journal of Applied Behavior Analysis,* 1976, *9,* 315–322.

Wodarski, J. S. The application of cognitive behavior modification techniques to social work practice. *International Social Work,* 1975, *18*(3), 50–57.

——— The modification of electrical energy consumption. *The Behavior Therapist,* 1978, *1*(4), 21–22.

Zifferblatt, S. M., & Hendricks, C. G. Applied behavioral analysis of societal problems: population change, a case in point. *American Psychologist,* 1974, *29*(10), 750–761.

A CURRICULUM TO TRAIN
BEHAVIORAL SOCIAL WORKERS

Within the last five years there has been significant incorporation of social behavioral theory into the social work school
curriculum. However, most of the curricula offer, at best, only
an introductory course in behavior modification which is most
unfortunate if the desire is to train social workers capable of
implementing behavioral techniques reviewed thus far in the
text. Obviously, offering one or even two courses pertaining to
the application of behavioral techniques to human difficulties is
insufficient for preparing a clinician for effective practice. At
this point it should be apparent to the reader that behavioral
social work is indeed complex. This complexity necessitates
intensive study, practical application, and structured sequential
learning experiences. Before social behavioral theory may be
properly implemented, certain tasks must be mastered in succession whether the interventions are on an individual, group,
organizational, institutional, or a societal level (Green & Morrow, 1972; Howe, 1974; Shorkey, 1973; Wodarski, 1974). Likewise, behavior modification is an applied science, definitely a

practice experience, wherein the opportunity for students to try out the techniques discussed in the classroom and to gain appropriate feedback to sharpen their practice skills before engaging in actual clinical practice is imperative.

This chapter outlines a specific training program for the preparation of students for social behavioral practice. Although the chapter focuses on training students, the procedures set forth can be easily modified to train practitioners in agencies. Initially the number and the nature of courses that should be allotted in the social work curriculum are discussed. Course training should center primarily around five areas. Courses entitled "The Empirical and Theoretical Foundations of Behavior Modification" and "Empirical Foundations of Effective Interviewing and Relationship Formation" are considered prerequisites for the following seminars: "Behavior Therapy with Children," "Behavior Therapy with Adults," and "Seminars in Critical Issues in Behavior Therapy." Objectives for each course are outlined. Tasks such as making diagnoses from videotapes and choosing appropriate change techniques and experimental designs to evaluate clinical interventions, which students must master in each course, are reviewed along with performance criteria for each task.

Specific educational goals for the practicum experience are delineated, such as viewing a variety of client behaviors which have been defined as problematic either by clients themselves and/or significant others; applying a variety of techniques after behavioral diagnoses are made; having the opportunity for feedback on implementation of techniques through videotapes, empirical observational data provided by trained behavioral observers, or data derived from other inventories measuring worker behaviors; witnessing actual demonstrations of techniques among students and practice instructors; watching seasoned practitioners implement techniques; and devising programs to ensure the transfer and maintenance of behavior.

Next, the use of videotapes to demonstrate the various techniques and to increase the precision with which the techniques are applied is discussed. The chapter concludes with a discussion pertaining to decisions regarding admissions to training programs in behavior modification. Specifically, what characteristics should admitted individuals possess, such as empathy, unconditional positive regard, verbal congruence, self-adjustment, and verbal ability? How may these skills be enhanced? What organizational requisites are pertinent to continued professional development of those trained in social behavioral theory? When is a worker prepared to practice?

ORGANIZATIONAL ASPECTS OF THE CURRICULUM

The number of courses to be devoted to training is the first consideration in designing a behavior modification specialization for schools of social work. Usually, two foundations courses are required. The first centers on learning theory, especially as it relates to human learning and social conceptualizations of personality formation, and how the various learning theories form the foundation blocks of behavior modification practice. The second concentrates on effective interviewing and training in the essentials of relationship formation. Three seminar courses generally are allocated in addition to a practicum experience involving behavior modification. Obviously, however, the number of courses necessary to adequately prepare students for behavior modification practice depends ultimately on the background of students.

The educational prerequisites for the second foundations course and seminar courses should focus on two areas: background in the theoretical foundations of the various learning theories that provide the empirical bases for social-behavioral practice and actual application of learned theoretical constructs through simulation exercises such as watching videotapes, observing and recording behavior, executing $N=1$ designs, keeping a diary on their own behaviors, and recording antecedents and consequences. Through these exercises students are trained to identify those antecedent conditions and consequences that have produced the target behaviors and to assess those environmental conditions that support, reinforce, and maintain them and that can lead to alteration of behavior. The carrying out of simulation exercises prior to clinical practice enables the student to experience the various properties of the constructs and to observe how they relate to behavior change, thereby facilitating the application of the various concepts to practice with clients.

Students having adequate backgrounds can go directly into the second foundations course and then proceed to the seminar courses. A review of the students' backgrounds will be necessary to determine whether or not they are adequately prepared. If they are not, the decision must be made as to whether the school will provide the prerequisites to inadequately prepared students or whether they should direct them to departments of psychology prior to admission to the specialization.

COURSES

The Empirical and Theoretical Foundations of Behavior Modification

This course deals with learning theories and their application to human development, personality formation, and individual functioning. A solid theoretical background in learning theories, especially social learning theories, is presented to students. The material presented is based on the empirical findings regarding the nature of human behavior and behavior change. The opportunity for operationalization and application of these principles is offered to students through supervised experimentation which employs simulation exercises. This offers not only the opportunity for applying the theoretical concepts the student has learned but also helps ensure that he has adequately mastered the application of these principles prior to clinical practice with human clients. In addition, students are required to learn how to objectively evaluate their own intervention practices and how to use corrective feedback in designing effective treatment strategies and programs.

Since this course emphasizes the social learning approach to human behavior, it focuses on behavioral assessments and thereby eliminates the practice of psychiatric diagnosis and stigmatization. Students are trained to identify those antecedent conditions and consequences that have produced the undesirable target behaviors and to assess those environmental conditions which support, reinforce, and maintain them.

A major goal is to help students see the interrelationship of social learning theory and the basic principles of learning upon which behavior modification techniques rest. Moreover, they see how the theoretical orientation not only provides a paradigm for the description and explanation of behavior but also for the accurate prediction and successful modification of undesirable responses in clients.

OBJECTIVES OF THE COURSE.

1.   To explore the historical development and theoretical basis of modern learning theory and to introduce the students to the empirical foundations of learning theory and its application. To elucidate the various types of learning paradigms, for example, the classical, the operant, and the observational paradigms of learning.

2.   To demonstrate how these theoretical principles have been used to explain normal and deviant human behavior, personality formation, individual differences, and intraindividual consistencies. To develop an understanding of how the various principles of learning can be used to predict and modify human behavior.

3.   To develop an understanding of the various treatment approaches used in behavior modification and the theoretical principles upon which they rest.

4.   To elucidate how these various paradigms provide a rationale for the treatment of a variety of clinical problems.

5.   To show how scientific investigation, theoretical development and testing lead to the advancement of effective clinical practice.

OUTLINE OF TOPICS COVERED.

1.   Introduction to learning theory

2.   The scientific method and how it relates to learning theory

3.   Respondent model

4.   Operant model

5.   Observational model

6.   Exchange theory: A holistic conceptualization of the social learning process

7.   Concepts in mathematical and cognitive processing theory

8.   Application of these models to human development, personality formation, and behavior

9.   The social learning paradigm of human behavior.

10.   Human interaction as a system of contingencies, reinforcements, discriminative stimuli, and punishments, and as a reciprocal bargaining process

11.   Human interaction as a sharing process composed of approach and avoidance learning

12.   The relationship between learning theory and the acquisition of socially desirable and undesirable behaviors

13.   The relationship between learning theory and behavior modification practice

14.   Learning theory, the development of clinical practice and evaluation: A unitary corrective-feedback process

15.   Summary: Emerging issues in modern learning theories

PERFORMANCE CRITERIA.   Students are required to demonstrate their understanding of the various learning models presented to them in this course by their performance in the supervised laboratory practicum. For example, a student wishing to demonstrate his or her knowledge of operant conditioning might design a project which depicts the relationship between various schedules of reinforcement and response acquisition and resistance to extinction. Similar projects are required for evaluating students' learning of both the classical and observational models.

TEXTS.

1.   Albert Bandura. *Principles of behavior modification.* New York: Holt, Rinehart and Winston, 1969.

2.   Albert Bandura. *A social learning theory.* Englewood Cliffs, New Jersey: Prentice-Hall, 1977.

3.   Albert Bandura & R. M. Walters. *Social learning and personality development.* New York: Holt, Rinehart and Winston, 1963.

4.   Walter Mischel. *Personality and assessment.* New York: John Wiley, 1968.

5.   Robert L. Karen. *An introduction to behavior theory and its application.* New York: Harper and Row, 1974.

6.   John Gottman & Sandra Lieblum. *How to do psychotherapy and how to evaluate it: A manual for beginners.* New York: Holt, Rinehart and Winston, 1967.

7.   John W. Thibaut & Harold H. Kelley. *The social psychology of groups.* New York: John Wiley, 1959.

8.   Peter E. Nathan & Sandra L. Harris. *Psychopathology and society.* New York: McGraw-Hill, 1975.

9.   K. J. Gergin. *The psychology of behavior exchange.* Reading, Ma.: Addison-Wesley, 1969.

Empirical Foundations of Effective Interviewing and Relationship Formation

This course is practical and didactic in nature and as such it offers the student both a knowledge base as well as a practice experience. The knowledge bases are:

1.   The historical conceptualizations of the nature of behavior change and its relationship to clinical intervention
2.   The empirical literature available on interviewing behavior and its application to verbal conditioning
3.   The effectiveness of traditional forms of clinical intervention
4.   The relationship between certain client variables and therapeutic outcomes
5.   The relationship between certain therapist characteristics and therapeutic outcomes.

The practical component of this course will focus upon the training of students in the development and utilization of those necessary characteristics of genuineness, nonpossessive warmth, congruence, accurate empathic understanding, and so forth that were identified in Chapter 2 as being necessary conditions for behavioral change. The educational techniques employed to reach this end will include the use of models, positive corrective feedback, peer supervision and feedback, coaching by the instructor and other students, successive approximations, shaping of desired responses through the use of feedback, in-class practice, out-of-class practice to ensure transfer and generalization of the required behavioral responses, behavioral ratings by trained behavioral observers, self-observation through the use of videotapes and films, and the development of self-monitoring devices to maintain critical therapeutic skills and to ensure their continuance and generalization to practice contexts following completion of the course.

OBJECTIVES OF THE COURSE.

1.   To understand the relationship between the various theories of intervention and their underlying assumptions concerning the nature of the person, the process of development, and behavior change, and how this influences the formation of the therapeutic relationship.

2.   To become acquainted with and proficient in the available techniques in the area of clinical intervention which are based on empirical data.

3.   To become versed in the existing body of empirical research that evaluates the effectiveness of traditional forms of verbal psychotherapy, clinical social work, and behavior therapy.

4.   To become proficient in those skills necessary to bring about and maintain a helping relationship between the social worker and the client.

5.   To understand the relationship between specific factors, such as client variables and therapist characteristics, and positive therapeutic outcomes.

6.   To become proficient in the use of those empirically validated interviewing practices and techniques that are known to produce positive changes in clients and which facilitate relationship development, e.g., genuineness, nonpossessive warmth, accurate empathic understanding, immediacy, concreteness, and respect.

7.   To review the literature on interpersonal attraction and demonstrate how the procedures can be incorporated into effective behavior change principles.

8.   To develop such behaviors as eye contact, body position, and verbal congruence which all increase the attractiveness of a change agent.

9.   To develop programs for the use of the aforementioned skills in various settings and to ensure their continued practice upon completion of formal training.

10. To devise a variety of projects to facilitate the generalization and transfer of these skills from the classroom to clinical settings.

OUTLINE OF TOPICS COVERED.

1. Overview of the field of clinical social work, psychotherapy, and behavior therapy

2. Effectiveness of the various forms of traditional verbal therapy and clinical casework intervention

3. The effectiveness of the various forms of behavior therapy

4. Theoretical conceptualizations and philosophical assumptions concerning the nature of people and the nature of induced behavior change

5. A review of the literature on verbal conditioning and other variables that affect verbal behavior

6. Review of the various programs and theoretical conceptualizations of relationship training

7. Research evaluation of therapist effectiveness: therapist characteristics, interpersonal skills, and interpersonal attraction

8. Review of research on client characteristic variables associated with behavioral change

9. The future of clinical intervention in terms of different models of delivery of services

PRACTICAL EXPERIENCES.

1. Demonstration of skills to be learned through the use of films and live and videotaped models

2. In-class practice of such various skills as empathy, congruence, and acceptance under the observation of the instructors and peers

3. Use of peer and instructor feedback for corrective purposes

4.   Homework assignments wherein behavioral skills are practiced and evaluated by peers and by the student himself

PERFORMANCE CRITERIA.

1.   Upon completion of this course the student is expected to present a detailed program devised to ensure the transfer and maintenance of skills learned in the course to settings outside the classroom, such as the agency in which he has been placed for his field practicum.

2.   Upon completion of the course the student is required to conduct an initial interview with another student. The degree to which the student has mastered those behavioral skills taught in the course, as well as the degree to which he appropriately applies those skills are assessed by a panel of trained behavioral raters.

TEXTS.

1.   Alan E. Bergin & Sol L. Garfield. *Handbook of psychotherapy and behavior change.* New York: Wiley, 1971.

2.   Robert R. Carkhuff. *Helping and human relations* (Vols. I and II.) New York: Holt, Rinehart and Winston, 1969.

3.   Stephen J. Danish & Alan L. Hauer. *Helping skills: A basic training program.* New York: Behavioral Publications, 1973.

4.   Mark Knapp. *Non-verbal communication in human interaction.* New York: Holt, Rinehart and Winston, 1972.

5.   Charles B. Truax & Robert R. Carkhuff. *Toward effective counseling and psychotherapy.* Chicago: Aldine, 1967.

6.   A. S. Gurman & A. M. Razin. *Effective psychotherapy.* New York: Pergamon, 1977.

7.   A. E. Ivey. *Micro counseling: Innovations in interviewing training.* Springfield, Ill.: Charles C Thomas, 1971.

8.   M. M. Berger. *Videotape techniques in psychiatric training and treatment.* New York: Brunner/Mazel, 1970.

9.   A. Kadushin. *The social interview.* New York: Columbia Press, 1972.

Behavioral Approaches to the Treatment of Children and Adults

These have been conceptualized as two separate courses focusing on the modification of undesirable behaviors of children and of adults in a variety of contexts. The modification of troublesome behaviors in the natural environment as well as in clinics, agencies, and institutional settings is stressed. The use of behavioral techniques with individuals, with groups and with families is a major focus.

The primary emphasis of these courses is the understanding of human behavior in the context of the social environment. The student develops an understanding of how social reinforcers are used to develop, shape, maintain, and to modify human behavior. The development of complex behaviors such as thinking and concept formation are presented. The use of reinforcements, models, and contingency contracts between individuals, families, and groups is dealt with extensively.

SEMINAR ON BEHAVIOR THERAPY WITH CHILDREN. COURSE OBJECTIVES.

1.   To become acquainted with and proficient in the available knowledge derived from the operant, respondent, and modeling paradigms for intervention with children classified as autistic, hyperactive, delinquent, retarded, antisocial, and so forth.

2.   To become proficient in behavior modification methodology as applied to clinical assessment. This includes knowledge of how to operationalize the target behaviors to be changed, treatment interventions, choice of appropriate treatment, and choice of adequate designs to assess whether treatment interventions were effective.

3.   To apply knowledge learned in class to one case in the practicum experience.

OUTLINE OF THE TOPICS COVERED

1. Experimentally based clinical methods
2. Behavioral assessment
3. Techniques for behavioral intervention
4. Evaluation of interventive attempts
5. Focus of interventional level: individual, group, societal, organizational, and/or institutional
6. Understanding complex behavior through shaping, chaining of responses, higher order conditioning process, and complex schedules of reinforcement
7. Application of behavior therapy to antisocial children
8. Application of behavior therapy to hyperactive children
9. Application of behavior therapy to autistic children
10. Application of behavior therapy to retarded children
11. Application of behavior therapy to inner-city children
12. Application of behavior therapy to normal children
13. Application of behavioral principles with children in group contexts
14. Application of self control techniques with children

PERFORMANCE CRITERIA.   Students are expected to treat at least one case through the use of behavior modification. Students continually present their cases to the class to secure feedback. Students are required to develop a paper on the case chosen for modification which involves the specification of the experimental design used to evaluate whether the treatment interventions were effective.

Upon completion of this course the students are able to:

1.   Write a specific behavioral analysis of a presenting problem including a:

a.   statement of the problem in specific behavioral terms;
b.   statement of the conditions which precede, parallel, or follow the problematic behavior;
c.   statement of the reinforcing stimuli or events that control the problematic behavior;
d.   specific behavioral statement of treatment goals consisting of those:
    1.   behaviors to be decreased
    2.   behaviors to be increased
    3.   behaviors to be acquired
e.   specific behavioral treatment plan including rationale for choices which consists of:
    1.   a list of techniques to be used,
    2.   the means of intervention, i.e., individual, group, organizational, or societal,
    3.   a statement regarding who will carry them out,
    4.   where the changes will be implemented,
    5.   a statement of what contingencies will be used,
    6.   a plan for monitoring the treatment and its outcome.

TEXTS.

1.   John B. Krumboltz & Helen B. Krumboltz. *Changing children's behavior.* Englewood Cliffs, N.J.: Prentice-Hall, 1972.

2.   Robert L. Hamblin, David Buckholdt, Daniel Ferritor, Martin Kozloff, & Lois Blackwell. *Humanization process.* New York: John Wiley, 1971.

3.   Robert Browning & Donald O. Stover. *Behavior modification and child treatment.* Chicago: Aldine-Atherton, 1971.

4.   Leo A. Hamerlynck, A. C. Handy, & Eric J. Mash (Eds.) *Behavior change, methodology, concepts and practice.* Champaign, Ill.: Research Press, 1973.

5. Gerald Patterson & Elizabeth Gullion. *Living with children: New methods for parents and teachers.* Champaign, Ill.: Research Press, 1968.

6. G. A. Tharp & Ralph J. Wetzel. *Behavior modification in a natural environment.* New York: Academic Press, 1969.

7. Anthony Graziano. *Behavior therapy with children* (Vol. 2) Chicago: Aldine, 1975.

8. Roger Ulrich, Thomas Stachnik, & John Mabry (Eds.) *Control of human behavior: Behavior modification in education* (Vol. 3) Glenview, Ill.: Scott Foresman, 1974.

SEMINAR ON BEHAVIOR THERAPY WITH ADULTS. COURSE OBJECTIVES.

1. To become acquainted with and proficient in the available knowledge derived from the operant, respondent, and modeling paradigms for intervention with adults classified as neurotic, psychotic, antisocial, retarded, and so forth.

2. To become proficient in behavior modification methodology as applied to clinical assessment which includes learning how to operationalize the target behavior to be changed and treatment interventions, choosing appropriate interventive techniques, choosing adequate designs to assess treatment intervention, and developing means for evaluating data to see whether treatment interventions were effective.

3. To apply knowledge gained in class to the treatment of one case in the practicum experience.

OUTLINE OF TOPICS COVERED.

1. Assessment of adult behavior
2. Choice of interventive strategies
3. Evaluation of interventive strategies
4. Focus of interventive level: individual, group, societal, organizational and/or institutional

   5.   Progressive relaxation training
   6.   Systematic desensitization
   7.   Adversive conditioning
   8.   Token economies
   9.   Modeling procedures
  10.   Assertive training
  11.   Operant techniques applied to marital and family
interaction
  12.   Cognitive behavior modification
  13.   Behavior modification of selected somatic conditions
  14.   Application of behavioral principles with adults in
group contexts
  15.   Application of self control techniques

PERFORMANCE CRITERIA.   Students will be expected to treat
at least one case from the behavioral modification perspective.
Students will present the case to the class to secure feedback
throughout the duration of the course and develop a paper on
the case chosen for modification that would involve the specification of the experimental design to evaluate whether the treatment interventions were effective.
   Upon completion of the course the students are able to:

   1.   Write a specific behavioral analysis of the presenting
problem including a:
   a.   statement of the problem in specific behavioral
terms;
   b.   statement of the condition which precedes, parallels,
        or follows the problematic behavior;
   c.   statement of the reinforcing or adversive stimuli or
        events that control the problematic behavior;
   d.   specific behavioral statement of the treatment goals
        consisting of:
        1.   those behaviors to be decreased,
        2.   those behaviors to be increased,
        3.   those behaviors to be acquired;

e. specific behavioral treatment plan including rationale for choices which consists of:
1. a list of techniques to be used,
2. the means of intervention: individual, group, organization, or societal,
3. a statement regarding who will carry them out,
4. where the changes will be implemented,
5. a statement regarding what contingencies will be used,
6. a plan for monitoring the treatment and its outcomes.

TEXTS.

1. Joseph Wolpe. *The practice of behavior therapy.* New York: Pergamon Press, 1973.
2. Alan E. Kazdin. *The token economy.* New York: Plenum Press, 1977.
3. S. Rachman & J. Teasdale. *Aversion therapy and behavior disorders, an analysis.* Coral Gables, Fla.: University of Miami Press, 1969.
4. David Knox. *Marriage happiness: A behavioral approach to marriage counseling.* Champaign, Ill.: Research Press, 1971.
5. Douglas A. Bernstein & Thomas D. Borkovec. *Progressive relaxation training: A manual for the helping professions.* Champaign, Ill.: Research Press, 1973.
6. Edwin J. Thomas (Ed.). *Behavior modification procedures: A sourcebook.* Chicago: Aldine, 1974.
7. William J. DeRisi & George Butz. *Writing behavioral contracts.* Champaign, Ill.: Research Press, 1975.
8. K. D. O'Leary & G. T. Wilson. *Behavior therapy application and outcome.* Englewood Cliffs, N.J.: Prentice-Hall, 1975.
9. A. J. Lange & P. Jakubowski. *Responsible assertive behavior.* Champaign, Ill.: Research Press, 1976.

Seminar on the Critical Issues in the Field of Behavior Therapy and Clinical Intervention

This course, although focusing upon the various ethical, moral, and legal issues involved in the use of behavioral techniques with clients, is in no way limited to behavior therapy alone in that it centers upon relevant issues requiring resolution by all professional clinicians. It therefore deals with the rights, obligations, duties, and responsibilities of both clients and therapists alike.

COURSE OBJECTIVES.

1.   To provide an in-depth focus on the various issues in the utilization of behavior modification techniques in social work practice.

2.   To require a detailed investigation by each student of one issue in the utilization of behavior modification in social work practice. Issues are developed according to the students' interests. In addition, clinical materials and media such as television, films, etc. are used to illustrate the issues discussed.

OUTLINE OF TOPICS COVERED.

1.   The steps involved in terms of organizational requisites in the application of behavior modification techniques in open settings, such as community centers, mental health clinics, and juvenile courts.

2.   Values: what behaviors ought to be increased, decreased, and altered?

3.   What types of reinforcers are effective for various client groups?

4.   Focus of intervention: individual, group, society, and/or organizational.

5. Programming for the generalization and transfer from the laboratory to the clinic.

6. Utilization of modeling as a potent behavior modification technique.

7. Adversive versus positive control of behavior.

8. Cognitive conditioning.

9. Architectural control of behavior.

10. Training for sociobehavioral practice.

11. Role of expectations in sociobehavioral practice.

12. Use of paraprofessionals as change agents.

13. Legal issues in the use of behavior modification.

14. Application of behavioral techniques to energy conservation, pollution control, and so forth.

15. Future developments in behavioral technology.

PERFORMANCE CRITERIA.   Students choose an issue in behavior modification practice, develop a paper setting forth the pros and cons of the issue, and orally present their findings to the class and defend their presentation.

TEXTS.

1. Kathleen Kinkade. *A Walden Two experiment.* New York: William Morrow, 1973.

2. B. F. Skinner. *Beyond freedom and dignity.* New York: Bantam, 1971.

3. Carl E. Thoresen & Michael J. Mahoney. *Behavioral self-control.* New York: Holt, Rinehart and Winston, 1974.

4. Anne E. Freedman. *The planned society: An analysis of Skinner's proposal.* Kalamazoo, Mich.: Behaviordelia, 1972.

5. Dale M. Breathower. *Behavioral analysis in business and industry.* Kalamazoo, Mich.: Behaviordelia, 1972.

6. Arnold A. Lazarus. *Behavior therapy and beyond.* New York: McGraw-Hill, 1971.

7.   Harvey Wheeler (Ed.) *Beyond the Punitive Society.*
San Francisco: W. H. Freeman, 1973.

BEHAVIORAL INTERNSHIP

Organizational Considerations

A practicum experience occurring concurrently with other
courses in behavior modification provides students with an immediate opportunity to implement techniques discussed in the
classroom and thus facilitates the acquisition of skills through
the provision of more feedback channels. If it is impossible to
structure such a curriculum it is imperative that organizational
ties are developed between courses taken before or after the
fieldwork experience. Close coordination between the classroom and the practicum instructor will be necessary to enable
the student to secure relevant data on their cases in order that
they might use this data in the classroom discussions or be
permitted to practice the implementation of the techniques previously covered in the classroom.

A basic training objective is to provide beginning students
with the necessary tools to evaluate their practice endeavors
through the collection of data. The feedback provided by data
collection should prove influential to practice behaviors. As an
added benefit, the skills they develop in evaluating their practice behavior should enable them to improve their practice
behaviors throughout their professional careers. During the
practicum three requisite evaluation skills have to be mastered:
data collection techniques, observational techniques, and appreciation of experimental design applications.

Methodological Practicum Experiences

TRAINING IN DATA COLLECTION.   Before the student imple-
ments any influence attempt, he reviews a tape of clients' interactions, makes a behavioral assessment, designs a cor-

responding intervention plan, and specifies how he will evaluate the success of the intervention plan. It is of utmost importance that the behaviors to be modified are defined in terms of observable referents and that treatment interventions to be used to achieve the modification are clearly explicated. The criterion for determining whether the behaviors and treatment interventions are adequately explicated is evaluated in terms of whether two persons can consistently agree that the selected behavior has occurred. Usually consistent agreement is determined according to the following formula which yields a ratio of interobserver agreement according to the intervals of time chosen to observe various client and worker behaviors:

$$\frac{\text{Ratio of interobserver}}{\text{agreement}} = \frac{\text{Number of agreements}}{\text{Number of agreements} + \text{Number of disagreements}}$$

Ninety percent agreement is usually considered adequate and indicates that the behaviors have been explicated sufficiently. These behavioral procedures require that students are trained in the collection of data on the behaviors to be changed and the techniques to be employed in changing the behaviors. The requirement necessitates that they become skilled in observational techniques.

OBSERVATIONAL TECHNIQUES.   Data in Figure 1 provide an example of prosocial, nonsocial, and antisocial behavior for each of 14 two-hour group sessions for 10 antisocial children participating in a group at a community agency. The exact definitions of prosocial, nonsocial, and antisocial behavior are provided in Table 1. The acquisition of observational data on behaviors entails determining a specific time wherein the target behaviors are counted. The behaviors may be counted by certain time intervals, such as at the beginning of each 10-second interval, every time they occur within a 10-second interval, and

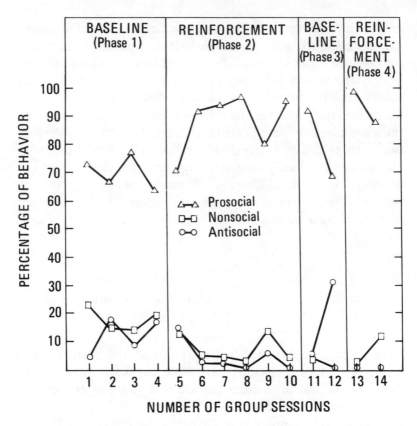

Figure 1   Average percentage of prosocial, nonsocial, and anti-social behaviors exhibited by 10 children, according to number of group sessions.

so forth. The type of measurement process chosen depends upon the behavior chosen for modification, availability of technical equipment, context of measurement, the frequency of the behavior, and so forth.* Various behaviors that may be exhib-

*For an excellent discussion of measurement techniques see, Bijou, S. W., Peterson, R. F., Hanes, F. F., Allen, K. E., & Johnston, M. W. Methodology for experimental studies of young children in natural settings. *The Psychological Record*, 1969, *19*, 177–210. Thomas, E. J. (Ed.) *Behavior modification procedure: A source book.* Chicago: Aldine, 1974.

Table 1 Children's Behavior Categories

Prosocial behavior is defined as any behavior directed toward completion of the group task or toward participation in the group activity. Nonsocial behavior is defined as behavior which is not directed toward the completion of the group task but which does not interfere with another child's participation in the group task or activity. Antisocial behavior is defined as any behavior exhibited by a group member that prevents the other group members from participating in the group task or activity. The following behavioral descriptions were used in the initial training and then for actual observation.

Prosocial behavior occurs when a child:

(a) actively engages in the group activity;

(b) asks the change agent about the group activity; (For example, the activity is arts and crafts and the child asks how to select certain paints for his picture.)

(c) hands another child a material object, such as a basketball or hockey stick, which the latter needs to participate in the group activity;

(d) asks the change agent or another child to help someone participate in the activity;

(e) works together with another on the same activity; For example, one child shows the other how to saw a board or helps the other to overcome difficulties so that they may jointly execute an activity, such as lifting lumber to build a tree hut.)

(f) helps another to participate in a discussion by making a comment that elicits continued verbal behavior; (For example: One child is telling about drugs and the other says "good point," "please continue," "elaborate on that," "tell us more," and so forth.)

(g) engages in the decision-making process verbally or nonverbally; (For example, nods his head, pats another child for engaging in the process, smiles, listens or sits quietly, or has eye contact with the change agent or another child.)

(h) makes an appropriate comment; (For example, the activity is hockey and the child says "Let's choose sides.")

(i) tries to help someone, shares something with another child, stops other children from arguing or fighting, helps children to be friends with one another, or tries to do something nice even though nobody expected it;

(j) says nice things to another, such as "I like you";

(k) helps other group members to tidy up their belongings, solve a problem, or fix something that was broken;

(l) helps the group change agent by paying attention to him, cooperating with him, or carrying out reasonable instructions.

Table 1   (continued)

Nonsocial behavior occurs when a child:

(a) looks out the window or stares into space;

(b) plays with some object but does not interact with the other children;

(c) does not engage in appropriate tasks for the interactional situation; (For example, the children are playing basketball but he sits in the corner)

(d) lays his head on the table or furniture;

(e) pulls at his hair or clothing;

(f) cleans or forages in a desk without disturbing another child;

(g) draws on the desk or table;

(h) bites his nails or sucks his thumb or other objects;

(i) engages in other motor activities which do not disturb his peers; (For example, takes off his shoes, rocks in a chair, moves a chair in place, sits out of position)

(j) lies down on the ground;

(k) digs in the dirt or plays with the grass;

(l) isolates himself from the group members so as to preclude the possibility of social interaction.

Antisocial behavior occurs when a child engages in any of the following behaviors.

(a) *Verbalizations* Talks to another child and thus disrupts the other's participation in the group activity; talks to another and thus disrupts someone else who is trying to participate in the group activity; speaks without directing the conversation toward anyone; engages in name calling, crying, screaming, laughing loudly, coughing loudly, disruptive singing, disruptive whistling, and so forth.

(b) *Gross motor behaviors* If the children are seated around the table or in a circle a child is out of his seat or position without the others' approval, or he runs, jumps, skips, stands up, hops, moves a chair, or walks in a manner that disrupts the group's activity.

(c) *Object interference* A child plays with some object that interferes with another's participation in the group, taps a pencil on the table or slams things on furniture.

(d) *Physical contacts* Disruptive contact is initiated by one child toward another who is participating in the group activity. Such contact may include hitting, kicking, shoving, pinching, slapping, striking with an object, biting, pulling hair, touching, patting, or disturbing another child's property.

(e) *Distracting behaviors* A child engages in physical movement that attracts another child's attention and causes the latter to stop participating in the group activity; the former may turn his head or body to look at another child, show an object to another, rock in a chair, sit out of position, clean or rummage in furniture, and so forth.

ited by the practitioner working with groups are listed in Table 2. These behaviors were derived from a five year "Group Integration and Behavioral Change" research project wherein one of the goals was to assess behaviors exhibited by group workers in terms of different treatment methods employed.*

The actual behaviors that are measured in the context for behavioral change will depend upon the type of clients and the treatment strategy used by the students. Determining the types of client behavior to change will probably entail a baseline observational period. As mentioned in Chapter 3, this period prohibits interventions by the worker on a rational systematic basis to change the behavior of the client except in instances where psychological or physical damage might occur to another individual. This procedure ensures that the worker assess the natural behavior of the client and thus formulate the target behavior to be modified without undue bias from his own interventive efforts. If this period can be videotaped it will provide the opportunity for the worker to recheck his specification of target behaviors and, in addition, make it possible for other workers to provide their observations. One word of caution is necessary concerning the operationalization of client and worker behaviors. The task is not accomplished without ample expenditure of time and energy, and workers should be prepared to meet this requirement.

EXPERIMENTAL DESIGN APPLICATIONS.   Once students have been introduced to the observational techniques, they are provided with information regarding the use of experimental designs to determine if their interventions are having an effect on

*This scale that measures prosocial, nonsocial, and antisocial behavior of children and various change agents' behaviors may be obtained from the authors or is available in Wodarski, J. S. & Feldman, R. A. Behavior observational scale for children and therapist interacting in a group. In Orval G. Johnson (Ed.) *Test and measurements in child development: Handbook II.* San Francisco: Jossey-Bass, 1976.

Table 2 Therapist Behaviors

Single interventions
Individual single interventions
Group single interventions
Time out or unknown (no *I* or *G*) single interventions
Individual single interventions directions
Individual single interventions positive contact
Individual single interventions praise
Individual single interventions positive attention
Individual single interventions holding
Individual single interventions criticism
Individual single interventions threats
Individual single interventions negative attention
Individual single interventions time out or unknown
Group single interventions directions
Group single interventions positive contact
Group single interventions praise
Group single interventions positive attention
Group single interventions holding
Group single interventions criticism
Group single interventions threats
Group single interventions negative attention
Group single interventions time out or unknown
Multiple interventions
Individual multiple interventions
Group multiple interventions
Individual multiple interventions directions
Individual multiple interventions positive contact
Individual multiple interventions praise
Individual multiple interventions positive attention
Individual multiple interventions holding
Individual multiple interventions criticism
Individual multiple interventions threats
Individual multiple interventions negative attention
Individual multiple interventions time out or unknown
Group multiple interventions directions
Group multiple interventions positive contact
Group multiple interventions praise
Group multiple interventions positive attention
Group multiple interventions holding
Group multiple interventions criticism
Group multiple interventions threats
Group multiple interventions negative attention
Group multiple interventions time out or unknown

the behavior. A major strength of behavior modification technology has been the development of various experimental procedures that are economical in terms of money, energy required to implement them, administrative concerns, and manpower, and their accessibility to practitioners for the evaluation of their practice interventions. Likewise, administration of these procedures is relatively simple.

The classical design in behavior modification is the A, B,A,B, design that consists of four basic phases where behaviors are observed for a specified time period. In the first phase the clients are exposed to a baseline period. During this period the worker does not rationally plan interventions that are likely to influence the display of target behaviors. After the client's observed incidence of target behavior reaches a stabilized, or "natural" level, the behavior change strategy is introduced and clients' behaviors are monitored (phase two) until they are once again stabilized. A behavior is considered stabilized when the average of its measurements do not vary more than 10 percent for 3 to 5 days. After the behaviors are stabilized, a baseline conditon is reintroduced (phase three). This condition is termed the reversal period. The procedure enables the students and others evaluating the changes to determine whether the influence attempt was responsible for the various changes in behavior. Immediately after it becomes evident that the treatment strategy has been effective in reducing target behavior the reinforcement procedures are applied once again (phase four). Figure 1 illustrates the use of this design by a worker with 10 antisocial children, ages 11 and 12, in a group context.

In some situations the A,B,A,B, design may not be feasible due to the types of behaviors being modified and/or for various ethical reasons. The primary reason for utilizing an alternative design is when in the A,B,A,B, design the modified behavior will not reverse itself, i.e., since it now is maintained by natural reinforcements existing in the client's environment, or when in many instances reversals would be too damaging to the client or significant others in his life. For example, when fighting is brought under control in a home it would not be feasible to do a reversal on this behavior since in the past physical harm has been inflicted on others. A design that may be utilized in lieu of the A,B,A,B design is the multiple baseline design wherein a series of behaviors for modification are operationalized. Predictions are made on how the various techniques will affect different behaviors. Each behavior is then modified according to a time schedule. Usually one or two behaviors are modified at a time. For example, the worker might want to decrease such behaviors as yelling, fighting, throwing objects, straying from the group; and increase prosocial behaviors, such as task participation and appropriate verbal comments. The worker in this instance might choose first to ignore the yelling and use positive reinforcement to increase appropriate verbal comments. Once the yelling decreases and the appropriate verbal comments increase he would sequentially modify the second, third, and fourth behaviors. In Table 3 an outline is provided on how such a process operates. The technique being employed becomes more efficacious every time the behaviors change in the direction predicted for each child.

Another design that can be used is the A,B design. In actuality it is the first half of the A,B,A,B design. It involves securing a baseline and introducing treatment after the behavior to be altered is stabilized. This is a minimum prerequisite for proving the interventions effective.

In summary, all of these designs can be easily implemented in clinical practice; that is, they are economical in terms of money, energy required to implement them, and administrative execution. Above all, they provide data that will enable a worker to determine if his interventions have had an effect on client behaviors. It is not practicable to indicate what design should be used. This depends on the context of the behavioral change situation in terms of behaviors to be modified, time considerations, administrative concerns, and so forth.*

Clinical Practicum Experiences

The clinical practicum is designed as a highly structured and closely supervised learning experience requiring considerable time and effort on the part of the students. Students are required to observe a variety of client behaviors in different situational contexts. Students are asked to make accurate behavioral assessments of these clients and to formulate appropriate intervention programs based upon these behavioral assessments. They are expected to master and to apply a wide range of behavioral techniques directed toward the modification of undesirable target behaviors. Corrective feedback is given immediately to the students regarding their performances once the specific assessment and intervention techniques have been outlined. Audiovisual tapes, observations by trained behavioral raters, and other measurement inventories are utilized toward this end. Demonstrations of the behaviors to be mastered by the students are achieved through the use of filmed and live models of competent clinical practitioners.†

BEHAVIORAL ASSESSMENTS OF A VARIETY OF CASES.   Each practicum experience should take place in an agency that provides students the opportunity to view a variety of presenting behav-

---

*For a detailed description of the various designs that might be used to evaluate group work interventions see Gottman, John M. N-of-one and N-of-two research in psychotherapy. *Psychological Bulletin,* 1973, *80,* 93–105; Browning, R. M. & Stover, D. P. *Behavior modification in child treatment.* Chicago: Aldine-Atherton, 1971, pp. 75–110; Barlow, David H. & Hersen, M. Single case experimental designs: Uses in applied clinical research. *Archives of General Psychiatry,* 1973, *29,* 319–325; Hersen, M. & Barlow, D. H. *Single case experimental designs.* New York: Pergamon, 1976; Howe, M. H. Casework self-evaluation: a single-subject approach. *Social Service Review,* 1974, *48,* 1–23.

†A listing of films that can be used in training students is available upon request from the Association for Advancement of Behavior Therapy, 420 Lexington Ave., New York, N.Y. 10017.

Table 3. Example of Procedure for Multiple Baseline Design Using Extinction to Decrease Antisocial Behavior and Positive Reinforcement to Increase Prosocial Behavior*

Behavior to be modified	I	II	III	IV
1. Not staying with group—task participation	Modification plan instituted			
2. Yelling—making appropriate verbal comments		Modification plan instituted		
3. Fighting—increasing helping behaviors, such as sharing, working together on a task, and so forth			Modification plan instituted	
4. Throwing objects—cleaning up after group meeting				Modification plan instituted

*Length of time periods are not specified; this depends on how rigorous one wants to be in showing the effects of the modification plan. Usually a period lasts until the behavior stabilizes at a variance of less than 10 percentage points variability for 3 to 5 days.

iors defined as problematic by the client and/or by significant others. Likewise, a variety of different age levels should be incorporated, such as children, youth, adolescents, young adults, middle-aged adults, and the aged. If such a practicum experience is impractical a student might be placed in more than one agency where it would be possible to assess a variety of problems, or if it is necessary in order to secure experience with a greater variety of cases, students might view tapes of different clients and make the appropriate behavioral assessments and treatment intervention plans. These plans should be evaluated on the following criteria:

1.   Has the target of intervention been decided?
2.   Has the most appropriate change agent been chosen?
3.   Are the behaviors of the worker and client operationalized sufficiently?
4.   Has an adequate baseline of client behaviors been executed?
5.   Have data collection procedures to enable the evaluation of the intervention procedures been delineated?

If the modification plan cannot be implemented the minimum requisite for an adequate learning experience would involve discussion among practicum instructors and students to provide feedback regarding the feasibility of their plans.

The practicum experience also should provide the opportunity for students to assess the client's behavior in groups in the natural environments where the problematic behaviors are exhibited. Through gaining a perspective on how peers can influence behavior a student can deduce whether behavioral modification plans should be aimed at changing the group reinforcement patterns and/or the individual reinforcement patterns in order to secure client change. For example, if a child's problems center around his misbehavior at school, the student who was able to observe the child in the school is more likely to secure an accurate assessment of his presenting problem.

Moreover, the truly sophisticated and effective practice experience would enable the student to implement the treatment plan.

A substantial portion of the student's time should be spent assessing what interventions could be employed at the societal, organizational, and institutional levels. This focus would minimize one of the dysfunctional aspects of social work education, i.e., inadequately training students to choose whether change strategies should be aimed at modifying the individual's behavior or be applied to changing the groups, organizations, and/or institutions wherein the individuals interact.

DEMONSTRATIONS.   Demonstrations of students working with practicum instructors to illustrate the techniques are excellent learning experiences and help the learner to discriminate the essential behavioral components of the particular behavior modification techniques. Role playing by combinations of a student and student or student and instructor will depend on the educational requirements of the practicum experience. Students also can make videotapes of the implementation of behavioral techniques that can be shown to others in the student units. This same procedure can be used by the practicum instructor while he is working with clients. An invaluable technique in training students is the use of the one-way mirror, where students can observe either practicum instructors or other students implementing techniques with clients. Additionally, films depicting various means of implementing behavior modification techniques are available.

APPLYING A VARIETY OF TECHNIQUES AND FEEDBACK.   The practicum experience should provide a diversity of learning experiences along with opportunites for students to apply such various behavior modification techniques as relaxation, token economies, adversive conditioning, and various techniques derived from the cognitive conditioning model. A sharpening of behavior skills requires that the behavioral therapist secure feedback on his implementation of the techniques. Thus, every practicum experience should have the organizational mechanisms to enable a student to secure feedback on making a behavioral assessment and formulating a treatment plan, role playing the implementation of these various techniques, and working with a client. Periodic videotapings of the student's implementation of behavior therapy techniques with his clients is extremely beneficial. Tapes provide a medium wherein various techniques of the model can be replayed and examined again, client-worker interventions can be accurately recorded, and likewise, with proper analysis, the tapes can be used to sharpen practice skills. Other forms of feedback include observations by students and practicum instructors of implementation of techniques through a one-way mirror and various self- and observational rating scales on therapist behavior that provide pertinent data. These feedback mechanisms provide the learner with the necessary data to assess whether he has been successful in achieving his goals of mastery of the various behavior modification procedures.

UNRESOLVED ISSUES

The acquisition of skills necessary to apply sociobehavioral theory to social work practice rests on the assumption that behavior modification training is a sequential type of learning experience. That is, certain behaviors must be mastered before others may be acquired. Thus, the proposed sequential training contradicts much of the current social work educational philosophy that permits students flexibility and freedom of choice with the curriculum (Block, 1972; Carlson, 1974; Greenblatt & Katkin, 1972; Guzzetta, 1972; Horowitz, 1971; Katz, 1971; Mann, 1971; Richan, 1971; Walker, 1972). The training procedure, however, need not work against the core curriculum idea of many schools of social work. Actually, the training in behavior modification can occur concurrently with the core curriculum training, or directly afterwards. In the future behavior modification will be coordinated with social policy, macrolevel interventions, and so forth that will increase the effectiveness of the training. It is hard to imagine a training program in behavior modification in which the individuals who are trained as behavioral social workers are not also trained in the essentials of relationship formation, systems analysis, and so forth. The question is, however, how does one ensure that students who graduate from such a program possess those essential skills for effecting positive behavior change in clients?

Perhaps the most crucial question for training in behavior modification centers around which characteristics should be possessed by competent behavioral change agents. The existing literature in psychology and social work indicates that workers should have empathy, unconditional positive regard, and verbal congruence (Carkhuff, 1969, 1971; Carkhuff & Berenson, 1967; Truax & Carkhuff, 1967; Wells & Miller, 1973). Thus, a critical issue which must be decided before any applicant is considered for admission to this program specialization is whether he or she demonstrates the potential for acquiring those therapist characteristics which have been found to produce positive changes in clients (Anthony & Carkhuff, 1977; Fischer, 1975; Luborsky, Chandler, Auerbach, Cohen, & Bachrach, 1971; Truax & Mitchell, 1968, 1971). The preparation of competent behavioral social workers must include a basic skills preparation with the goal of developing and utilizing these core conditions that have been found to produce positive change in clients and that can be coupled with powerful techniques of behavior change. The following evaluation and screening procedures are recommended for all applicants.

Evaluation and Screening

Each applicant whose academic credentials are found to be acceptable for admission to the program specialization will be required to conduct an interview with another student who has already been admitted to the program. This interview will be videotaped and evaluated by a panel of behavioral raters. These raters using reliable inventories will ascertain the degree to which each applicant possesses those core qualities of genuineness, nonpossessive warmth, accurate empathic understanding, the ability to reinforce others, and so forth. Those applicants who are judged to possess these qualities to a medium or higher degree will be admitted to the program; others will be disqualified at this time or will be given the opportunity to achieve higher levels of skills through additional training.

There are studies which suggest that, in addition to these skills, the motivation to help others change, self-adjustment on the part of the worker, and verbal ability are also essential qualities possessed by effective therapists (Berkowitz & Graziano, 1972; Gruver, 1971; Suinn, 1974). Most of these studies have focused on training in techniques other than sociobehavioral therapy. Thus, it is postulated with caution that the development of such personal attributes along with skills in implementing potent behavioral change techniques leads to efficacious therapeutic practice. Future research should enable us to concretely specify the characteristics that when combined with specific techniques facilitate behavior change in the most expeditious manner.

It should be kept in mind that only one in three people who apply to graduate programs in clinical psychology and counseling possesses these skills to an acceptable degree (Garfield, 1971). Therefore, any school wishing to screen applicants in this manner must be prepared to offer a training program similar to the one outlined above and to reject a substantial number of applicants. Clinical educators need not despair, however, since the techniques for achieving sufficient levels of core qualities is based on a number of studies reviewed by Truax and Carkhuff (1967) which show that trainees can be brought up to accurate levels of genuineness, nonpossessive warmth, and accurate empathic understanding in less than 100 hours of supervised clinical training and practice.

This chapter centers on the initial training of students who will implement behavioral technology; however, an issue of equal significance for the continued professional development of students is what takes place after they leave schools of social work. Agencies must be prepared to provide such mechanisms as videotapes, one-way mirror viewing facilities, inventory data on worker behaviors provided by trained observers, and data derived from various other inventories measuring worker behaviors, all of which make possible the provision of feedback on the practitioner's implementation of techniques and thus enable the worker to continue sharpening his practice skills throughout his professional career. Moreover, incentives must be provided for practitioners to keep abreast of new developments in sociobehavioral theory through reading journals and attending conferences, to view filmed or actual demonstrations of new techniques by seasoned practitioners, and to become proficient in implementing techniques through appropriate feedback mechanisms.

Finally, the difficult question of deciding when an individual is prepared to independently practice techniques from sociobehavioral theory must be approached. Accomplishment of all tasks described above is essential. However, the major criteria is the empirically demonstrated ability to effect positive change in the target behavior. Research efforts in the coming years will make possible the delineation of various other parameters of competence in social behavioral techniques. Only when these additional criteria are identified will it be possible to ensure the consistent application of sociobehavioral theory.

Summary

With very few exceptions, theoretical frameworks employed by the social work profession have been descriptive about training processes and have lacked specifications as to what behaviors the worker should exhibit in order to deliver services to clients. Furthermore, a majority of the knowledge bases are characterized by poorly developed programs for the training of workers, i.e., programs being a sequential series of steps workers should master before they are considered trained, and by their obvious lack of clearly defined objectives for evaluating the training process. Perhaps the greatest deficiency in the training process is the lack of a rational and empirical base for the programs. This is due to poorly operationalized sequences for training and to the lack of research on the appropriate means of facilitating the training of workers. These limitations in the training process preclude the possibility of determining whether or not workers are prepared to provide service to social work's clientele. Such difficulties do not characterize the training for the implementation of behavior modification techniques in social work practice. Behavior modification technology offers a specific means of evaluating students' training since this body of knowledge includes a methodology for defining objectives, specifies steps in the training process, and provides means for evaluating various aspects of the training process.

REFERENCES

Anthony, W. A., & Carkhuff, R. R. The functional professional therapeutic agent. In A. S. Gurman, & A. M. Razin (Eds.), *Effective psychotherapy*. New York: Pergamon, 1977.

Berkowitz, B. P., & Graziano, A. N. Training parents as behavior therapists: a review. *Behavior Research and Therapy*, 1972, *10*, 297–317.

Block, A. M. The dilemma of social work education: restructuring the curriculum. *Journal of Education for Social Work*, 1972, *8*(1), 19–23.

Carkhuff, R. R. *Helping and human relations*. New York: Holt, Rinehart and Winston, 1969.

————. Training as a preferred mode of treatment. *Journal of Counseling Psychology*, 1971, *18*, 123–131.

————, & Berenson, B. G. *Beyond counseling and therapy*. New York: Holt, Rinehart, and Winston, 1967.

Carlson, R. W. Expanding educational assumptions for social work education. *Journal of Education for Social Work*, 1974 *10*(3), 17–24.

Fischer, J. Training for effective therapeutic practice. *Psychotherapy; Theory, Research, and Practice*, 1975, *12*(1), 118–123.

Garfield, S. L. Research on client variables in psychotherapy. In A. Bergin, & S. Garfield (Eds.), *Handbook of psychotherapy and behavioral change: An empirical analysis*. New York: John Wiley, 1971.

Green, J. K., & Morrow, W. R. Precision social work: general model and illustrative projects with clients. *Journal of Education for Social Work,* 1972, *8*(3), 19–29.

Greenblatt, B., & Katkin, D. Prolegomena to a curriculum for some occasions. *Social Work Education Reporter,* 1972, *20*(3), 55–61.

Gruver, G. G. College students as therapeutic agents. *Psychological Bulletin,* 1971, *76*(2), 111–127.

Guzzetta, C. Curriculum alternatives. *Journal of Education for Social Work,* 1972, *8*(1), 24–30.

Horowitz, G. New curriculum policy statement: freedom and/or regulation –1. *Journal of Education for Social Work,* 1971, *7*(2), 41–46.

Howe, M. M. Casework self-evaluation: A single-subject approach. *Social Service Review,* 1974, *48*(1), 1–23.

Katz, A. J. New curriculum policy statement: freedom and/or regulation –2. *Journal of Education for Social Work,* 1971, *7*(2), 47–54.

Luborsky, L., Chandler, M., Auerbach, A. H., Cohen, J., & Bachrach, H. M. Factors influencing the outcome of psychotherapy: a review of quantitative research. *Psychological Bulletin,* 1971, *75*(3), 145–185.

Mann, M. W. Restructuring social work education: knowledge, curriculum, instruction. *Journal of Education for Social Work,* 1971, *7*(2), 31–38.

Richan, W. G. New curriculum policy statement: the problem of professional cohesion –3. *Journal of Education for Social Work,* 1971, *7*(2), 55–60.

Shorkey, C. T. Behavior therapy training in social work education. *Journal of Behavior Therapy and Experimental Psychiatry,* 1973, *4*(2), 195–196.

Suinn, R. M. Traits for selection of paraprofessionals for behavior-modification consultation training. *Community Mental Health Journal,* 1974, *10* (4), 441–449.

Truax, C. B., & Carkhuff, R. R. *Toward effective counseling and psychotherapy: Training and practice.* Chicago: Aldine-Atherton, 1967.

————, & Mitchell, K. M. The psychotherapeutic and the psychonoxious: human encounters that change behavior. In M. Feldman & H. M. Bachrach (Eds.), *Studies in psychotherapy and behavioral change* (Volume I). Buffalo.: State University of New York Press, 1968.

————, & Mitchell, K. M., Research on certain therapist interpersonal skills in relation to progress and outcome. In A. Bergin, & S. Garfield (Eds.), *Handbook of psychotherapy and behavioral change: An empirical analysis.* New York: John Wiley, 1971.

Walker, W. L. Changing thought and action styles of students and faculty: imperatives for social work education. *Journal of Education For Social Work,* 1972, *8*(1), 56–63.

Wells, R. A., & Miller, D. Developing relationship skills in social work students. *Social Work Education Reporter,* 1973, *21*(1), 60–73.

Wodarski, J. S. A behavioral program for the training of social group workers. *Journal of School Social Work,* 1974, *1*(3), 38–54.

Chapter 12

SUMMARY: EMERGING TRENDS

In previous chapters we have reviewed various empirically based techniques derived from behavior modification theory that social workers can readily incorporate into their practice repertoires. In this chapter, we will review possible issues and developments in behavioral social work of the next decade. Included will be a review of the following: self-control, use of aversive techniques, biofeedback, generalization and maintenance of behavior, empirically based concepts of human behavior, comparative evaluation of various techniques, competency criteria for practice, legal actions, macrolevel analysis, and prevention of behavioral difficulties.

SELF-CONTROL

The coming years will witness increased emphasis on the use of self-control techniques. Sufficient data from social psychology indicate that when clients participate in the choice of therapeutic procedures and their implementation, their motivation and commitment to change is increased, a condition indicated by research to be necessary for behavioral change (Brehm, 1976; Feldman & Wodarski, 1975; Secord & Backman, 1964). The typical 55-minute interview with clients wherein therapeutic procedures are implemented and behavioral changes are exhibited does not allow for the generalization or maintenance of behavior. Although behavior may change in the therapeutic context, the process does not facilitate the generalization of behavior to other environments or assure its maintenance once it is achieved. When behavior modification techniques are applied only in the therapeutic context of an office, all of the stimuli of the office building, including the therapist's characteristics, become discriminative stimuli for the occurrence of the altered behavior (Stokes & Baer, 1977; Waters & McCallum, 1973). If clients can be taught how to covertly reinforce themselves through use of cognitive procedures, that is, offering themselves appropriate consequences, they can actually practice the modification of their behavior in their homes, in the office, or any other relevant context. Furthermore, if clients can relax themselves not only at the therapist's office, but at their jobs and their homes, the probability of generalization and maintenance increases. The increase in the number of practice trials results in greater learning and enlarges the number of discriminative stimuli that control the behavior thereby increasing the probability of the client actually exhibiting the behavior in the desired context (Staats, 1975).

A variety of issues concerning self-control techniques must be addressed. For example, who can apply them and what variables influence the self-control process? Variables to be investigated might include verbal, intellectual, and cognitive abilities of clients, e.g., internal and external focus of control, expectations about the therapeutic process, and self-consistency. Similar questions can be asked about the therapists: What are the essential characteristics of the therapists who can apply self-control techniques? Is there a certain type of therapist who likes to work with people in this way and who is effective? Possibly the therapist who does not have to be very authoritative to function effectively with people, who is flexible, and who believes in the ability of the clients to control their own behavior may find self-control techniques easy to implement in their practice.

We also must ask what it is about self-help groups, such as Alcoholics Anonymous, Convicts Anonymous, Addicts Anonymous, Smokers Anonymous, Weight Watchers, and so forth that produces and maintains behavioral change. What do all of these groups have in common? How do they differ? Are there any characteristics of these self-help groups that are analogous to self-control techniques, such as the ability to use positive reinforcement, stimulus control, contingency contracts, and punishments, self-consistency, ability to think about behavior and its consequences, and monitoring of behavior. The investigation of these procedures should help isolate other variables that can be incorporated into behavioral technology to facilitate the alteration of behavior and its maintenance.

Use of Aversive Techniques

The use of aversive consequences or punishment in behavior modification currently is occurring less frequently due to certain political, legal, and social issues, and this decrease should be significant in the future (Bandura, 1975). There is evidence of misuse of certain aversive procedures and punishment in many of our institutional settings such as prisons, residential treatment centers for children, and psychiatric facilities. However, much of the blame for the lack of acceptance of aversive techniques and the adverse publicity comes from the behavioral field itself. We have not done an adequate job of educating the public as to the appropriate use of the techniques. For example, empirical data indicate that aversive techniques used in conjunction with positive reinforcement techniques are more efficient and expedient than others in altering certain self-destructive behaviors (Johnston, 1972; Romanczyk & Goren, 1975). Moreover, we have not ensured the appropriate use of the techniques in that we have failed to develop criteria for determining who is sufficiently trained to implement aversive techniques.

The general commercialization of aversive conditioning such as in the popular novel and film *Clockwork Orange* and other popular media conceptions of it, have not facilitated the public's image of the field. Behavior modifiers in the future will be charged with getting out and educating the public about behavioral modification if the image is to improve.

In the future we will see more of an emphasis on the use of techniques to increase prosocial behaviors, such as providing positive reinforcement after a prosocial behavior occurs to increase the probability of its occurring in the future and using punishment and aversive techniques as a last resort with clients who exhibit severe self-destructive behaviors. In all instances where aversive procedures are employed the following procedures should be implemented to ensure against their misuse: The client or his guardian must grant consent, the clients must be informed of their rights to terminate treatment at anytime, and the procedures must be approved by an institution's Human Rights Committee, preferably composed of a constituency of doctors, lawyers, patients, and so forth. In all instances the treatment must be related solely to the client's resocialization and cannot be used to control the client for the sake of institutional maintenance.

BIOFEEDBACK

Another area that will witness substantial development is the use of biofeedback techniques to alter various types of physiological conditions, such as migraine headaches, hypertension, cardiac-arrhythmias, and epilepsy. A word of caution is in order, however. The data on the effectiveness of such techniques are in the preliminary stages of development. Although the application of these techniques is increasing, classic articles in Franks and Wilson's (1975) *Annual Review of Behavior Therapy Theory and Practice* suggest that little data exist to support wide use of these techniques at this point in time. (Blanchard & Young, 1974; Elder, Ruiz, Deabler, & Dillenkoffer, 1973).

The wide use of biofeedback raises serious issues for the helping professions. In one respect, researchers should move to develop biofeedback techniques that may enhance our dealing with daily anxieties. However, it seems that behavior modification has taken the same approach as have the majority of therapeutic approaches (Brown, 1974; Glenn & Kunnes, 1973; Ryan, 1971), to wit, to do something to help individuals control anxiety and deal with stress while perhaps a more rational approach would be to do an analysis of the society to isolate how we could identify and modify or eliminate the *causes* of anxiety and stress. It seems senseless to teach remedial coping procedures such as relaxation and systematic desensitization without at the same time stressing a preventive approach of moving in the direction of a society that creates less stressful and anxiety-producing experiences for individuals, e.g., alleviating poverty, overcrowding of cities, poor transportation, working in dehumanizing institutions, and setting unrealistic expectations of ourselves. Behavioralists have fallen into the same trap as many traditionally oriented psychotherapists whose goal is adjustment to society as it exists and whose target of intervention is the individual and not the society. Thus, biofeedback is another coping strategy that focuses on altering the individual's behavior and not the contribution provided by societal entities involved in the production of anxiety. Due to the education social workers receive which emphasizes how social system variables affect behavior, behavioral social workers are in a unique position of applying the behavioral approach at the macrolevel of intervention to isolate those societal items that cause stress and anxiety for individuals and to modify them accordingly.

GENERALIZATION AND MAINTENANCE OF BEHAVIOR

Probably the most important issue confronting the field of behavioral social work is the generalization and maintenance of behavior change once it is achieved (Koegel & Rincover, 1977; Stokes & Baer, 1977; Waters & McCallum, 1973). No one can argue that behavior therapy does not modify behavior. The data show that behavioral techniques are appropriate with a wide variety of populations, e.g. autistic, retarded, hyperactive, antisocial and inner-city children who have deficient reading, verbal and arithmetic skills, and with adult clients who have been traditionally classified as neurotic and psychotic, antisocial, and retarded. We have the technology available to change behavior. Now we must investigate and develop procedures that ensure maintenance and generalization of behavior to relevant contexts.

The generalization question will have to focus more on how the social system determines and how it maintains behavior. How does it reinforce people in terms of type of reinforcement and schedules? Once behavior is modified, is the therapist ethically bound to ensure that the social system provide a sufficient level of reinforcement to maintain it? Various procedures that can be implemented to ensure generalization have been discussed in this volume. We can apply the basic principles of variable schedules of reinforcement toward the end of therapy; fading procedures, that is, trying to incorporate the natural consequences of the environment to facilitate the behavior coming under the control of such; and practicing the behavior in various contexts to increase the number of stimuli that control it (Kazdin, 1975). The role of social workers in the process of ensuring generalization and maintenance will be substantial. We are the professionals who are in the best position to program the individual's environment to ensure that sufficient reinforcements are provided and to help the individual practice the requisite behavior in the desired contexts.

We also need to develop a whole technology for treatment termination. While much is said about termination, in the social work literature no criteria exist that can guide the process of terminating an intervention. We need to establish appropriate criteria for determining what are appropriate levels of frequency and quality of behaviors to facilitate the decision making process of termination.

EMPIRICALLY BASED CONCEPTS OF HUMAN BEHAVIOR

We will witness in behavioral social work the incorporation of new concepts of human behavior. The traditional S-R theory, or the classical Skinnerian paradigm which posits that one only responds to external stimuli, will have to be modified in the future to include cognitive processes, such as what clients are saying to themselves, what they perceive, what they expect, and how such processes affect behavior (Guttman, 1977; Lazarus, 1977; Mahoney, 1977). The inclusion of cognitive variables will see an increased emphasis on a theory of learning that relates coherently to the following items: how does the organism select stimuli; how does the organism process stimuli; how does the organism determine what response it will exhibit; how does one evaluate the rewards and costs for exhibiting or learning new behaviors; and how does this appraisal of behavior and its consequences affect behavior change? Thus, to be an effective theory of human behavior change, behavior modification will have to incorporate new empirically based knowledge of human cognition and information processing theories.

As discussed above, new variables must be isolated and new types of theories will have to be developed in order for us to effectively alter complex human behavior. Another development for social work practitioners will have to be the incorporation of not only behavior modification theory in social work practice, but additional theories of human behavior and behavior change that are empirically based, such as the work of Truax and Carkhuff on accurate empathic understanding, nonpossessive warmth, and genuineness as mentioned in Chapter 2. Many graduate programs in social work will incorporate into their curricula current theories of interpersonal attraction, attribution, and relationship formation, game theory and decision theory, and theories on how organizations affect behavior, nonverbal communication, and so on.

In the past, employment opportunities for social workers in the following fields were uncontested: criminal justice, marriage and family counseling, and human services. If social workers are to compete with other nontraditional human services programs that are also preparing individuals with such empirically based knowledge to enter the helping professions, the curricula of schools of social work will have to incorporate knowledge bases of social psychology that will provide an empirical base for practice techniques (Wodarski, 1978).

THE EVALUATION OF DIFFERENT TECHNIQUES

We have accumulated data to indicate that behavior modification works but how does one know how to select the appropriate procedures to use with a given individual, i.e., operant techniques, modeling procedures, or techniques based on respondent conditioning, when adequately developed criteria are not available to facilitate a choice. For the selection of appropriate techniques we still rely upon the creative abilities of the worker rather than on criteria developed from empirical data. In the future more research will have to be undertaken to provide information about what client problems are best treated by what techniques, with what type of therapist, and in which therapeutic contexts. Moreover, a component analysis of each successful behavior modification treatment package will occur

(Paul, 1969). For example, in systematic desensitization we will try to determine its critical elements, such as: 1) Do you need to relax clients every time? 2) Do you need to construct a hierarchy? 3) Are the expectations of the client and therapist important? 4) Are the cognitions that the client has important in systematic desensitization? 5) What are the effects of therapists' characteristics such as warmth, unconditional positive regard, and empathy?

What are the critical components in assertive training? Are they the actual practicing of assertive behavior; developing an assertive belief system; expectations of change; feedback from the therapist; the models used; or perceptions of demand characteristics for assertive behavior? More effort will be placed on conducting experiments where the effects of these previously mentioned variables can be isolated. Only then can we begin to make statements such as, "modeling works better than operant conditioning for certain types of behaviors," and begin to streamline the interventive package by eliminating unnecessary components (Wodarski & Buckholdt, 1975).

COMPETENCY CRITERIA

As the demand for behavioral social workers increases, the training of such practitioners will have to be formalized and competency criteria will have to be developed. Few places in the country offer concrete behavior modification training. We will have to streamline existing training programs since behavior modification is an extremely complex technology to apply and substantial time is needed to develop requisite skills for implementing the procedures in a comprehensive and competent manner. We must determine where to train practitioners and what level of skills must be acquired at each educational degree level. That is, what are the basic training functions at the undergraduate level, at the master's level, and the doctoral level? We will need to develop entrance criteria for students who will become behavioral social workers as well as appropriately defined objectives for training. Also, testing procedures will have to be developed and incorporated into training programs to ensure that students meet appropriate standards. Such an assessment process will ensure that the individuals who call themselves behavior therapists are in fact competent to practice the techniques (Arkava & Brennen, 1975; Armitage & Clark, 1975; Peterson, 1976).

LEGAL ISSUES

Legal issues regarding appropriate reinforcers, what contingencies can be utilized, and so on will continue to be recognized. Behavioral social work can be practiced within the constraints of the Constitution and certain legal decisions that are being made may even facilitate the utilization of behavioral techniques since these decisions emphasize stating treatment objectives concretely and in such a manner that they can be measured. Under the legal doctrine of equal protection, i.e., constitutionally all individuals are entitled to the same privileges, that is, the same social services, and the doctrine of least restrictive alternatives, treatment technologies that restrict the client's civil liberties the least and demonstrate superior effectiveness over other approaches will have to be utilized. Thus, if two or more technologies are available that achieve the same results, the technology that restricts the client's liberties the least in terms of personal resources such as money, time, and energy must be used. If data continue to accumulate that attest to the efficacy of behavior modification approaches the legal precedence for their wide scale usage will be set. These two criteria have been used in legal cases in the past and judges have based their rulings concerning treatment issues on this basis. Thus, clients have a right to the most efficacious social services and the ones least restrictive of their civil liberties (Martin, 1974, 1975; Wodarski, 1976).

MACROLEVEL ANALYSIS

It is likely that future research will begin to unravel the complex relationship between societal experiences and human behavior. How we can construct a society with macrolevel interventions as opposed to individual interventions to prevent or facilitate certain behavior has been virtually ignored by the field. For example, social policies with provision of incentives for welfare clients who can work to secure and maintain employment, designing physical environments in such a manner that the probability of criminal behavior is decreased, and so on must be examined. One example of an environmental design to facilitate the occurrence of a particular behavior is the "open schools" concept. In the open classroom the purpose is to increase social interaction among children and adults. The crucial questions center on how to structure environments that will support behavioral change achieved through interpersonal approaches, that is, provide enough reinforcers to maintain prosocial behavior, and what behaviors can be altered directly through macrolevel intervention (Kelly, Snowden, & Muñoz, 1977).

PREVENTION

Behavioral social work will place more emphasis on prevention, a major issue to be considered as the helping professions have a history of dealing with individuals only *after* they have exhibited problematic behaviors rather than *before* problematic behavior occurs. Some may wonder if we can really alter clients' behaviors after 20, 40, or 60 years of learning. Our task, therefore, is to facilitate the preventive and educative roles that can be assumed by social workers. We should develop criteria for early intervention. Prototypes of such an approach may be found in courses on parental effectiveness, sex education, marital enrichment, and so on. Such courses should focus on helping parents develop better communication and consistent child management skills, two variables research has shown are necessary conditions for successful child rearing (Hoffman, 1977), and helping prepare young adults for the requisites of marriage, with effective communication skills, problem-solving strategies, and conflict resolution procedures (Collins, 1971; Ely, Guerney, & Stover, 1973; Lederer & Jackson, 1968; Rappaport & Harrell, 1972; Satir, 1967). The use of behavioral techniques in preventive medicine is an exciting application of behavioral analysis. Prevention of coronary heart disease is illustrated by efforts to identify high-risk individuals and apply behavioral techniques designed to decrease weight and increase exercise, stop smoking, and reduce serum cholesterol (Meyer & Henderson, 1974).

We will have to evaluate how the different reinforcement strategies, i.e., cooperative or competitive, that schools employ affect the development of children's self-concepts and their attitudes toward adults in society, traditional societal values, norms, and institutions and how they facilitate the development of relevant prosocial behaviors and a sense of belongingness in the child (Buckholdt & Wodarski, 1978; Hoffman, 1977).

SUMMARY

Over the last 15 years we have seen a revolution take place in the helping professions. Behavior modification provides a totally new way of looking at clients and offering assistance. It is one of the most humane approaches since it assumes that behavior is learned and therefore can be unlearned, that is, individuals at any time in their lives can change their behaviors. The collection of data to determine whether the techniques are working to produce client change provides the behavioral approaches with the necessary feedback to ensure their continued development. That is, if the worker's interventions are not enabling a client to change, he or she tries other empirically based

techniques and collects the necessary data to evaluate the interventive attempts until behavioral change is achieved.

REFERENCES

Arkava, M. L., & Brennen, E. C. Toward a competency examination for the
    baccalaureate social work. *Journal of Education for Social Work,* 1975,
    11(3), 22–29.
Armitage, A., & Clark, F. W. Design issues in the performance based cur-
    riculum. *Journal of Education for Social Work,* 1975, *11*(1), 22–29.
Bandura, A. The ethics and social purposes of behavior modification. In C.
    M. Franks, & G. T. Wilson (Eds.), *Annual review of behavior therapy,
    theory and practice (1975).* New York: Brunner/Mazel, 1975.
Blanchard, E. B., & Young, L. D. Clinical applications of bio-feedback trai-
    ning: a review of evidence. *Archives of General Psychiatry,* 1974, *30,*
    573–589.
Brehm, S. S. *The application of social psychology to clinical practice.* New
    York: John Wiley, 1976.
Brown, P. *Toward a Marxist psychology.* New York: Harper Colophon
    Books, 1974.
Buckholdt, D. R., & Wodarski, J. S. The effects of different reinforcement
    systems on cooperative behaviors exhibited by children in classroom
    contexts. *Journal of Research and Development in Education,* 1978, in
    press.
Collins, J. D. The effects of the conjugal relationship modification method on
    marital communication and adjustment. Unpublished doctoral disserta-
    tion, The Pennsylvania State University, 1971.
Elder, S. T., Ruiz, Z. R., Deabler, H. L., & Dillenkoffer, R. L. Instrumental
    conditioning of diastolic blood pressure in essential hypertensive pa-
    tients. *Journal of Applied Behavior Analysis,* 1973, *6,* 377–382.
Ely, A. L., Guerney, G. G., & Stover, L. Efficacy of the training phase of
    conjugal therapy. *Psychotherapy: Theory, research and practice,* 1973,
    10, 201–207.
Feldman, R. A., & Wodarski, J. S. *Contemporary approaches to group treat-
    ment.* San Francisco: Jossey-Bass, 1975.
Franks, C. M., & Wilson, G. T. Bio-feedback and other strategies in self-
    management. In C. M. Franks, & G. T. Wilson (Eds.), *Annual review of
    behavior therapy, theory and practice (1975).* New York: Brunner/Ma-
    zel, 1975.

Glenn, M., & Kunnes, R. *Repression or revolution.* New York: Harper Colophon Books, 1973.

Guttman, N. On Skinner and Hull: a reminiscence and projection. *American Psychologist,* 1977, *32)(5), 321–328.*

Hoffman, M. L. Personality and social development. In M. R. Rosenzweig, & L. W. Porter (Eds.), *Annual review of psychology.* Palo Alto, Ca.: Annual Review, 1977.

Johnston, J. M. Punishment of human behavior. *American Psychologist,* 1972, *27*(11), 1033–1054.

Kazdin, A. E. *Behavior modification in applied settings.* Homewood, Ill.: Dorsey, 1975.

Kelly, J. G., Snowden, L. R., & Muñoz, R. F. Social and community intervention. In M. R. Rosenzweig, & L. W. Porter (Eds.), *Annual review of psychology.* Palo Alto, Ca.: Annual Review, 1977.

Koegel, R. L., & Rincover, A. Research on the difference between generalization and maintenance in extra-therapy responding. *Journal of Applied Behavior Analysis,* 1977, *10,* 1–12.

Lazarus, A. A. Has behavior therapy outlived its usefulness. *American Psychologist,* 1977, *32,* 550–554.

Lederer, W., & Jackson, D. *The mirages of marriage.* New York: Norton, 1968.

Mahoney, M. M. Reflection on the cognitive learning trend in psychotherapy. *American Psychologist,* 1977, *32,* 5–13.

Martin, R. *Behavior modification: human rights and legal responsibilities.* Champaign, Ill.: Research Press, 1974.

———. *Legal challenges to behavior modification.* Champaign, Ill.: Research Press, 1975.

Meyer, A. J., & Henderson, J. B. Multiple risk factors reduction in the prevention of cardiovascular diseases. *Preventive Medicine,* 1974, *3,* 225–236.

Paul, G. L. Behavior modification research. In C. M. Franks (Ed.), *Behavior therapy: Appraisal and status.* New York: McGraw-Hill, 1969.

Peterson, G. W. A strategy for instituting competency based education in large colleges and universities: a pilot program. *Educational Technology,* 1976, *16*(12), 30–34.

Rappaport, A., & Harrell, J. A behavioral exchange model for marital counseling. *The Family Coordinator,* 1972, *21,* 203–212.

Romanczyk, R. G., & Goren, E. R. Severe self-injurious behavior: the problem of clinical control. *Journal of Consulting and Clinical Psychology,* 1975, *43*(5), 730–739.

Ryan, W. *Blaming the victim.* New York: Vintage Books, 1971.

Satir, V. *Conjoint family therapy.* Palo Alto, Ca.: Basic Books, 1967.

Secord, P. F., & Backman, C. W. *Social psychology*. New York: McGraw-Hill, 1964.

Staats, A. W. *Social behaviorism*. Homewood, Ill.: Dorsey, 1975.

Stokes, T. F., & Baer, D. M. An implicit technology of generalization. *Journal of Applied Behavior Analysis*, 1977, *10*, 349–367.

Waters, F. W., & McCallum, R. N. The basis of behavior therapy: mentalistic or behavioristic? A reply to E. A. Locke. *Behavior Research and Therapy*, 1973, *11*, 157–163.

Wodarski, J. S. Recent supreme court legal decisions: Implications for social work practice. Paper presented at the 102nd Annual Meeting, National Conference on Social Welfare, Washington, D.C., June, 1976.

———. Critical issues in social work education. *Journal of Education for Social Work*, 1978, *14*, in press.

———, & Buckholdt, D. Behavioral instruction in college classrooms: a review of methodological procedures. In J. M. Johnston (Ed.), *Behavior research and technology in higher education*. Springfield, Ill.: Charles C Thomas, 1975.

INDEX